WHO'S TO BLAME?
CHILD SEXUAL ABUSE AND
NON-OFFENDING MOTHERS

Anyone familiar with current literature on child sexual abuse knows that non-offending mothers are routinely blamed for allowing their children to be victimized. This book analyses and challenges this orthodoxy. It explores why mothers are held responsible when they are not themselves offenders, and documents the institutionalized sexism they encounter in their dealings with intervening agencies.

Central to the study are the cases of twenty-four mothers whose children disclosed incidents of sexual abuse. Betty Carter follows the experiences of these women in detail, documenting the treatment they received from police, child-protection workers, counsellors, schools, courts, physicians, co-workers, and family members. She traces the tendency to blame mothers of sexually abused children to the specific wording of legislation, to the implementation of agency policies, and to front-line practices.

Using a feminist analysis, and drawing on her years of experience as a child-protection workers and child-abuse specialist, Carter argues that the procedures and policies of various institutions reproduce and maintain patrearchal ideology and sexist practices.

BETTY JOYCE CARTER is Assistant Professor Emeritus, School of Social Work, University of British Columbia.

BETTY JOYCE CARTER

Who's to Blame?
Child Sexual Abuse and
Non-Offending Mothers

UNIVERSITY OF TORONTO PRESS
Toronto Buffalo London

© University of Toronto Press Incorporated 1999
Toronto Buffalo London
Printed in Canada

ISBN 0-8020-2847-0 (cloth)
ISBN 0-8020-7727-7 (paper)

Printed on acid-free paper

Canadian Cataloguing in Publication Data

Carter, Betty
Who's to blame? : child sexual abuse and non-offending mothers

Includes bibliographical references and index.
ISBN 0-8020-2847-0 (bound)   ISBN 0-8020-7727-7 (pbk.)

1. Child sexual abuse – Canada.   2. Mothers – Legal status, laws, etc. –
Canada.   3. Sexually abused children – Canada.   4. Sexually abused
children – Services for – Canada.   I. Title.
HV6570.4.C3C37 1999   362.76'3'0971   C99-930063-3

University of Toronto Press acknowledges the support to its publishing
program of the Canada Council for the Arts and the Ontario Arts Council.

This book has been published with the help of a grant from the Humanities
and Social Sciences Federation, using funds provided by the Social Sciences
and Humanities Research Council of Canada.

Contents

Preface

The world of child victims of sexual abuse and their male offenders has changed significantly over the past fifteen years. Sadly, the world of mothers of children who disclose sexual abuse has changed very little. Women are still blamed for 'allowing' the sexual abuse to occur. Even when women are absent or have had no knowledge of or participation in that sexual abuse, they are blamed by both the public and the professional community. It is not unusual to still hear the question: 'Why did that mother not protect her child?'

There is now a small but growing body of literature on the experiences of mothers whose children have been sexually abused, but what is different about this book is that it clearly documents institutionalized sexism in all of the intervening systems (medical, police, school, court, workplace, child welfare, and group counselling), based on the experiences of the twenty-four mothers interviewed. The practices of child welfare workers and others involved in the intervention process of child sexual abuse examined in this research reveal that the mothers themselves became victims of the broader legal, educational, and social service systems, since those systems blamed the non-offending mothers for allowing the sexual abuse to happen to their children.

This book, then, is about how women responded after they learned about their child's disclosure of sexual abuse, how they identified helpful and unhelpful relationships and contacts, and how they endured and survived throughout the difficult period that followed the disclosure. But this book is also about the various professional groups and intervening institutions involved with the women and how their well-intentioned practices and policies reproduced and maintained the status quo.

I met many women just like the strong and courageous women in this book when I worked in the child welfare system as a social worker in various provinces across Canada. In the 1970s and the early 1980s, we had no language and little understanding of the dynamics of child sexual abuse. When it was specified in the legislation that we had to intervene in sexual abuse cases, I recall how frightened I felt for the women whose husbands were the alleged offenders. Not only were most of the women afraid of their husbands, but they were confused about the expectations placed on them by society to be loyal to their husband and yet, at the same time, to be responsible for protecting their children. In particular, the child welfare literature emphasized the importance of respect and autonomy of the family unit where the male was seen as the head of the household.

When I later attempted to search out knowledge that would help me to train other social workers in this area, and to develop group programs for sexually abused children, I recall my discomfort with the traditional social work literature, which focused on the collusive mother and the seductive child. At that time, however, I did not question the theories that informed our practice. It was only much later, after being exposed to feminist literature, that I was able to develop a political analysis of the mainstream approach to child sexual abuse.

A feminist analysis offers a world-view of equality that benefits not only women, but also children and men. Unfortunately, feminism still remains marginal in the work of most child welfare agencies.

Without the work of the women's movement, child sexual abuse, rape, violence against women, sexual harassment, child pornography, and female sex slavery would have remained a hidden epidemic. Feminist and pro-feminist theorists and researchers are mainly responsible for the considerable literature now available on the topic of violence against women and children. My own work in this area has been influenced by the early work of Sandra Butler, Diana Russell, Judith Herman, Linda Gordon, David Finkelhor, Charlotte Bunch, Rebecca and Russell Dobash, Jane Gilgun, Kathleen Faller, Lena Dominelli, and Christine Courtois, to name but a few.

During my doctoral studies, I was greatly influenced by the feminist scholars at the Ontario Institute for Studies in Education, located next door to my own Faculty of Social Work building in Toronto. I took courses there, audited classes, attended many evening lectures and weekend workshops, and became totally immersed in feminist methodology, policy analysis, theory, and action. I benefited greatly from the scholarly work of Margrit Eichler, Mary O'Brien, Dorothy Smith, Paula Caplan, Geri Wine, and Kathleen Rockhill.

When I first started collecting data, the overwhelming number of cases of child sexual abuse being reported concerned female children; my research reports on twenty-seven females and only four males. Since that time, the sexual abuse of male children and youth has come to the attention of child welfare authorities and police officers, as well as the public, through the news media.

Clearly, there have been gains made over the past twenty years in our knowledge base, training, programs, and policies with respect to child sexual abuse. We continue to struggle with some of the consequences of our earlier decisions and reforms, however, such as our placing children in the criminal courts as witnesses, and the inclusion of post-traumatic stress disorder in the DSM (Diagnostic Symptom Manual) and whether that inclusion has been a help or a hindrance to survivors of sexual abuse. We continue to mobilize against the backlash of the false memory syndrome lobby group, and to deal with new developments in our research, practice, and training agendas, such as developing effective programs for sexually intrusive children who victimize other children. We also continue to try to protect our colleagues and other professionals experiencing secondary trauma from working closely with the victims of sexual abuse.

One major area in which we have made little progress is understanding and supporting the experiences of mothers whose children are sexually abused. For example, the twenty-four women I interviewed for this study all appeared to have suffered vicarious traumatization as a result of their children's victimization. The entrenched ideology of a patriarchal society that devalues and subordinates all women – especially mothers – suggests it will take many more years to bring about the desired change. Women are cast in the ideal or 'perfect mother' role, and then harshly sanctioned when they are unable to fulfil the impossible expectations placed on them by society.

Although this research was conducted in Ontario, Canada, I do not believe the situation in other provinces in Canada or in the United States differs greatly, since many of the research, practice, and policy initiatives in this area have been shared throughout North America.

In summary, this research derives from the perspective of twenty-four mothers' experiences. It includes both male and female child-victim experiences and describes both father-daughter incest and situations where children were sexually abused by other relatives and trusted family, friends, and neighbours. The research draws on secondary data from interviews with fifteen key informants and the examination of the families' child welfare records. The book looks at all the major intervening institutions and offers a feminist analysis of child sexual abuse.

Although my work supports much of the current feminist literature now available in this area, it also differs from, and in some instances contradicts, other feminist studies. For example, this study shows that child welfare services can provide help to mothers of sexually abused children, and mothers do need that help; also, much feminist scholarship does not hold a realistic view of mothers (any more than mainstream scholarship does) regarding the possibility of the 'perfect' mother.

My hope is that this book will help to create a better understanding of the day-to-day struggles in the lives of those women who are faced with the aftermath of their children's sexual abuse. I also hope it will help to establish a greater appreciation of the complexity of the social relations that dominate the policy and practice area in sexual abuse interventions. As well, those who are looking for a pedagogical tool to increase their sensitivity and understanding of sexual abuse in their work with women and children will, I believe, benefit from reading this book.

Acknowledgments

My doctoral dissertation at the University of Toronto Faculty of Social Work forms the basis of this book. I owe a special debt to the twenty-four women who shared their post-disclosure experiences with me. Each of the women spoke candidly despite the very sensitive nature of the content. I am also grateful to the key informants who participated in the study, and to the staff of various agencies who made it possible for me to obtain volunteer participants and authorized access to their clients' files.

The academic guidance and thoughtful critiques provided by Drs Ralph Garber, Sheila Neysmith, Margrit Eichler, David Locker, and Linda Davies shaped my original dissertation and therefore made this book possible.

Thanks to all those friends and colleagues who influenced and supported my work, such as Jane Aronson, Lynn Kearney, Maureen Jessop Orton, Imogen Taylor, Sally Palmer, Barbara Chisholm, Linda Page, Sandy Butler, Freda Robertson, and members of Margrit Eichler's thesis group.

I thank the various anonymous readers for revision suggestions, as well as the editorial staff of the University of Toronto Press for their guidance. I especially wish to express my deep appreciation to Virgil Duff, executive editor, for his patience and support during the long process of bringing this work forward for publication.

Financial assistance throughout the entire period of my original study was gratefully received from the University of Toronto's Open Fellowship Program and the Ontario Graduate Scholarship Program. A University of British Columbia research grant provided computer equipment that was invaluable in producing the manuscript. I also wish to thank the University of British Columbia School of Social Work for the clerical support needed to produce this book. I thank those friends and colleagues at the UBC

School who contributed to my work with their ongoing support, and especially Drs Kathryn McCannell and Paule McNicoll.

My family members have had confidence in my ability and have supported my work over the years, especially my sister, Margaret MacDonald, and my son, Paul Curran. My mother, who was responsible for my interest in the area of violence against women and children, died before this work was completed. She was of the generation of women who were taught to keep silent about such oppressions as violence against women and children in the family. Her courage, endurance and spirit have left an indelible mark on my life, although I was late in appreciating her many acts of resistance.

My greatest feeling of appreciation is to Anne Bullock, who made an enormous contribution to the process of writing this book and to whom this book is dedicated. Her reading of various drafts, insightful and scholarly commentary, and support and encouragement were invaluable.

The long process from dissertation to book was one in which editors, readers, and various individuals along the way made valuable comments, offered support, and helped in the publication process. Still, I take responsibility for the final product; any errors or shortcomings in this book are mine.

WHO'S TO BLAME?
CHILD SEXUAL ABUSE AND
NON-OFFENDING MOTHERS

1

Introduction

Research completed by Weinberg (1955) estimated that there would be one case of child sexual abuse per one million population per year in the whole of the United States of America. Weinberg's prediction lost its credibility completely eighteen years later when a single mandated agency in San Jose, California, received 31 validated cases of sexual abuse by 1973 (Giarretto and Giarretto 1981).

Since the late 1970s, we have witnessed an unprecedented number of child sexual abuse reports to child-welfare agencies despite research findings that many incidents of sexual abuse are never reported to mandated agencies (Badgley et al. 1984; Finkelhor et al. 1997; Russell 1986). Whether there were as many children victimized two decades ago is difficult to say, and indeed there is considerable controversy in the literature on this topic. Most researchers, however, would agree that there is more sanction for children to disclose sexual abuse (especially female children) within recent years, and that there is better documentation and action on reported cases.

This does not mean that this crime against children is in any way under control, or that children are now safer at home or on the streets in the 1990s than they were in the 1970s. From my own experience in this work, I do know that in Toronto, the largest metropolitan area in Canada, those of us working in the child sexual abuse area in 1980 could identify only 100 cases of validated child sexual abuse that was documented. Nine years later, a reasonable guesstimate of 1,000 cases of child sexual abuse opened for protection service in the Toronto Metropolitan area supports the Giarrettos' prediction (1981) that we would see a major increase in reported cases, given the 2.5 million population at the time.[1] I do not believe this phenomenon is peculiar to any one province or state but is typical of the situation in most societies around the globe (Gelles and Cornell 1983).

A variety of prevention programs are now available in the schools and within the social, health, and judicial ministries to educate children and parents regarding sexual abuse risk factors. We still appear to be engaged in pioneer work with respect to various stages of intervention, treatment, and prevention of this social problem, however.

Differing opinions exist in the literature as to how to explain the increase in the number of reported cases of sexually abused children. Russell (1986), on the basis of her random sample of 930 women interviewed in San Francisco, California, argues that we are indeed experiencing a real increase in the number of children being sexually abused. Finkelhor (1984; Finkelhor and Assoc. 1986), on the other hand, argues that increases shown in statistics reflect increased public awareness, which results in better reporting and an improved documentation of the problem. It is not clear exactly what the increases represent. What is clear, however, is that such increases continue to challenge child welfare workers and police departments, as well as others involved in the intervention and treatment aspects of child sexual abuse.

Why did child sexual abuse become a 'public' issue in the 1970s? Again, there are various opinions discussed in the literature to explain this phenomenon, including the influence of the civil rights movement, the children's rights movement, sensitivity groups (which encouraged individuals to share personal information previously held private), the professional child advocate movement led by pediatricians (which brought the physical abuse of children to public attention), and the women's liberation movement. Although it is difficult to be certain of the exact process that brought child sexual abuse to public attention in the 1970s, it is reasonable to assume that it was a combination of a number of influences and factors. It is my position that feminists were the most influential in putting child sexual abuse on the public agenda. Feminism has provided the most challenging questions and compelling insights into the reasons why children are sexually abused.

Despite differences of opinion about who placed child sexual abuse on the public agenda, there was little question that governments and mandated agencies needed to know how to deal with what were becoming extensive and widespread criminal offences in Canada. The federal government's response was to attempt to determine the scope and nature of the problem by commissioning the first committee ever to conduct research in this area in Canada (Badgley et al. 1984). Closely following on the heels of the Badgley Report was the Fraser 1985 Report, examining another aspect of child sexual abuse (pornography and prostitution).

Both of these committees were mandated by the minister of justice and attorney general. A third committee, mandated by the minister of national health and welfare (Rogers), reported in 1990 on possible solutions to eradicate the sexual abuse of children and youth.

Robin Badgley's committee examined approximately 10,000 cases of sexual abuse of both children and youth in fourteen separate studies across Canada, and their principal conclusions were that 'these crimes occur extensively and that the protection now afforded these young victims by the law and the public services is inadequate' (1984, 1). The report included 52 recommendations for change. In one of the fourteen studies completed using a random sample of 2,008 Canadian adults in 210 communities, the findings indicated that 22 per cent of girls and 9 per cent of boys will have been sexually abused before they reach the age of seventeen years. These figures were calculated using a definition in which the acts committed are violations of the *Criminal Code of Canada* (Bagley 1985). These Canadian figures are supported by similar research fingings in the United States by Russell (1986), Wyatt and Peters (1986), and Finkelhor (1994).

Paul Fraser's committee recognized that the long-range task of re-educating and reshaping attitudes in society is critical in terms of achieving equality. In order to bring about the necessary reallocation of economic and social resources, however, there would have to be considerable social adjustment. A reform of existing legislation could not wait until those changes in attitude were completed. The committee found little support for 'repression of sexuality as a means of eliminating what people found offensive about pornography and prostitution' (1985, 26). In fact, it was found that 'young people often turn to pornography, soft or hard core, in the search for information about their developing sexuality, because good sex education courses and healthy erotic literature are unavailable to them' (26). Fraser et al. (1985) made 108 recommendations to the minister, which included changes to the Criminal Code, Canada Customs, Canada Post, and in areas related to broadcasting and communications, human rights, hate literature, film classification and censorship, and education.

A third major federal study on child sexual abuse was a report to the minister of health and welfare Canada in 1990 (Rogers). The mandate was 'to prepare for the Minister a report on the long-range direction of federal child sexual abust initiatives, their implementation and co-ordination' (1990, 7). One of the major conclusions of the report was the need to change the underlying, deeply rooted attitudes of sexism in Canadian society. On the basis of the contributions of approximately 1,600 persons across Canada, the special adviser, Rix Rogers, proposed 73 recommendations for change. Although Roger's report does not deal with the incidence and prevalence of child sexual abuse, he was quoted at a public meeting where he described the situation in Canada as an epidemic, given the large number of children who are sexually victimized each year (Platiel 1989).

The most recent statistics from a random sample in Canada are from a study completed by the Canadian Panel on Violence Against Women, *Changing the Landscape: Ending Violence – Achieving Equality* (1993). Based on interviews with 420 women, the study found that 54 per cent of girls under age 16 years experience some form of unwanted or intrusive sexual experience. It should be noted that the definition included in this study was very broad, and did not use the Criminal Code of Canada as the guideline. That rationale was that any girl under age sixteen years could define her own terms of reference as to what she considered unwanted or intrusive sexual behaviour.

Also in 1993, Statistics Canada conducted telephone interviews with a random selection of 12,300 women aged eighteen and over. These women were asked about physical and sexual violence against them since the age of sixteen. The findings of the *Violence Against Women Survey* revealed that as of 1993, 48 per cent of all women who had ever been married or lived common law reported that their ex-partners had assaulted them (Trainor, Nromand and Verdon 1995, 104).

The definition of 'child' used in my study includes those under the age of sixteen years. The definition of 'child sexual abuse' used here is broader than that used within child welfare in most provinces in Canada. It includes cases of both intrafamilial (where the child was sexually abused by a relative or relatives within the family system, blood and/or relationship) and extrafamilial (where the child was sexually abused by perpetrators not part of the child's family life, including authority figures, neighbours, and acquaintances) abuse. This research, however, does *not* include sexual acts committed by strangers. The definition, then, includes sexual abuse perpetrated only by known males who were trusted by the child-victims.

This book addresses one of the most heated debates in the area of child sexual abuse, namely, mothering and the responsibility that mothers are given by society to protect their children from all harm, including sexual abuse. The state, professionals and the public continue to hold mothers responsible for their children's sexual victimization. In other words, the 'ethic of blame' with respect to mothers remains prevalent in our society

(Butler 1978; Caplan et al. 1985; Courtois 1988; Dempster 1992; Herman 1992; Hooper 1992; Johnson 1992; Krane 1994; Russell 1986).

During the past decade, we have witnessed changing attitudes towards perpetrators and child-victims. Negative attitudes towards mothers in cases of child sexual abuse, however, appear to be solidly entrenched in the conscious and unconscious minds of professionals and the public, according to the results of my research conducted with twenty-four mothers whose children disclosed sexual abuse. Although the size of my sample does not permit me to generalize my results to that of the experiences of all mothers whose children were sexually abused, it does provide the type of rich data that allows the reader to know about the experiences of these particular mothers whose characteristics, in my opinion, do not differ greatly from those of other mothers in the same geographical location.

Since women are the main caregivers of children, with almost exclusive responsibility for the child's day-to-day care, they are the ones most seriously affected by the child's disclosure of sexual abuse. Disclosure creates a period of crisis in any family, but when the perpetrator is the child's father, it places an added burden and trauma on both the child and on the mother, often resulting in dramatic changes within that particular family (Russell 1986; Williams 1993).

I became interested in the area of child sexual abuse in the 1970s, when those of us who were involved in child welfare work began intervening in families before we even knew the consequences of our interventions. I recall the dilemmas of the mothers who were left to pick up the pieces after their children made their disclosures. Most of these women were confused and frightened by the intervention process. Meanwhile, the father would be vehemently denying any responsibility for the abuse and the mother would be forced to make decisions for herself and her children based on limited choices, with little understanding or support from intervening authorities. The mothers with whom I was involved had few marketable job skills to compete in the workplace, a number of children in the home to support, and little financial independence from their husbands/partners.

We have made progress in this area since the 1970s. The social and judicial systems do reflect a change in the attitudes of professionals and the public with respect to both victims and perpetrators of sexual abuse. Child-victims are assumed to be telling the truth in most instances and are emotionally supported much more now than they were in the past, while perpetrators are more frequently expected to accept the responsibility for their crimes. The sentencing of offenders, however, does not yet reflect the seriousness of the crime, and treatment programs do not reach all offenders in prison. Many offenders refuse treatment (if it is available to them) and are subsequently released back into the community. In many instances, the perpetrators are likely to be reoffenders.

For the most part, non-offending mothers are still being 'blamed' for allowing the child to be victimized. Blame is defined here as placing the responsibility on the mother, censuring and condemning her for allowing the sexual abuse to occur.

It is worth noting here that I recognize that the men, women, and children referred to in this study all have whole lives and are not simply victims, survivors, mothers, offenders, and non-offenders. When I use such language, it is for purposes of clarity and brevity and not to diminish any human being to a label.

The underlying assumptions at the basis of current policy formulation and program development in both legal and social services tend to reflect the prevailing beliefs and values of professional 'experts' about mothers of victims of child sexual abuse. These derive from psychiatric and psychological notions, including Freudian theories about the motivations of women, rather than knowledge arising out of women's lived experiences. According to a leading researcher in child sexual abuse, David Finkelhor (Finkelhor et al. 1997), there is a need to learn more from parents who have had the experience of having their children disclose sexual abuse. Current literature reviews reveal little research focused specifically on the experiences of non-offending mothers. Although mothers themselves have been interviewed about their children's sexual abuse, the major focus of much of the research has been in other areas.[2]

My study differs, however, from others focused in this area (Dempster 1992; Hooper 1989; Johnson 1992; Krane 1990), in that it covers the responses of the workplace, the actual tracking of mother-blame to the wording of specific legislation, the implementation of agency policies, and the practices of intervenors. It focuses on the women's relationships with their husbands/partners, and examines the insensitivity of some of key informants to the rights and needs of women and children.

Empirical research indicates that the initial effects of child sexual abuse can be painful and confusing for the child and the long-term effects can have very serious consequences (Badgley et al. 1984; Bagley and King 1990; Courtois 1988, 1991; Finkelhor and Assoc. 1986; Herman 1992; Russell 1986; Wyatt and Powell 1988). In a study of 117 adults who were survivors of child sexual abuse, 86 per cent met full DSM-III criteria for a posttraumatic stress disorder diagnosis (Rodriguez et al. 1996). Non-offending mothers of children who disclose sexual abuse can also be severely traumatized by this experience (Figley 1995; Green et al. 1995; McCann and Pearlman 1990).

This book looks at the experiences of twenty-four non-offending mothers whose children were victims of sexual abuse. The major theme in the analysis is the commonality of their experiences. All the women experienced feelings of blame for not protecting their children from the abuse. These feelings were manifested in their contact not only with professionals in the network of services provided after the child's disclosure, but also with partners, family members, and friends. The women also blamed themselves. Although these women said that they could not and should not be blamed for their children's victimization, they continually engaged in such self-blame. Numerous examples are provided to illustrate this point.

Although this work stresses the important role ideology plays in keeping women in their place, it also points out that material and economic considerations sometimes make it difficult for women to leave abusive situations.

I have attempted to extend my inquiry into women's experiences after the disclosure of the sexual abuse of their children beyond the twenty-four in-depth interviews I conducted. I also conducted an empirical examination of past practices and policies of child welfare by analysing twenty-two agency records of the families of this study. In addition, I interviewed fifteen key experts in the areas of child welfare and women's issues.

On the basis of the above three sources of data collection, I was able to support the findings of current feminist studies in a number of areas, including: the mother-blaming that women experience from the child welfare and the broader legal and social service systems; the secondary trauma mothers experience; the complexity of decision-making following disclosure; the lack of emotional support mothers receive from their partners; the financial burdens faced by women who chose to leave their husbands and partners (when they were the offenders); and the degree of violence experienced by mothers separate and apart from the sexual victimization of their children.

The second chapter of this book allows the reader to 'meet' the women interviewed, but first the circumstances under which the study was conceptualized and the interviews conducted are described. This provides a brief snapshot of the 'behind the scenes' preparation for this study, describing how I went about the work of locating the women to interview. I also discuss my feminist framework for the study. The profile of the mothers includes information such as country of birth, ethnic heritage, religion, education, occupation, marital status, household income, and number of children. The interaction between myself as the researcher and the mothers is also discussed.

Chapter Three reviews relevant literature on such topics as motherhood, the concept of blame, the ideology of the family, and theories of child sexual abuse. It looks at mainstream and alternative views in the literature with respect to these concepts. Most mainstream theories on motherhood hold both mothers and children more culpable for the abuse than the offenders themselves. By contrast, alternative theories and practices seek to empower women and children by providing space for them to speak for themselves. This review of both mainstream and alternative literature allows the unpacking of some of the philosophical assumptions underlying theories and practice with respect to motherhood.

The concept of blame is central to this study. The reader is provided with the thinking of leaders in the field in the 1960s and 1970s that greatly influenced child welfare practice. Again, using the framework chosen for critiquing the literature, I present mainstream and alternative views on this concept. This is followed by a discussion on the ideology of the family from traditional clinical literature to various feminist perspectives. The chapter ends with an examination and analysis of the various theories of child sexual abuse that have informed and are informing agency practice, from the traditional clinical (mainstream) to radical feminist (alternative) perspectives.

Chapter Four provides a framework of the women's experiences that is critical in helping the reader to understand the context in which these children's disclosures take place. The women describe the violence in their own lives. This is followed by a section on the children and the nature and effect of their sexual abuse, utilizing the Finkelhor and Browne (1985) framework (which is described in the chapter) to illustrate the harm caused by the abuse. The chapter ends with a brief discussion about the men who sexually abused the children in this study.

In Chapter Five, I examine how mothers responded to the disclosure events and how their experiences contradict many of the prevalent myths surrounding such responses; their beliefs in their children's stories; who it was the children told first; the action taken by the women; who reported to the child welfare authorities; and the support (or lack of support) given to mothers by significant others.

Chapter Six describes how the mothers experienced the intervention of the child welfare professionals, following a brief historical overview of the child welfare system in Ontario in order to provide a clear understanding of the mandate and responsibility of the workers involved in the protection of children.

In Chapter Seven, the mothers speak of their experiences after disclosure with the following intervening institutions: medical, police, workplace, counselling/support groups, schools, and courts; each section includes case illustrations.

Chapter Eight provides the reader with information about the key informants' attitudes and views.

Chapter Nine provides an analysis of agency records, examining the intended and unintended consequences of intervention. The analysis demonstrates institutional complicity in defending male power in families.

A feminist analysis in Chapter Ten reveals institutionalized abuse of mothers. This chapter is a discourse on the major theme of the book; it draws on the findings throughout the preceding chapters, including the literature review, the interviews with the mothers, the examination of agency records, and interviews with key informants.

The final chapter examines the implications of this book's findings for professionals working in the area of child sexual abuse, and proposes ideas for social action and change.

Definition of Terms

Before moving on to Chapter Two, I will clarify the various definitions to be used for child sexual abuse throughout this book. They were chosen on the basis of the research location and time-frame, and include, first, how broadly I am defining sexual abuse for the purposes of this study; second, the operational definition being used; third, the legal definition used in the Ontario child welfare legislation; and fourth, the Criminal Code of Canada definitions.

There appears to be no universally accepted definition of child sexual abuse, and, indeed, any definition is culture- and time-bound (Mrazek 1985). For purposes of this study, child sexual abuse includes incest (sexual contact between biologically related family members) and is defined as any form of sexual activity, such as intercourse, anal-genital contact, fondling, or other encounters with a child under the age of sixteen years designed to lead to the sexual arousal and/or gratification of the adult or mature individual involved.

The definition used here is broader than that used in the legislation of the province of Ontario, where the research was conducted. In Ontario's definition, only the person 'having charge of the child' at the time of the sexual abuse is considered for legal purposes. My definition includes cases of both intrafamilial and extrafamilial sexual abuse, but does not include sexual acts committed by strangers. This definition includes sexual abuse perpetrated only by known males who were trusted by the child or in an authority position over her or him. The perpetrator did not, however, need to be 'in charge' of the child at the time. For example, my study includes neighbours, boarders, friends of the family, and others who had access to the child.

The definition of sexual abuse for the purposes of this study is an adapted operational definition included in *Child Abuse: A Child Protection Manual for Hospitals of Ontario*:

Sexual abuse is the involvement of a child with or without the child's consent, with an adult (or age-inappropriate adolescent) within the family (intrafamilial), or outside the family (extrafamilial) in sexual behaviour designed for the gratification of the adult or older adolescent whether heterosexual or homosexual. It includes manual, oral, anal, buttock or breast contact or the use of objects for sexual penetration, fondling or stimulation. It also includes sexual exploitation of the child for pornographic purposes, and making a child available to others as a child prostitute. Inappropriate solicitation, exhibitionism and exposure of erotic material for the purposes of stimulation of a child are also included in this definition (Carter 1987b, 27).

The legal definition of child sexual abuse when I conducted my interviews is as follows:

s. 37 (2). A child is in need of protection where ...:
(c) The child has been sexually molested or sexually exploited, by the person having charge of the child or by another person where the person having charge of the child *knows or should know* of the possibility of sexual molestation or sexual exploitation and fails to protect the child; (emphasis added)
(d) There is a substantial risk that the child will be sexually molested or sexually exploited as described in clause (c) ... (*Child and Family Services Act*, 1984) Ontario

The Criminal Code of Canada (1988) covers seventeen offences that could apply to child sexual abuse. They are: sexual interference, invitation to sexual touching, sexual exploitation of a young person, anal intercourse, beastiality, parent or guardian procuring sexual activity of a child, householder permitting sexual activity, exposing genitals to a child, vagrancy, living off the avails of child prostitution, attempting to obtain the sexual services of a child, incest, corrupting children, indecent acts, sexual assault, sexual assault with a weapon, threats to a third party or causing bodily harm, and aggravated sexual assault (Wells 1990, 28).

Legally, children under twelve years are never able to consent to sexual activity. Children between twelve and fourteen are only able to consent with their peers. Young persons between fourteen and eighteen cannot give valid consent if the person approaching them sexually is in a position of trust or authority over them (Wells 1990, 15).

2

Meet the Mothers

What follows is a description of some of the background work that went into locating the women to be interviewed, and to discuss my research method, thinking, and rationale. This chapter addresses all of these areas and gives a profile of the mothers as a group.

My Approach

I examined the effects on the experiences of each of the mothers after her child's sexual abuse disclosure through in-depth interviews. I will discuss the details of my selection process and the interviews themselves later on in this chapter. I also interviewed key informants, who provided not only what might be termed 'the official and formal' view of this phenomenon, but also alternative views. I examined agency records in order to verify certain dates and time frames of services provided, as well as to ascertain the ways in which the women's experiences were defined and managed by agency professionals.

My research method, therefore, consisted of listening to respondents and examining records, with primacy given to the women's accounts. I chose a qualitative methodology with a feminist perspective rather than a mainstream (traditional) methodology because, in my opinion, it is more suited to examining the issues I wanted to focus on from women's experiences.

My feminist framework for this research basically covers six guiding themes as developed by Judith Worell and Claire Etaugh (1994, 446–50):

(1) *Challenging the Tenets of Traditional Scientific Inquiry*
This theme reminds me to recognize that our values enter into all scien-

tific scholarship and should therefore be explicitly stated. As a feminist, I reject the assumption of an objective science that can be free from the history, culture, values, and experiences of the researcher. Part of my research agenda is to identify and correct the various elements of sexism, bias, and omissions in scientific research procedures. Mainstream researchers have too frequently focused their studies on white, middle-class university students, whereas feminist researcher's principles extend the populations to those relevant to the questions being asked. Although I have selected a qualitative method of gathering data for my study, I recognize and accept that a range of research methods is needed for different purposes.

(2) *Focus on the Experience and Lives of Women*
I value women as a legitimate target of study, and do not accept the notion of male as norm. For me, it is important to explore research questions that are relevant to women's lives such as incest, sexual abuse, physical assault, rape, sexual harassment, discrimination, and so on. In this study, guided by feminist principles, I try to avoid the 'context-stripping' approaches that reduce the complexity of women's lives. Most of the interviews were conducted in their natural milieu. Although my study does focus on women's problems, I also address their strengths and capabilities.

(3) *Viewing Power Relations as the Basis of*
Patriarchal Political Social Arrangements
I support the feminist principle that women's subordinate status in society is based not on women's deficiencies, but on the unequal distribution of power. It is critical that feminist scholars work toward shifting attribution of responsibility and blame from victims to perpetrators. My research deals with this issue and, in fact, this is the central theme of my work. Recognizing the power of patriarchal political social arrangements, my strategies and recommendations for social change and social action are based on the need for women's empowerment.

(4) *Recognizing Gender as an Essential Category of Analysis*
My study acknowledges gender as a social construction that is based on power arrangements, and my analysis emphasizes that the situational context of gender is a process that has structured the social interactions of the women interviewed for this research.

(5) *Attention to the Use of Language and the Power to 'Name'*
Feminists have created public awareness of hidden phenomena such as

child sexual abuse by identifying and naming it. Language frames thought and is therefore critical in terms of excluding or including women. My research rejects the generic masculine language which we have all been taught in public schools and universities. I strive to promote a gender-free language system.

(6) *Promoting Social Activism toward the Goal of Societal Change*
I am fully cognizant of how mainstream research in the past (but also the present) has resulted in the oppression of women, and I would therefore like to see social work theories and methods reconceptualized to benefit women and promote gender justice.

These six feminist themes and the sub-themes and issues discussed are taken up in most chapters, and related ideas are interwoven throughout this book.

Harding suggests that traditional theories have been applied in ways that make it difficult to understand women's participation in social life or to understand men's activities as gendered. She further points out that epistemology is the theory of knowledge, especially as it relates to methodology and validation. This raises such questions as 'who can be a "knower?"'; 'Can women be knowers?'; 'What kinds of things can be known?'; and 'Can subjective truths count as knowledge? Mainstream research (intentionally or unintentionally) has systematically excluded the possibility that women could be 'agents of knowledge,' whereas feminist research chooses to validate the perspective of women's experiences, and uses these experiences as significant indicators of 'reality' against which propositions are tested (1987, 3).

Mary Hawkesworth's (1989) article, 'Knowers, Knowing, Known: Feminist Theory and Claims of Truth,' suggests that, 'precisely because feminists move beyond texts to confront the world, they can provide concrete reasons in specific contexts for the superiority of their accounts' (p. 557). The 'truth' of women's reality in my study lies in just such 'concrete reasons in specific contexts,' meaning the experiences after disclosure in the day-to-day lives of the women interviewed.

My research method was greatly influenced by my feminist knowledge and experience of consciousness-raising (CR) groups, which is really only 'talk in small supportive groups about women's experiences' (Kramarae and Treichler 1992, 105). However, the contribution made to the women's movement by CR groups was significant. CR groups were modelled on a practice used by revolutionary Chinese called 'speaking bitterness,' and opened up the sharing of personal information between females, which was the beginning of women obtaining recognition that something was true because they lived through it. In these groups, personal experiences were validated and had authority (Eisenstein 1983).

The CR groups were associated with the radical feminist agenda, and first documented at the First National Women's Liberation Conference near Chicago in 1968 (Redstockings 1975, as quoted in Kramarae and Treichler 1992, 105).

CR groups quickly became a widespread practice and were instrumental in uncovering some of the very painful truths of women's daily lives such as battering by husbands, and sexual abuse by fathers, uncles, brothers, and other males. The CR groups became an attempt to put feminist theory into practice. In these groups, the feminist slogan, 'the personal is political' took on real meaning for women.

Consciousness-raising groups were instrumental in women's distrusting professional 'experts,' as they challenged established theory and practice. The groups were later criticized for both class and race bias, since they relied on verbal skills in which white middle-class women were comfortable. Although they have not totally disappeared, CR groups are often referred to as education groups or just women's groups. Such groups offer advantages not available from individual therapy or other services (NiCarthy et al. 1984).

The theoretical framework used in this study was informed by the experiences of the women who were interviewed. The feeling of 'being blamed' exemplified for them the treatment they received after their children disclosed. 'Being blamed' appears to be integral to the concepts of motherhood and family, as developed in academic and professional discourses and in the wider society through the public press.

My framework also draws upon the interdisciplinary work of feminist scholars and researchers whose social and political analyses assert that 'patriarchal relations' (rather than men) are central to the problem of violence against women and children. Much of the work of mainstream scholars and researchers has been 'gender-blind,' and has taken as received wisdom the blaming of mothers, as well as their idealization. Although this study focuses on the relations of domination and subordination arising out of gender inequality, this is not to imply that other types of inequality, such as race, class, sexual orientation, disability, and so forth, are less important. Since aspects such as class, race, and gender structure any individual's understanding of reality, it follows that they inform all claims to knowledge (Hawkesworth 1989).

In order to further illustrate my methodology and aims, it might be useful to further clarify my feminist perspective. Under the heading 'Principles informing feminist social work,' Dominelli and McLeod outline their first principle of feminist social work:

We are all equal irrespective of our gender. Social relations that obliterate this fact must therefore be transformed and recreated in ways that reflect equality in terms of gender. In keeping with this, a feminist stance endorses egalitarianism across all social dimensions ... and against social divisions which reflect dominance and subordinat[ion] such as rac[ism], class[ism], heterosexism, ageism and 'ablebodieism' (1989, 1–2).

And according to Kelly, 'For research to be feminist it must be predicated on both the theoretical premise and the practical commitment: its purpose being to understand women's oppression in order to change it. Feminism is, therefore, both a mode of understanding and a call to action' (1988b, 4).

In 'A Feminist Perspective on Research: What Does It Help Us See?' author Joan Cummerton discusses what a feminist perspective should include: 'a description of the researcher's involvement, value stance, and experience related to the problem or issue. In addition, researchers would share how they know what they do about the research situation and the people in it' (1986, 87). The author goes on to say that feminist research is political and should improve the quality of life for women, and that the research should be *for* women rather than research *on* women.

The need for one-sex studies is suggested in Eichler and Lapointe: 'It is important to note that studies involving only one sex are legitimate and justifiable. In particular, studies involving women compensate for the many gaps in knowledge, errors and omissions which characterize the social sciences and humanities (1985, 21).

The major focus of my research is on women only and it aims to fill in some of the gaps and omissions mentioned above. Also, as discussed earlier, most traditional clinical literature has been about women rather than arising out of women's experiences. Again, Eichler and Lapointe suggest: 'Each sex can speak *about* but not for the other' (emphasis added), and therefore when conducting research there must be a clear indication 'that at best these responses convey the opinion of one sex about the other, rather than the reality experienced by the other' (12).

This is not to say, however, that same-sex sensitivity is ensured, or that opposite-sex sensitivity is impossible. Although this particular study is concerned with gender, this member-oriented, qualitative guideline could be generalized to other situations, such as persons with disabilities or other oppressed groups.

Locating the Twenty-Four Women to Interview

Because of the sensitive nature of the topic, I anticipated some delay in locating women who would be willing to discuss their experiences. Given my own background of working in the area, however, I felt confident that I would succeed within a reasonable period of time. I was not prepared for the stance taken by some of the agencies I approached, whose gatekeepers put every obstacle possible in my way. These gatekeepers refused to give me access to the women in their programs. I believe they had little respect for the qualitative/feminist approach of the study.

My initial strategy for finding research participants (mothers) was to approach the three largest organizations that provided counselling groups for mothers of child-victims of sexual abuse. These three particular organizations were involved in delivering other types of services to children, adolescents, family members, and their communities throughout the Metropolitan Toronto area. Running crisis-support groups for mothers and children was therefore not their major focus.

The executive director of the first organization I contacted gave me the impression that she would not be supportive around my request to locate potential participants from her groups; however, she did not refuse my request outright at that initial appointment, but referred me to the program director of the groups for a final decision. After several unsuccessful attempts to discuss my work with staff, I suggested that perhaps I should write a letter and enclose my research materials to their board of directors for a decision. At this point, I was advised that the executive director would have veto power over such a request. I considered this a refusal and made no further attempts to locate respondents in that particular organization. No clear reason was ever given for this lack of interest or support, although a suggestion was made that too many research projects were already underway in that organization. On checking this statement, I learned that only one master's level social work student from another part of the province was engaged in a study, and his study was totally unrelated to mine. Perhaps there was a lack of trust in an unknown person such as myself being involved, as these new programs were highly political at the time, and the lack of continued funding was a constant threat. Criticisms of the program made public might jeopardize the survival of the group-work for mothers. These are only speculations, as I never learned the real reason for refusal from this, the largest organization I approached.

I then contacted the second largest of the three agencies, a publicly funded centre, where I was again refused access to potential participants for my study. Bogdan and Biklen (1982) have suggested that qualitative approaches in research are dismissed by some researchers as being just 'fluff,' owing to their lack of measurement and quantification. This, I believe, was the reason for the negative response from this second centre. After investing over a year of writing letters, providing the centre with my materials, sending key papers on which my proposal was based, documenting and clarifying points within my proposal, and making numerous phone calls and two personal visits, it became obvious that the researchers on the ethics committee of this centre were not prepared to accept the fact that there were no formal 'hypotheses to be tested' in my study. I was therefore unable to approach any mother from that particular treatment centre.

Such difficulties are not uncommon in this field of study. Janis Tyler Johnson (1992), an American researcher, discusses a similar delay in locating participants. She originally wanted to interview twenty mothers whose children had disclosed sexual abuse, but after one and one-half years, located only six mothers.

After such a disappointing beginning, I changed my strategy for locating participants and wrote a letter to the editor of the local (Toronto) newspaper, giving a description of my research and requesting that any mother who saw herself as fitting within the study guidelines contact me if she was interested in participating. This method proved to be relatively successful, as my first interview was with a mother who had responded to my letter. Later, I was successful in obtaining immediate and ongoing support for my study from a third agency, which subsequently provided the largest number of participants for the study (fifteen).

In an attempt to diversify the participants in the study, I approached a private consultant and a private psychotherapy centre. Although both acknowledged the need for such research with women, and supported the approach I was taking, neither was able to make referrals, since no mother from these private centres volunteered to be interviewed.

Financial assistance in the form of a research grant was sought to cover travel and other expenses involved in the collection of the data. The particular funding body I approached rejected my request for a research grant partly on the grounds that I chose to place my 'emphasis ... on mothers only,' partly because it was 'questionable whether the proposed research is relevant to ... [their] research priorities' (child-abuse prevention), and partly because I had not 'specified the study's hypotheses.' The response received from the potential funding body with respect to the approach of my study indicates once again that a quantitative methodology was considered the proper approach in conducting research, even in this particular situation where little basic data had been gathered from mothers themselves about their own experiences after disclosure (that particular agency no longer exists).

Clearly, the difficulty in accessing participants appeared to be connected to the qualitative methodology I planned to use and the feminist perspective, although this was not stated. This anti-feminist sentiment was never expressed in formal letters of response to the University of Toronto with respect to my doctoral research, however, those of us who were engaged in feminist research in the Toronto area were well aware of the identification of agencies and administrators who were anti-feminist in their approach, and valued only the work of mainstream researchers, as they were the ones who benefited from grants, available positions, contracts, and recognition. Agencies questioned whether the mothers themselves were the appropriate focus for such research.

All the rejection I experienced from these organizations created considerable sadness and defeat with regard to my research, and dampened my outlook for ever completing the work which had originally excited me so. At no time, however, did I ever question changing my methodology. I was convinced that using a qualitative, feminist approach was the only reasonable way to learn about the experiences of women whose children had been sexually abused. I should also mention here that I had the on-going support of all my feminist colleagues and friends, and also support from those on my dissertation committee, some of whom were feminist scholars. I was advised that what I was attempting to accomplish would not be an easy undertaking, and that I should expect resistance from mainstream professionals. The refusals were not accepted with acquiescence. Every attempt was made to convince the gatekeepers of these organizations and agencies by me and by the acting chair of my committee that I should have access to the women involved in their groups for my study. I did everything possible (within the academic setting) to overcome the resistance encountered, but eventually had to seek other sources because of the long delays involved.

Twenty-four volunteer participants were eventually located from thirty-four referrals received from the following sources: eight from child-welfare agencies within the Metropolitan Toronto area; two from child-welfare agencies outside Metro Toronto; fifteen from crisis/support groups; one from a volunteer organization; and eight from responses to a letter placed in the *Toronto Star*. The ten individuals who did not participate in this study were either unable to be located, had changed their minds about participating, or did not fit the criteria for the study. Once engaged in the interview process, however, no participant quit the study.

Each of the mothers received a letter explaining the purpose of the study and an assurance that participants' and other family members' names and all information shared would be held in strict confidence. Eighteen of the twenty-four women chose to be interviewed in their own homes. Of the remaining six, two were interviewed at the university offices, one in a nearby park, one in a motel room, one at her place of work, and one was interviewed in my car (in a parking lot near her workplace).

An attempt was made to conduct the interviews with the mothers in the most relaxed and permission-giving environments possible, since discussion of such an emotional topic (it was presumed) would cause a great deal of pain and discomfort for most of the mothers interviewed. Gilgun's (1987) non-coercive method was used in interviewing the women. This is an interviewing method based on the Rogerian concepts of non-directiveness, empathy, unconditional positive regard, and congruence. Gilgun's method helps to provide an environment where participants can choose freely to share or not to share important life stories with a sensitive interviewer.

Every effort was made to keep the integrity of Reinharz's (1992) qualitative method of an active participation of the interviewees rather than a passive one, and the adoption of a non-hierarchical, non-authoritarian, and non-manipulative relationship with the women interviewed. I support Siedman's view that, 'interviewing is both a research methodology and a social relationship ...' (1991, 72).

Characteristics of the Mothers Interviewed

The characteristics of the twenty-four women who participated in the study are presented in group form. The age of the mothers when interviewed ranged from 26 to 54 years, with an average age of 35.1 years.

Birthplace and Ethnic/Racial Background

Twenty-one of the twenty-four mothers were born in Canada. Of those born outside the country, one was born in Israel, one in England, and one in South Ireland. Sixteen of the twenty-one mothers born in Canada were born in the province of Ontario, where the study was conducted; the remaining five mothers were born in other Canadian provinces. Nine of the sixteen mothers born in Ontario were born in Toronto, while the remaining seven were from rural areas and smaller cities outside of the metropolitan area. This mix in locations provided various types and levels of experiences for analysis, including communities where access to services differed from that of a large city.

The women come from a variety of ethnic backgrounds, including British (the majority), Irish, Israeli, Portuguese, Japanese, Dutch, German, and French. Three of the women interviewed identified themselves with First Nations heritage, although only one of the three was raised within First Nation's culture. It is interesting to note that these three mothers indicated that they had little information about that part of their heritage because it was not discussed freely and openly within their families when they were growing up. Other women did not make similar comments about silences perceived in other ethnic backgrounds during the interviews.

Religion

The religious identification and practices of the women in this study did not appear to be significant in terms of the response or the impact on the mothers. Two of the mothers did indicate, however, that they had chosen to discontinue practice of their religious faith for reasons of sexual abuse (Salvation Army and Pentecostal). One was related to an unwanted sexual experience a mother had as a child with a member of her clergy; the other incident was in relation to advice one mother received from a member of her clergy after her child had disclosed. The advice was interpreted by this mother as blaming her for her child's victimization.

Fifteen of the women were Protestant, six were Roman Catholic, one was Jewish. Two indicated they had had no religious affiliation. Only seven said they were currently practising their religion (that is, attending religious services on a regular basis). The various denominations represented in the Protestant category included Anglican, United Church, Pentecostal, Salvation Army, Presbyterian, Baptist, and Jehovah's Witness.

Education

With respect to the mothers' formal education levels, nine of the mothers interviewed had not completed high school; nine had completed high school and had additional education at the community college or business level; six mothers had attended university; two of the six were full-time students at the graduate level. Since approximately one-third of students in Ontario drop out before finishing high school, these women do not appear to differ greatly from the general population (Radwanski 1987).

Occupation

The occupations of the women interviewed generally reflected the educational level they had achieved. Six of the women were full-time homemakers, six worked in clerical positions, two were in service occupations, one was in the technical field, and nine were in business management or professional occupations.

Marital Status

Twelve of the twenty-four women were either married or had male live-in partners when I interviewed them. I did not specifically ask whether any of the women were in same-sex relationships and none indicated they were. At the time of disclosure, however, seventeen were married or had live-in partners, while seven were sole-support mothers. According to the women, all of their partners were employed.

Number of Children in the Home

There were a total of thirty-one child-victims in the study, with an additional twenty-four children living at home. A total of fifty-five children were living with the mothers when I interviewed them. Fifty were biological children and five had been adopted. An additional ten children were in these twenty-four homes on a part-time and sporadic basis. Only one biological child (under age sixteen) was living elsewhere (with relatives) at the time I interviewed the women.

Household Income

A breakdown of the household income and marital status of the twenty-four women interviewed is shown in Table 2.1.

As indicated earlier, twelve of the women interviewed were married or had a live-in partner, and the other half (twelve) were sole-support mothers at the time I interviewed them. As shown in Table 2.1, fifteen of the twenty-four households (ten of the twelve sole-support mothers and five of

TABLE 2.1
Annual Household Income and Marital Status of Mothers of Victims of Child Sexual Abuse, N = 24

Household Income ($)	Single SSM	LIP	Married	Divorced SSM	LIP	Separated SSM	LIP	Widow SSM	LIP	Total
Under 10,000	1			1		1				3
10,000–19,999			1	2	1	2				6
20,000–29,999		1	2	2		1				6
30,000–39,999				1						1
40,000–49,999								1	1	2
Over 50,000			5			1				6
Totals	1	1	8	6	2	4	1	1	0	24

SSM = sole-support mother
LIP = live-in partner

the two-parent families) received less than $30,000 per year household income. Three of the ten sole-support mothers received less than $10,000 per year to support themselves and their children. Only three mothers in the separated category and three mothers in the divorced category received financial support from the children's fathers. None of the unmarried mothers received financial support from their children's fathers.

The majority of the twelve two-parent households in this study (seven) received over $40,000 annually. The average sole-support mother in this study received approximately $20,416 per year. It can be said that most of the sole-support mothers in this study were living at the poverty line (National Council of Welfare 1990).

Some of these mothers already had the responsibility of maintaining a home and, in most cases, other children in addition to the child-victims, on inadequate incomes. The financial aspects need to be factored in for mothers in any analysis of child sexual abuse as it increases the vulnerability of women.

Both the current and potential financial situation of the individual household and the type of emotional support given by others were important indicators of an individual mother's response to the disclosure.

The Interviews

Unlike traditional paradigms, feminist research, with which I identify, attempts to bring together a better fit between theory and practice, illustrated in interviewing techniques that validate women's experiences as women and as people (Aronson 1988; DeVault 1991; Harding 1987; Oakley 1982; Reinharz 1992; Smith 1987; Swigonski 1993; Worell and Etough 1994).

My commitment to these feminist principles resulted in there being considerable verbal interaction between the mothers and myself during the interviews. The interviewing situation was not a one-way process in which I elicited and received, but did not share, information. Influenced by the work of Oakley (1982) and Roberts (1985), I responded to questions about information on the various aspects of the problem of child sexual abuse when I knew the answers. I also answered questions the women asked me about myself and my studies, which usually took place at the end of the interviews. In addition to the exchange of information, all but one of the mothers shared food and beverages with me. One woman insisted I stay and have dinner with her, which I did, and we continued the interview after the meal. Sharing food, drink, and conversation in such an informal manner with the participants differs significantly from methods of data collection in a more conventional or positivist approach, which emphasizes the prediction and control of events and things, rather than understanding subjective experiences. In a conventional research model, emphasis is placed on detachment, a value-free orientation, and being objective, whereas the approach used here encourages the researcher to be involved, have a sense of commitment, to be value-oriented, and acknowledge a subjective orientation. Thus, I appear in my work not as, 'an invisible, anonymous voice of authority, but as a real, historical individual with concrete, specific desires and interests' (Harding 1987, 9).

Most of the interviews with the women took place during weekday evenings and on weekends. The actual interviews with the twenty-four mothers were enjoyable and rewarding experiences that changed my views. In a number of the visits, I felt unsafe both coming and going to where some of these women and their children lived (both public housing and private rentals) and in just being on the premises. I was especially nervous during evening visits when leaving the premises after dark, but sometimes it also felt unsafe during the day. For example, one morning I visited a mother in a public-housing building for an interview. The interior of the building was quite a frightening sight, with its gouged walls, obscene graffiti, and damaged apartment doors. The back stairwell showed signs of drug use, and reeked of urine. Not, I thought, as I walked cautiously through the halls, a place where any woman should have to raise her children in a rich country such as Canada.

During another daytime visit in a high-rise apartment, I experienced such a degree of fear due to an incident with a man on the elevator that it was impossible for me to begin my interview with the participant for at least fifteen minutes after I arrived at her apartment. I shared my obvious discomfort with this woman and she made us a cup of tea, which had a calming effect upon me. I learned later that living in such a place was also frightening for her, and that she was often afraid to allow her daughter to play outside of their own apartment building.

I was introduced to twenty of the thirty-one child-victims in this study and also to a number of their siblings. This took place when the children returned home while I was still there or before bedtime on my evening visits.

Because of the nature of the interview questions, which covered such emotional topics, some women appeared to be noticeably upset during particular parts of the interview. In keeping with the non-coercive method of interviewing (Gilgun 1984), I attempted to give permission for the women to not talk about situations that made them uncomfortable, but most insisted on continuing anyway. In only one instance did a mother remain quiet until I changed the topic to a less sensitive area.

At the end of each interview, I asked the women what it was like for them to be interviewed. Anita Marshall's and Bridget Hesse's (not their real names) quotes illustrate the general feedback in response:

It was fine ... I guess it was sort of an anger release for me ... They [those in decision-making positions] have to understand that the mother is in the middle ... they are getting it from the courts ... from the child ... I don't think people understand ... life doesn't end in a file ... it goes on ... the whole situation was totally devastating for me ...

I guess it's enlightening in a way because ... it brings back what I went through ... because you really don't go back and think it through ... I guess you are too busy dealing with the present ... and I guess it has helped me to get some of my things out that I think are important ... and they should be acted upon ... and it is something to help us mothers ... and we need it.

Research 'for' Women – Interpretation and Analysis

Three of the women who were part of the second in-depth interview phase were asked (because of their availability) to read over the transcribed notes from the taped interviews and decide whether these were an accu-

rate reflection of what they had wanted to convey in the interviews. All
agreed with the content of the notes, and no changes were made.

A grounded theory method (Strauss and Corbin 1990) within a feminist
framework allowed me to understand and interpret the data. Strauss and
Corbin define a grounded theory as: 'one that is inductively derived from
the study of the phenomenon it represents. That is, it is discovered,
developed, and provisionally verified through systematic data collection
and analysis of data pertaining to that phenomenon. Therefore, data
collection, analysis, and theory stand in reciprocal relationship with each
other. One does not begin with a theory, then prove it. Rather, one begins
with an area of study and what is relevant to that area is allowed to emerge'
(1990, 23).

Bogdan and Biklen suggest that, '[d]ata analysis is the process of systematically searching and arranging the interview transcripts, fieldnotes and
other materials that you accumulate to increase your own understanding
of them and enable you to present what you have discovered to others'
(1982, 145).

According to Strauss, this can be partly achieved when 'both the complex interpretations and the data collection are guided by successively
evolving interpretations made during the course of the study' (1987, 10).
Another important aspect in the interpretation process is the conducting
of a very detailed and intensive examination of the data, in order to grasp
the complexity of what lies behind the data (10). Some of my data analysis
took place concurrently with the data collection, but mostly it took place
after the data were in, when there was time for concentration on what I
had collected, and for mulling over ideas. I searched for single or recur-
ring themes, attempted to determine the women's levels of self-revelation,
thought about the complexities upon which decisions were made, and
considered the costs of those decisions psychologically, economically, and
socially to the women.

While I was involved in thinking over the ideas and working with the
data to decide what would become the major focus of analysis and what
would remain in the background, the theme that most stood out was how
mothers were obliged (legally) to turn to various institutions for help in
resolving the problem of their children's victimization; however, when
they did so, they encountered responses that left them feeling almost
solely responsible for the abuse. This was selected as the central theme of
the study.

In her discussion of doing research, Dorothy Smith talks about 'making
sociology for women,' and points out the need for a method that does not

'turn women into objects and produce their lives in abstractions' (1987, 215). Smith presents some of her ideas related to conducting research with women as 'a strategy that takes as central that women should speak from themselves and their own experience and that the comments of their oppression are to be discovered in a discourse that can expand their grasp of their experience and the power of their speech by disclosing the relations organizing their oppression (215).

The women in this study were willing to speak in considerable detail about their experiences of their children's disclosures of sexual abuse and the relations that organized their oppressions. One might ask: How can such a method provide anything but a one-sided view of the event? And, why would it not be assumed that mothers might be dishonest about their own behaviour in responding to the disclosure events? The answer is that we cannot be certain. Given existing related research, however, it has been found that women are more willing to explore their own actions than are men (Dobash and Dobash 1979; Herman and Hirschman 1982; Kelly 1988b; Russell 1986).

Dobash and Dobash conducted 109 interviews with women residing in refuges for battered women in Edinburgh and Glasgow, and found that the women did not fail to note their own behaviours relating to violent episodes with their partners. Many of the women in my study were helped to recognize that they were blaming themselves, since the widespread tendency is for society to make mothers feel responsible for their children's sexual abuse.

Swigonski argues that feminist researchers must take marginalized and oppressed groups 'out of the margins and place their day-to-day reality in the centre of the research' (1993, 172). The mothers' voices are moved out of the margins and made central in this study.

Oakley suggests that, 'the goal of finding out about people is best achieved when the interviewer is prepared to invest his or her own personal identity in the relationship' (1982, 41). Moreover, Stanley and Wise argue 'that the researcher's own experiences and consciousness will be involved in the research process as much as they are in life, ... all research must be concerned with the experiences and consciousness of the researcher as an integral part of this research process' (1983, 48).

My 'point of entry' (Smith 1987) in this study involved my experiences not only as a mother, but also as a professional social worker for more than twenty years in child welfare. I am familiar with 'mainstream' literature and have grown increasingly aware of how state policies and practices, informed by family ideology, shape services to women and children. The state mandate to protect children frequently involves us in adversarial relations with mothers in which they are blamed for failure to care properly for their children. Some feminist scholars argue that child neglect should be eliminated as a child-welfare category, since we, as professionals, spend more time policing mothers than we do providing services to them (Callahan 1993; Swift 1995). In reality, some children are placed in the state's care not because of inadequate maternal care but because of the lack of appropriate housing, which is more of a commentary on how our economic and social priorities are structured than it is on adequate 'mothering.' A recent survey shows that in 18.4 per cent of the cases of a large child welfare agency, the family's lack of adequate housing was one of the factors that resulted in placement of the children (Cohen-Schlanger et al. 1995). The consequences of such actions against women by child-welfare workers who are themselves women (in the majority of cases) can be devastating for those women whose children are targeted, but can also negatively affect men.

During the interviews with the twenty-four women, I identified myself as a mother and a woman who is fully aware of oppressive experiences not only as a professional, but also from my own personal life experiences. I recall as a young child seeing adult men exposing their genitals, as I'm sure many other girls who grew up in my era did. Such sights were part of the landscape during my daily walks to and from school through a park with many bushes. Today these same events would have been considered sexual exploitation of children and criminal investigations would be instigated. No such action was taken in the 1940s. Sharing some of my personal information during the interviews, as suggested by Oakley (1982) when appropriate, seemed to increase the comfort level of the women. My own mother raised seven children under extremely difficult circumstances, and having been the youngest of this large working-class family, I have vivid memories of how burdened my mother was living with a violent husband and how responsible she felt for every problem that developed within our family. More important, I remember how she coped and how she endured during those difficult years. I feel that such experiences in my own life have increased my understanding and empathy of the lives of women and children who are victims of male violence.

In the transcribing of the women's stories in this study, I attempted to keep their meaning and sound alive by not editing their language, and by using punctuation that would reflect their emphasis. On occasion, I went back to the tapes and listened to the women's voices again and again to pick up the subtleties and nuances.

Some Strengths and Weaknesses of This Study

Babbie (1983) discusses the strengths and weaknesses of qualitative research and suggests that, compared to other approaches, qualitative research generally has more validity but less reliability and cannot be generalized as safely as that based on rigorous sampling and standardized questionnaires. Since I did obtain data from a number of sources (twenty-four women, fifteen key informants, and twenty-two agency records), this triangulation of data sources increased the validity of my study (Olesen 1994). The participants interviewed for this study were self-selected, however, and not randomly selected, and therefore do not constitute a representative sample. The results cannot be generalized, but the analysis can be transferred to other cases or situations (if others choose to do so), as I have provided thick descriptions of rich data (Guba and Lincoln 1989).

The focus of this study was to get a full and in-depth view of the women's' subjective experiences and to reach a comprehensive understanding of their lives after disclosure, rather than to be able to make general statements about a large population (although I do not believe these women are remarkably different from other women whose children have been victims of sexual abuse). The qualitative approach and feminist framework have been particularly appropriate to use for this study.

Historically, women's experiences were never taken into account or considered as an important part of the knowledge base, therefore, such experiences not only constitute legitimate knowledge but crucial knowledge that is needed to counterbalance the existing traditional male perspective of women's experiences (Eichler and Lapointe 1985; Reinharz 1992; Smith 1987; Spender 1985).

3

Literature Review of Relevant Concepts

The meaning of motherhood has usually been interpreted by societal institutions which, as far as we know have always been under male authority. (Barbara Christian 1994, 95).

Motherhood, if conceived as a taken-for-granted dimension of women's normal adult role, becomes one of the key sources of women's oppression. (Gimenez 1984, 287).

Motherhood

What is the connection between an understanding of motherhood from a mainstream perspective and an understanding of motherhood from an alternative perspective?

I have chosen to divide the literature in this way in order to provide a framework for critiquing the relevant literature for this study. 'Mainstream literature,' for purposes of this work, is taken from the common under-standing of the word: the dominant opinion expressed in the dominant journals and textbooks on the subject by recognized experts. Alternative perspective is defined here as that literature that represents the views of those other than mainstream views. I include here feminist literature and a body of literature that is considered pro-feminist because it is the work of men or women who would not necessarily consider themselves feminists, but still assert that women are in an unequal position in our society and that this situation must change. Neither of these perspectives frees women from the all-powerful myth that there is such a thing as a 'perfect' mother. Our cultural ideology has continued to idealize and blame mothers. The differences between the two perspectives lies in the degree of understanding of a woman's role as a mother.

This chapter attempts to illustrate how mainstream literature (especially the early material) views a woman's role as one that should be totally devoted to the nurturing of children and a husband, with her own wishes for growth and development subordinated to what is deemed her most important focus in life. Alternative perspectives, on the other hand, demonstrate a greater recognition and understanding of the struggles faced by women in their roles as mothers and caregivers in society. Feminist scholars include in their analysis a structural view of motherhood that points out the tremendous burden placed on women to do motherwork, and the need to encourage men to nurture their children.

Mainstream perspectives continue to expect women to provide all of the caregiving in the family. This is totally unrealistic, given the number of women in the paid workforce. Alternative perspectives challenge the state and public and professional views on such expectations. Indeed, the critiques go all the way from advising women not to bear children, to demanding more recognition and celebration of childbirth, to suggestions that fathers take over one-half of the nurturing role of the children, to the notion that men are currently inadequately prepared for the role of nurturing children.[1]

The experience of mothering itself does not necessarily provide a full understanding of the concept of motherhood. To gain some insight into the social construction of motherhood, it is necessary to examine the historical context in which various theories on motherhood were developed. This changing concept differs depending upon the particular period in history, culture, socio-economic class, and/or gender of those articulating the ideology.

This literature review, then, tracks the concept of motherhood by dividing the literature into mainstream and alternative views, and considers the work of several well-recognized proponents for each on the subject.

My entry point is the period when particular theories about motherhood were first articulated and certain practices of mothering became higher profile for privileged families.

Brief History of Mainstream Views

Jean-Jacques Rousseau, who helped inspire the Romantic movement and the French Revolution, lost his own mother within a week of his birth and was 'mothered' by his aunt (Durant and Durant 1967, 5). Rousseau, held strong views on 'motherhood,' and also on how women should be taught to be good wives and mothers. Many of his theories on women's roles are expressed in *Emile*, written in 1762. 'The sole destiny that Rousseau accords to women is that of wife and mother' (Misenheimer 1981, 51). The following quote from his work illustrates his philosophy of women in their dual roles of mother and wife:

Thus the whole education of women ought to relate to men. To please men, to be useful to them, to make herself loved and honored by them, to raise them when young, to care for them when grown, to counsel them, to console them, to make their lives agreeable and sweet – these are the duties of women at all times, and they ought to be taught from childhood. (Rousseau 1979, Book V, 365).

According to Durant and Durant (1967), Rousseau's ideas have had more effect upon posterity than those of any other writer or thinker in the eighteenth century. Badinter's research (1981) shows that Rousseau's theories of motherhood were referred to until the beginning of the First World War. This idealized biological vision of motherhood influenced writers and philosophers of that pre-war period who set the moral tone for society.[2]

Badinter (1981) examined the nature of the relationship between mother and child in historical and literary documents. She argues that prior to the influence of Rousseau, 'mother love' was not a social and moral value of society. This is not to say that there were not loving mothers at the time, only that 'motherhood' was not a social convention that received particular notice or generated guilt for those women who did not adhere to a particular code of behaviour with their children.

Prior to the Industrial Revolution, there was little question about what women were doing in the home, eighteenth- and early-nineteenth-century rural women were making soap, candles, cloth, butter, preserves, beer, and cider, in addition they were caring for dairy cattle, breeding poultry, butchering livestock, operating wool carders and spinning wheels, and making medicines from herbs to heal their family members. At that time, there was no marking off of life into work/home, public/private; however, authority over the family was still vested in males (Badinter 1981; Ehrenreich and English 1979).

During the Industrial Revolution in the early nineteenth century, much of traditional women's labour was moved into factories. Sociologists reported that about four-fifths of the industrial processes carried out in the average American home was never to return after the Industrial Revolution, and the growth of the market economy. The industrial world no longer honoured women's traditional skills. Little by little wage labour and business replaced agriculture as the main way of life, and men became associated with the public realm and work outside the home, while women remained at home in the private realm. The dominant ideology at the time defined women as 'other,' while the home was seen as a refuge from the marketplace world of men. This ideology was known as sexual-romanticism and served the needs of the developing economy very well (Ehrenreich and English 1979).

Scientific theories began to replace earlier theories about motherhood. The dominant thinking about motherhood during that period was more in keeping with the industrial age, that is, with an emphasis on efficiency and the scientific method. The biological sciences became prominent in the 1870s and 1880s with Darwin's evolution theory. Between 1880 and 1920 the scientific method dominated medicine, management, public administration, housekeeping and child-rearing. Although women had previously been the traditional healers and mid-wives in the community they gradually lost that role, and by 1847 trained male doctors banded together to form the first national organization: the American Medical Association (Ehrenreich and English 1979).

By the turn of the twentieth century, women began to organize various clubs of their own. They wanted a new vision of the romantic ideal and, ironically that new vision became the housewife. Housework was made into a science between the late 1890s and before the 1920s. The keynote speaker at a 1897 meeting of Women's Suffrage Association focused on domestic science and the germ theory of disease; twenty years later, domestic science was incorporated into the public high-school curricula (Ehrenreich and English 1979).

The twentieth century became the century of the child with the first White House Conference on the Care of Dependent Children being held in 1909. The Conference delegates declared that home life was the best for children (Ehrenreich and English 1979).

In the 1920s and 1930s, we see the rise of psychoanalytic theory, and mothers had new child-rearing 'experts' from psychology and medicine to advise them on how to raise model children. Christopher Lasch (1979) argues that 'the helping professions' appropriated parental functions from about 1900 to the 1930s.

John Watson, a leading psychologist of that period, suggests in his *Psychological Care of the Infant and Child* that mothers should treat children like little adults. Watson discourages any emotional exchange between the mother and child and advises that although they should be kind and firm with their children, they should 'never hug or kiss them' (1928, 81–2).[3]

Maternal instinct was no longer considered acceptable as providing a practical guide to mothering. Compulsory education was a major influence on motherwork during this period. Education became the main vehicle for getting the new vision of 'motherhood' across to women through government pamphlets, family physicians, settlement houses, and so on (Ehrenreich and English 1979). This cognitive-educational approach differs from that of Rousseau as he supported biological theories that held that mothering was instinctual, and that all women are born with the knowledge of how to mother their children. Rousseau was also a moral reformer in terms of using education for female children to prepare them for what he saw as their natural duty. Girls were not to be educated in the same manner as boys according to his writings. It should be noted that Rousseau's message was directed to prominent families of the eighteenth century. The majority of mothers, at that time, were living in rural areas and were generally illiterate and therefore Rousseau's philosophy would have had little impact on their lives, since there were no organized physicians, social workers, media, or government bureaucracies to get the new vision of motherhood to the masses, as in the early twentieth century.

The influence of Sigmund Freud and his followers, cannot be underestimated in examining the next shift in the conceptualization of motherhood (A. Freud 1981). Although psychoanalytic influences contributed to focusing attention on mothers, giving them a central role in family life, these influences also established standards for judging 'good' and 'bad' mothers. We are now back to the notion of 'motherhood' as biological instinct. We see here the beginnings of 'motherhood as pathology' (Badinter 1981; Caplan 1984; Ehreneich and English 1979; Masson 1984).

The psychoanalysts following Freud began the process of breaking down maternal integrity even further and contributing to the 'no-win situation' of women through psychoanalytic theories about the development of the female personality. Natural maternal instincts soon became the focus of the specialists on mothering, such as Helen Deutsch, Melanie Kline, David Levy, and Rene Spitz.

This shift towards a new idea or notion of motherhood implied that if women did not perform their maternal role in line with psychoanalytic theory (i.e., the accepting mother rather than the rejecting mother or the overprotecting mother), then they were said to have defective instincts. The dilemma for women, according to Ehrenreich and English, was that if anything should go awry in the mother-child relationship or in the child's development, the finger of blame would no longer point at mother's faulty technique, but at her 'defective instincts' (1979, 226).

The notion of blame changed over time. Childhood disorders began to be traced to disorders of the mother and to mothering, and we see the focus on child rearing becoming more permissive. The popularity of Dr Benjamin Spock's (1957) and Dr D.W. Winnicott's (1957) best-selling books on how to raise healthy babies and children encouraged mothers to rely on their ordinary and 'natural' maternal sense.

For purposes of this review, the early work of Spock and Winnicott fits solidly into mainstream thinking because it embodies many assumptions and values widely held by the dominant society. Their manuals on child care were world-famous best-sellers. In the later part of his life (the mid-1960s until his death in 1998), Dr Benjamin Spock had developed alternative views about governments, the environment, and child-rearing, and, considered himself a pro-feminist. Spock was often criticized for what was referred to as his permissive attitude, since he presented an ambiguous and incomplete point of view regarding child discipline (Gordon 1974). Male theorists such as Winnicott (1957) and Bowlby (1963) ignored the mother's involvement outside her infant relationship (Chodorow 1978) and did not deal with parenting as a joint arrangement but expressed a fairly rigid sex-role conception of mother as the one who was to be continuously and intimately involved with the child (Rapoport, Rapoport, and Strelitz 1977).

Both Erik Erikson (1963) and John Bowlby (1963) manage to place mothers in the role of 'villain' in their theories of child development. Erikson's discussion on 'Mom' illustrates this: 'Mom is a woman in whose life cycle remnants of infantility join advanced senility to crowd out the middle range of mature womanhood, which thus becomes self-absorbed and stagnant' (291). Erikson's view of women can only be termed misogynist. Bowlby's work on rejection, as well as that of Joseph Rheingold (1964), describes a type of maternal destructiveness that provides the basis for 'maternal deprivation' theories, which were a 'scientific' form of mother-blaming.

Dr Burton L. White (1975), an American expert on the development of human intelligence and director of the Centre for Parent Education, talks about the learning and development process in the first three years of a child's life and assumes the total availability of the mother during this period of time. White argues that effective mothers are available to their children so they can react to their child's behaviour immediately. This discounts the participation of women in the workforce. He also implies that mothers should ignore their own needs and priorities when they arise and see to their child's needs immediately.

British psychologist Penelope Leach's recent book, *Children First* (1994), has a similar message to White's (1975). She states that mothers can be architects of perfect children, but it is critical that fathers make the home emotionally safe for mothers and babies. Like earlier mainstream experts, Leach perpetuates a stereotype of the mother which is rigid and constricting. Her analysis about how women, and in particular mothers, arrived at their current valueless location in society betrays her naivety as she suggests that '*accidents* of history have produced inequity for women not biological gender differences' (33–4, emphasis added).

I do support Leach's concern for the future of our children, whom she describes as 'not just failing in schools but terrorizing them' (xii). Her solutions, however, are totally unrealistic for women. Leach's solution for mothers being the architects of perfect children rests on the need for fathers to make the home emotionally safe. The reality, however, is sometimes very different. If there is anything we know from empirical evidence, is that many fathers have not been providers of emotional safety and protectors, but have beaten and terrorized their wives and children.

Leach argues that we should be trying to have femaleness validated in society instead of having women escape traditional female roles only to find themselves taking on traditional male roles and looking to the career world for focus and fulfilment. In short, Leach emphasizes biologically based differences between men and women. Like White, Leach encourages mothers to be available on a continuing basis for the first year of the new baby's life and not to place their babies in daycare. She does, however, suggest that 'older babies and toddlers do not need their mothers every minute' (1994, 83). Nurseries and daycare centres are not suitable in Leach's estimation because babies need one-to-one attention their first year for optimal development, and they are unable to receive such care in those types of facilities.

Without question, Leach is an excellent advocate for children in her stance against corporal punishment, where she states clearly 'there should be no punishment against children if it seen as the deliberate infliction of pain, physical or mental' (129); in her insistence that those in decision-making positions in governments must take action to eradicate child poverty; and, in her commitment to placing a high priority on the rights of children as Human Rights. Her views on women and gender equality, and on alternative types of families, however, are less admirable from this writer's point of view. Leach maintains that women who choose to remain childless, or delay or limit their childbearing, are giving in to an illusion of equal opportunities. For her, 'Being a mother is not less than male but uniquely, splendidly female' (40), while father's maleness makes him wonderful for a baby as 'he is a man fulfilling the exclusively male role of father' (46). Leach goes on to say that 'father is bigger (maybe), gruffer (certainly), different to feel and smell (always); because he is different.' She suggests that 'fathers really do not have to feel hurt if babies they have been playing with all afternoon cry for their mothers as they tire towards bedtime. That is part of what mothers are for' (46). She sees differences between women and men in parenting not just inevitable but positively desirable, and suggest that 'mothers or caregivers really do not have to feel hurt if the toddlers they have cared for and companioned all day abandon them the moment fathers come home. That is part of what fathers are for' (47).

Leach holds that every child needs both a mother and father and although extra mothering will help, it will not make up for lack of fathering. She regards it as normal and ideal for children to grow up with both their natural parents.

I clearly support Eichler's argument that 'emphasizing the biological differences between mothers and fathers has been a hallmark of many, if not most, attempts to support sex discrimination' (1997, 83). Leach's views on what she terms 'normal' and 'natural' parents could certainly be interpreted as a heterosexist bias.

These discourses on women, mothers, and motherhood have provided the major theoretical training for social workers and caseworkers. In agency casenotes, mothers are described as 'cold,' 'rejecting,' 'unresponsive,' and 'unloving' to their children more frequently than they are labeled 'warm,' 'loving,' and 'responsive.' This is partly due to the problem-oriented nature of the work, of course, but it is also a function of their training about mothers, which stresses individual casework and fails to address the material, structural conditions. While many factors enter into the relationships that workers establish with mothers, the knowledge base that informs their theory and practice about mothers, motherhood, and the larger social and economic system are critical factors affecting the type and focus of service women receive from these workers. The particular knowledge base described here from mainstream literature would tend to encourage dividing mothers into good/bad, warm/cold, and rejecting/accepting, with little analysis of structural problems faced by women in the real world.

Alternative Views on Motherhood

Over the past twenty years, feminist scholars have examined, researched, and analysed the questions of motherhood, mothering, maternal thought and behaviour and love. The work of Jessica Benjamin, Jessie Bernard, Jean Baker Miller, Carol Gilligan, Adrienne Rich, Nancy Chodorow, Anne Oakley, Barbara Ehrenreich, Deirdre English, Mary O'Brien, Elisabeth Badinter, and Helen Levine, to name a few, have addressed various aspects of motherhood mothering and mother love. Some of their views are discussed in this section.

More recently, a group of female psychologists, psychiatrists, and clinical social workers have been publishing their work from the Stone Center for Developmental Services and Studies at Wellesley College in Massachusetts on self-in-relation theory, or a relational approach based on their clinical experiences with women in treatment (Jordan et al. 1991; Surrey 1991; Miller 1994; Jordan 1995, 1997). Within this approach, the developmental goal for women is seen as an increased ability to build and maintain mutually enhancing relationships that will improve feelings of self worth and increase their personal agency in society. The Stone Center is known for its belief that women (unlike men) are deeply motivated to be connected and empathic with others and that this important skill is learned early through the mother-daughter interaction and bond. The work of the Stone Center has been criticized for praising women's relational abilities and failing to emphasize other areas of self-development such as agency, competence, and initiative (Benjamin 1992; Westkott 1997).

One belief that the aforementioned feminist authors share is that women's lives should not be defined or constrained by virtue of motherhood alone. Women should have choices regarding marriage, children, and career. Any or all of these choices should be seen as acceptable, recognized, respected, and legitimized by the state, with the appropriate infrastructure in place to support them.

De Beauvoir (1953) pointed out that caring is the category through which one sex is differentiated from the other. In our Western culture, being a doctor, an architect, or a judge is considered an important position in life, but being a 'mother' (one who cares for children) is not. Graham (1983) argues that it is difficult to categorize and qualify the components of mothering or caring and reduce them to a labour process because of their psychological affinity with femininity, and also because care typically involves looking after a loved one.

Baines et al. (1991) argue that a feminist approach to caring includes an analysis of the ideological context, since that is what shapes the relationship between those being cared for and those providing the caring. The authors emphasize the importance of developing strategies that will allow women to have choices and control over their own lives.

Chodorow (1978) argues through a psychoanalytic approach that the mothering role is produced through the dynamics of the mother-daughter relationship. In other words, 'women as mothers, produce daughters with mothering capacities and the desire to mother. These capacities and needs are built into and grow out of the mother-daughter relationship itself' (7). Chodorow goes on to say that mothers produce sons whose capacities to nurture are both curtailed and repressed systematically. This type of mothering (in the Western world) contributes to sexual inequality because of its effects on masculine personalities.

Bart, in her review (1983) of Chodorow's work, argues that she contributes to a further mystification of the female experience, rather than a demystification, which is the real goal of feminist scholarship. She further suggests that Chodorow's analysis reinforces the mother-blaming for which psychoanalytic theory is notorious (i.e., the male's inability to nurture is blamed on early socialization by mothers).

Jean Baker Miller's (1977) work suggests that it is through women's subordinate position that they develop the necessary psychological predisposition to provide for the caregiving in society. She argues that in order to survive in a patriarchal society, women have had to learn specific qualities, such as sensitivity, cooperation, and adaption and conformity to the wishes of those in power positions in the patriarchal order. Although these 'nurturing' qualities are devalued in our society, Baker Miller argues that these are the best qualities on which to build a more humane society.

Gilligan's (1982) research identifies a clearer representation of the development of women with respect to their moral development and identity formation. She examined those qualities previously labelled women's weaknesses and reframed them as human strengths.

Another important issue discussed in the feminist literature is not only blaming, but also the idealization of mothers. The traditional icons of motherhood, such as the images of the Madonna and Child, are no longer held in the same spirit of reverence in what is now considered a more secular society (Oakley 1981; Rabuzzi 1988). No longer is the institution of motherhood considered a sacred calling. The ideology of the 'perfect' mother, however, is still very much with us. Paradoxically, much of the feminist literature is similar to that of mainstream literature in its 'women-hating' and 'mother-glorifying' stance, according to Chodorow and Contratto (1982). In their analysis of 'the fantasy of the perfect mother,' the authors suggest that idealization and blaming the mother have become our cultural ideology, and are two sides of the same belief. The belief is that mothers are all powerful.

Rich in *Of Woman Born: Motherhood as Experience and Institution* (1986) suggests in her analysis that perhaps maternal perfection would emerge if we could overthrow the patriarchy; Flax (1978) points out the difficulties women face as mothers in a male-dominated society; Oakley (1981) suggests that the glorification of motherhood is probably the most important aspect of capitalist ideologies of femininity, as it justifies the restriction of women to the home and to mothering; Rossi (1973) argues that if mothers' pleasures were not interfered with by various factors, such as doctor-centred management, then it might be possible for mothers to fulfil their roles. These types of analyses, according to Chodorow and Contratto (1982), continue to perpetuate the myth that a 'perfect mother' is a possibility. Their analyses suggest that the problem is rooted in the 'unprocessed infantile fantasies about mothers.' The authors explain that growing up means appreciating mother's separateness, but that people have trouble doing this for two reasons: because the ideology condones and supports such notions about mothers; and because we are usually all mothered by one woman exclusively.

Chodorow and Contratto also point out that a theory of mothering requires theories of childhood and child development and that perhaps the child's 'felt desires' are not 'absolute needs' and might, in fact, represent unreasonable expectations from the caregiver. This suggestion seems to provide a far more flexible attitude towards child care and mothering than that previously mentioned in the mainstream literature by White (1975) and Leach (1994).

Chodorow (1978) points out that research suggests that children do not need the exclusive relationship of one person, but a small number of people in a stable relationship over time. The literature suggests that a revolutionary process must occur whereby men take on every aspect of child care and thereby truly share the parenting of children, as there are serious consequences of women providing exclusive mothering; consequences which affect children, men, and women themselves (Chodorow 1978; Oakley 1981, Ruddick 1982; Baker Miller 1977; Dinnerstein 1977). Other feminist scholars would suggest serious consequences of this proposed revolution of men 'mothering' children. They describe men as currently inadequate for the task of nurturing children (Bart 1983; Rich 1986; Westkott 1978).

Other important themes that appear in the feminist literature include the link made by some authors between motherhood and aggression. Some women say that they love their children, but they hate motherhood (Bernard 1974), not only because motherhood is so devalued in our society, but also because it is hard work and creates a great deal of depression and isolation in women's lives (Levine and Estable 1983).

In the work of Friday (1977), mothers are blamed for just about everything. According to Arcana (1979), the evil is in the patriarchy more than in mothers. In Dinnerstein's work (1977), mother is portrayed as the child's adversary and is the object of children's fury. The aggression theme is found in Rich's (1986) work where a depressed mother decapitates her two youngest children, and in Millett (1979) where a mother of seven children tortures a sixteen-year-old girl (the victim-mother creates a victim-child). Rich and Millett both describe maternal burdens and the subsequent aggression that sometimes results from such unsupported motherwork yet, according to Chodorow and Contratto, they do not condemn the aggression and violence in their own writing.

Another important discussion in the literature centres around maternal sexuality or asexuality. Firestone (1970) and Friday (1977) imply a split between motherhood and sexuality, while other feminists identify motherhood with sexuality. Firestone's view is that pregnant bodies are ugly and that motherhood is not at all compatible with sexuality. But Chodorow and Contratto suggest that such attitudes replicate those in the traditional clinical literature, which do not view the total woman positively. This contributes to the 'woman-hating' images prevalent in society.

Firestone (1970) argues that the very act of bearing children is at the basis of women's oppression, since it leads to the sexual division of labour. This view is not shared by other feminist scholars such as Chodorow (1978), O'Brien (1983), Baker Miller (1977), and Ruddick (1982). Rabuzzi (1988) considers it deplorable that only those women who engage in careers and relinquish motherhood are seen to be leading worthwhile and liberated lives. She argues that this viewpoint is as problematic for women as the patriarchal viewpoint, and that women should be able to have a range of choices in their lives.

In their critique, Chodorow and Contratto argue that there is a need to recognize mothers as women, and to respect the complexities in their lives, since women are also daughters, wives, and persons in their own right. The authors suggest that the overemphasis on the 'perfect mother' and on the early mother-infant relationship has led to a psychological determinism and reductionism in research since the work on bonding theories became prominent in the early 1950s, as if this early infant bonding is going to determine the whole history of society and our culture, and that failure of a child to bond to his/her mother is tantamount to abuse.

Mary O'Brien focuses on the lack of recognition and celebration of child birth and motherhood in our culture. She sees motherhood as 'despised, derided and neglected' (1983, 8), and points out that little attention has been given to a philosophy of birth.

A considerable literature has been developing on lesbian mothers over the past decade. Although lesbian mothers first came to the public attention during custody court battles over children conceived within heterosexual relationships, lesbians are now choosing parenthood by means of alternative insemination, adoption, and other options (Arnup 1995). 'These women resist restrictive definitions of family, motherhood and womanhood' (Boyd, quoted on back cover of Arnup 1995). Same-sex relationships in the growing number of alternative families (both lesbian mothers and gay fathers) promise to challenge the whole notion of motherhood.

In summary, prevailing alternative (feminist) views about motherhood include notions of women having free choices about motherhood and access to the type of concrete support services that would make motherhood a reasonable choice. Motherhood themes in the feminist literature include mother-hating and mother-glorifying; maternal sexuality and asexuality; the aggression theme; the process and politics of reproduction; the complexity of separating out the components of labour and care for a loved one; the mothering role as produced through the dynamics of the mother-daughter relationship; males socialized as non-nurturers; the female personality structure as the superior model for a more humane world; and lesbian mothering. The alternative literature thus provides a diversity of views on motherhood and mothering.

Next, I turn to an examination of two other central concepts important to the understanding of why mothers are blamed for the sexual abuse of their children: the concept of blame, and the ideology of the family.

The Concept of Blame

Rothman (1994) argues that motherhood is based on three deeply rooted ideologies that shape not only what we see, but what we experience: an ideology of patriarchy, an ideology of technology, and an ideology of capitalism. These are (briefly) explained as follows: 'motherhood in a patriarchal society is what mothers and babies signify to men. For women this could mean too many pregnancies or too few; trying again for a son ... The ideology of technology encourages us to see ourselves as objects; to see people as made up of machines ... Application has occurred in the medicalization of pregnancy and of child-birth' (140, 144).

The ideology of capitalism, that goods are produced for profit, is applied by the author to motherhood and to children (with children as commodities), since the family has always been an economic unit as well as a social and psychological one. Keeping in mind, then, mainstream and alternative views of motherhood as set out in the previous section of this chapter, as well as Rothman's three central threads that shape motherhood, this chapter moves on to examine a central concept that heavily influences our practice, theory, and research with respect to mothers and child sexual abuse.

The *Merriam-Webster Dictionary* defines blame in the following way: 'to find fault with; to speak ill of; to revile; to attribute responsibility to; to express disapproval of.' The reader is instructed to see synonyms for blameless under 'perfect.'

In the section on 'motherhood,' it became clear that part of the problem with theories developed about mothers and mothering is the notion of the 'perfect' mother. This form of idealization is found in both mainstream and alternative literature. With such unrealistic beliefs about mothers so deeply entrenched in our culture and in our conscious and unconscious minds, it is not surprising that mothers are singled out for blame if they don't measure up – and, of course, they cannot measure up, as it is not possible for any human being to be perfect.

As discussed in the previous section, since the idealization of mothers can be considered an infantile fantasy, it is not appropriate that fantasy material or unexamined notions about childhood development should inform theory or practice. As we have seen, however, feminist scholars have been trapped in the assumptions of the dominant culture so that while anti-feminists blame mothers, some feminists blame motherhood, the child, and having children as the problem (Chodorow and Contratto 1982).

As defined above, to blame someone is to attribute responsibility to them. Individuals often attempt to explain events that happen to them in their everyday lives, especially when they are important or unexpected events, such as the disclosure of child sexual abuse. The explanations described are what Weiner (1986) calls causal attributions. He argues that they have a direct effect upon that individual's subsequent cognitions, emotions, and behaviours. Weiner's attribution theory classifies all attributions into three distinct categories: (1) causes that are considered internal to the individual, such as abilities, or those external to the person that might be explained as chance or fate; (2) causes that are influenced by the person (i.e., controllable), or by other uncontrollable factors; (3) causes that are either stable (i.e., personality traits) or unstable (i.e., amount of effort). Weiner's theory argues that these three dimensions can potentially change an individual's beliefs and therefore the behaviours associated with a particular event in their lives.

Although the alternative literature noted previously described a much broader concept of motherhood and mothering than did the mainstream, both perspectives hold to the notion of the perfect mother. Since the concept of blame is a social construct constituted by the imputation of meanings to various observed or experienced situations, it has implications for those so labelled. One major consequence of being blamed is that it changes one's social status and self-concept. In other words, because mothers are blamed for much of what goes wrong with children, they are reviled by others in society.

To use Weiner's theory, the manner in which professionals, governments, and the public have defined the laws, policies, and practices with respect to child sexual abuse gives the impression that it is an event that is controllable by mothers, connected with her internal abilities, and that protection of children can be achieved by the amount of effort expended by those responsible for the child (mothers). In Chapter 10, I discuss how the women themselves tried to explain why their children were sexually abused.

Paula Caplan, in *Don't Blame Mother* (1989), discusses a study that was conducted with 121 women on their own opinions of their mothers. Only eight women saw their own mothers as admirable models to be emulated. Although this is a sad commentary on our collective opinion of mothering and mothers, it might be argued that it stems from the experience of female children reared in homes where they witness the subordination of their mothers by their fathers. The author documents more than anecdotes about the undervaluing of mothers. She produces facts, such as a U.S. department of labor's skill-level rating, where, on a scale of 1 to 887, the level of a homemaker, child-care attendant, or nursery-school teacher is rated at 878, while a dog trainer is placed at 228 (40). The mistaken notion that mothering tasks require no skills gets reproduced in the formal organization of the government's pay scales, and the consequences for women are not only inadequate recognition for their work, but also limited financial income for those who choose motherwork jobs in the paid workforce. It also brings into focus the low priority placed on children in our society by those in decision-making positions.

Caplan makes the point that along with support for mother-blaming is a taboo against father-blaming. Our cultural myths have been consciously or unconsciously constructed to set mothers up to be blamed and to avoid blaming fathers within the family context.

Caplan argues that fathers are not blamed for their children's problems the way mothers are blamed. Although fathers are preoccupied with their work, they do want the approval and respect of their children. On the other hand, mothers, in their caregiving role, are expected to be the enforcers, and most people resent those who impose rules. As the author points out, 'when you don't have the major responsibility for someone's behaviour, you can afford to be more lax about discipline' (1989, 73); therefore, fathers are seen by their children as more lenient, and as the ones who treat them better. This does not rule out those cases where fathers are the day-to-day disciplinarians in the family, but such cases are in the minority. In her discussion about mending the mother-daughter relationship, Caplan mentions nine myths about mothers which she attempts to debunk. The first four myths are about the 'Angel' or perfect mother and the remaining five are about the 'Witch' or bad mother. The first four myths set up standards that no mother could achieve, while the last five exaggerate our mother's real faults.

1. The measure of a good mother is a perfect [child]
2. Mothers are endless founts of nurturance
3. Mothers naturally know how to raise children
4. Mothers don't get angry
5. Mothers are inferior to fathers
6. Mothers need expert advice to raise healthy children
7. Mothers are bottomless pits of neediness
8. Mother-daughter closeness is unhealthy
9. Mothers are dangerous when they're powerful. (1989, 70, 96)

These nine myths are familiar to most of us. Paradoxically, we have been indoctrinated with some of these myths by our own mothers, and they appear to be part of the fabric of our whole culture. These notions are reproduced in the schoolroom, the church, the news media, and in most institutions, such as child welfare, the medical system, and the court system. Caplan helps to destroy some of these myths, and at the same time attempts to teach women how to more fully accept and value their own mothers and thus themselves. Caplan makes visible some of the social attitudes at the basis of mother blaming.

Marjorie DeVault in her book *Feeding the Family* (1991), discusses why women continue to accept their subordinate role; why they continue to take responsibility for the invisible work of planning, shopping, cooking, and serving meals for their families; how their work is never done; and how they struggle in silence with these roles. She argues that we will need to explore further how the experiences and consequences of caring are structured through race and class as well as gender relations.

Ruddick, in her discussion of mother-blame (1982), argues that maternal thinking becomes contradictory; in other words, such thinking betrays its own interest in the growth of the child. Mothers neither shape nor control the policies under which their children are raised. Their own values do not count, but rather they adhere to the values of the dominant culture. For a woman, being defined by a male-dominated society as subordinate means that the values of being obedient and 'good' are to be endorsed. This may mean training daughters for future powerlessness and sons for war or dehumanizing types of work. This is clearly an insupportable position if it were at the conscious level, but Ruddick suggests it is not. Given the damaging effects of 'prevailing sexual arrangements and social hierarchies on maternal lives,' she finds it, 'clearly outrageous to blame mothers for their obedience ... [since] obedience is largely a function of social powerlessness' (85).

According to Levine and Estable, 'guilt comes home from the hospital with the baby, along with many other emotions' (1983, 31). The authors go on to say that because mothers are made aware early in their lives of their central responsibility for children, they are constantly evaluating their own performance, but their goals are unreachable and what has been established is 'an unworkable job description. Knowing that others blame us, we in turn blame ourselves' (31).

Part of the problem as identified by the above authors is that most of the experts on childhood and the family are males who have the least direct experience in mothering themselves.

Caplan and Hall-McCorquodale researched mother-blaming by mental-health professionals, such as psychoanalysts, psychologists, psychiatrists, and social workers. They examined 125 articles in scholarly journals, published in 1970, 1976, and 1982, and found that regardless of the gender or occupation, all of the mental-health professionals were engaged in mother-blaming. Seventy-two different kinds of problems, ranging from bedwetting to schizophrenia in children, were blamed on mothers (1985, 47).

One area where mother-blame appears to be quite prevalent is in the area of child sexual abuse. Research in this area most closely related to my own includes the work of Dempster 1992; Heriot 1991; Hooper 1989, 1992; Johnson 1992; Krane 1990, 1994; and Myer 1984. All these studies conclude that mother-blaming persists into the 1980s and 1990s.[4] Three studies are selected for closer examination here, two British (Dempster and Hooper) and one American (Johnson).

Janis Tyler Johnson, in *Mothers of Incest Survivors* (1992), interviewed six mothers of female children who were victims of incest.

She had worked as a social worker in the area of public child welfare for a number of years and therefore had professional and personal contacts within that system in several nearby communities. She anticipated locating twenty incest-family mothers to interview through referrals from her colleagues. She also contacted (by letter) rape crisis units, abused women's shelters, the YWCA, and the local Planned Parenthood office. In addition, she placed an article in her local daily newspaper, and in various newsletters of women's organizations and the local hospitals. Over a period of a year and a half, however, she located only six mothers; four were referred by persons who knew the researcher personally, and two mothers referred themselves from the local newspaper and a community newsletter.

Johnson utilized the ethnographic interview, taped and transcribed all interviews, and developed a master matrix that showed the commonalities and differences among the mothers' stories. The author then wove together those perceptions, experiences, explanations, and meanings of the mothers. She found that what differentiates protective mothers from non-protective mothers in sexual abuse situations is the social context within which the disclosure takes place and the support from professionals and authorities within the system. Other interesting findings include the following:

- the six women all expressed feelings of guilt for what happened to their daughters
- two of the mothers had been sexually abused as children themselves
- all six mothers had encountered some form of physical or psychological abuse from their husbands/partners
- all the mothers mentioned that their daughter's pain was perceived as their own pain
- all the women defined their families as traditional as they were economically dependent on their husbands
- there was no indication of role reversal as is mentioned in most mainstream literature; role reversal between parent and child is a pattern in which a blurring of generational boundaries takes place, where the child is expected to and agrees to take on a spousal role (Goldsmith 1982)
- four of the six fathers had problems with alcohol

- it appeared that the women's newly discovered assertiveness contributed to the incest as it was seen to have undermined their husband's position of authority and caused them stress; for example, mothers in this study who went to work outside the home said this was a turning point as it involved making decisions on their own, and standing up to their husbands
- all the women indicated that they had poor sexual relations with their husbands
- the mothers found it easier to follow through with protective action when they had the emotional support of others
- four of the six mothers said they did not know their children were being sexually abused
- two women reconciled with their husbands
- all six women said they thought their husbands were 'sick' for molesting their own children
- three fathers were caught and held accountable: two went to prison and one was placed on probation; of the remaining three, one was not charged and two were found not guilty in criminal court
- three women felt their husbands got away with sexually abusing their daughters

Johnson insists that the women's experiences must be understood within a context that acknowledges roles women are socialized to play inside and outside the family.

Next we look at some of the highlights of the research completed by Carol-Ann Hooper in *Mothers Surviving Child Sexual Abuse* (1992). Hooper interviewed fifteen mothers of children who were sexually abused and examined thirteen child welfare records.

She designed her study within a sociological rather than psychological framework but draws on both perspectives for her analysis. Like my sample and those of Johnson and Dempster, Hooper's sample was not representative of all women whose children had been sexually abused. Given the sensitivity of the subject, the problems of obtaining a representative sample are, in her words, 'almost insuperable.' Her fifteen mothers participated on a voluntary basis after receiving a letter passed to them by social services departments.

Hooper made contact only after the mothers indicated their willingness to participate. Hooper's study was exploratory. Fourteen of the child victims were girls and one was a boy. They were all intrafamilial cases, with eleven of the children having been abused by the women's husbands/ partners, and four by other relatives. All seventeen perpetrators were male. Thirteen of the participants were white and of British origin, while two were Afro-Caribbean in origin. Eleven of the women were categorized as working class and four as middle class.

The central aim of Hooper's book was to demonstrate the complexity of the mother's response and the way it was embedded in the social relations within which the child sexual abuse took place. Her second aim was to help the mothers and their children by making known their true experiences. A central theme in the study was the secondary victimization that all the women experienced. Not all, however, had an opportunity to work through their grieving process and loss.

An important finding in Hooper's study was the notion that there is not just one course of action the women should be expected to take and therefore she does not consider it colluding with the sexual abuse if mothers do not leave their partners straight away or do not report to a mandated agency straight away. She contents that women need time to work out the situation as they do with other types of responsibilities of child-rearing. Other interesting findings include:

- four of the children were placed in care as a result of the disclosure
- two of the fifteen children were abused by their fathers
- the hoped-for family loyalty was not always forthcoming; families did not automatically provide the needed support for mothers after disclosure
- there was evidence of trauma with all mothers similar to a form of bereavement
- only two of the fifteen mothers said they had a confiding type of relationship with their partners
- the women found other family members and women friends to be the most supportive after disclosure
- eight of the fifteen women were survivors of sexual abuse themselves before the age of sixteen
- indications were found of a high degree of violence in the backgrounds of the mothers, as only two of the fifteen interviewed had experienced no form of direct violence
- in nine of the eleven cases where mother's partner sexually abused her daughter, those mothers had been victims physically, verbally, and/or sexually of that partner as well
- four mothers said there were years of unexplained difficult behaviours with their children before the children disclosed
- the women expressed guilt and self-blame
- thirteen of the fifteen cases were reported to the police

- four women did not press charges; nine did
- five cases were dropped in the courts because the men denied the allegations and there was a lack of evidence to convict
- four abusers were criminally charged, of which three pleaded guilty; one got probation; one received one month in prison; one offender received four years and served two.

Hooper (1992) ends her study with suggestions for change in the child welfare system that include policies intended to prevent abuse; to lessen the economic dependence of women on men; to remove abusive men instead of children from the home; to train all professionals involved in sexual abuse; to provide resources for both mothers and children to deal with treatment issues and grieving work; and to build partnerships between professionals and non-abusing mothers.

The third and final study to be examined in this section is Dempster's *The Aftermath of Child Sexual Abuse: The Woman's Perspective* (1992). Harriet Dempster, like Johnson and Hooper, describes her study as exploratory. She set out to explore the emotional responses of women when they discovered their children had been sexually abused. She interviewed thirty-four women from August 1988 to May 1989 who were recruited from one local authority social work department and a child psychiatry specialist child abuse team. Her interviews were loosely structured, and the women were encouraged to talk in their own words. All participants were white, and their ages ranged from 21 to 53 years. Ten of the women were employed at the time of the disclosure. Twenty-two women were living with partners when the abuse was discovered; the remaining twelve were single-parent families. The thirty-four women had a total of 102 children, of whom fifty-one had been sexually abused. Highlights of some of the findings of this study are as follows:

- all of the women took some form of action toward ending the abuse and protecting their children
- none of the children were placed in care as a result of the sexual abuse
- all of the abusers were male
- a key finding was that all of the women were devastated by the disclosure and all felt isolated and in shock
- the women frequently experienced extended families as unhelpful; however, other women who had been through a similar experience were very helpful and supportive
- fourteen of the thirty-four women disclosed that they had been sexually abused themselves as children

- the Finkelhor and Browne (1985) framework was used for analysis to explain the psychological impact and potential behavioural manifestations in women following the sexual abuse of their children
- one-third of the thirty-four women experienced domestic violence
- in two cases, the perpetrator took his own life
- approximately half of the women indicated that they felt quite differently about sex after the disclosure (less interested)
- over half of the women actively sought therapy for their children.

Dempster (1992) ends her study with recommendations for improved delivery of services to women. She suggests that child welfare services not be exclusively child-centred, but also woman-centred, which could be accomplished by the deployment of two separate social workers to deal with the competing needs. She emphasized the need for the type of group work that acknowledges the competing roles women in society face. Finally, Dempster, like Johnson and Hooper, argues that if we as helping professionals are going to be effective in helping women and children, then we must listen to the women and acknowledge the complexity and dynamics of their experience.

We have seen in the above three studies that all of the mothers interviewed expressed guilt and blame after they found that their children had been sexually abused, although they were all non-offending mothers. The literature on the concept of blame is clear. Women have been socialized to take on the total responsibility and protection of their children and they have internalized this notion very well. After disclosure, they know intellectually they had no part in the sexual abuse, and yet they still feel they failed as mothers in not protecting their children. Until the state, professionals, and the public are able to unhook mothers from these unrealistic responsibilities, they will continue to be blamed and blame themselves for a crime they did not commit.

The Ideology of the Family

Child victims and male offenders are all members of families, although not necessarily the same families. In this study, sixteen of the twenty-eight offenders were members of the same family as the children they sexually abused. It is important, therefore, to examine the discourse in mainstream and alternative literature to determine how ideology impacts the views of family members before discussing theories of child sexual abuse.

We have seen earlier how the role of mothers in families has changed over the years, and how professional and popular definitions have shifted in focus regarding proper methods of child rearing. Engels (1972) informed us that the family is not a 'natural' development, but is shaped by economic and social conditions.

It is impossible to discuss the ideology of the family without discussing the institution of the family, since they are mutually reinforcing concepts (Barrett and McIntosh 1982). It is equally difficult to speak of families without conjuring up a notion of the various bureaucracies that are part of the welfare state.

According to Reed (1972), the patriarchal family originated 'with the rise of state power to maintain the rule of the rich over the poor' (15). Throughout all its different stages (slavery, feudalism, capitalism) and forms (autocracy to democracy), the state has always kept 'social power in the hands of the exploiting class,' and has bolstered the patriarchal family (15). The state promotes mainstream views that will be demonstrated in the following pages; however, some proponents of patriarchy view the state as too intrusive into private family situations.

Mainstream Views

Both Lasch (1979) and Donzelot (1979) decry the erosion of traditionally based rights as a result of state interventions. For example, Lasch observes: 'Today the state controls not merely the individual's body but as much of his spirit as it can preempt not merely his outer life but his inner life as well; not merely the public realm but the darkest corners of private life ...' (1979, 189).

Donzelot (1979) also argues against state intervention into families and claims such intervention pathologizes the modern family.

Although the state does not present a unified voice on all matters, it has been influenced over the years by a variety of experts in the development of a child welfare system. Two important notions that have helped to shape modern families are related to child development. One such influence, which has affected the theory and practice of all members of the helping professions over the past seventy-five years, was developed from a basic principle that emerged during the period of transition, when the place of work was separated from the home. This shift took place during the period when countries in the Western world changed their bases of production from agricultural to industrial. Most women remained in the home caring for the children, while men worked outside of the home in paid work. The principle that 'children need home and *mother* to grow as they should' (emphasis added), had significant consequences for women, their work, and their position within the family (Pasick and Pasick 1985, 180). There is evidence, however, that working-class women continued to work outside the home, as they have always done.

Another highly influential theory central to the helping professions for over the past several decades is the acceptance of the psychoanalytic theory of Freud and his followers (Anna Freud, Karen Horney, Margaret Mahler and others) on early psychosexual experiences in childhood development as being crucial to subsequent adult adjustment. These theories are now being challenged by feminist scholars, but have had considerable impact on women's roles as mothers.

Child welfare workers learn from experts what are considered to be normal and/or natural relationships in families. A quote from Armin Grams, head of Human Development at the Merrill-Palmer Institute of Detroit, in an article published in 1970, illustrates the point: 'Parsons's classic division of sex role behavior into instrumental for men and expressive for women is still useful ... Mothering makes receiving possible and fathering encourages giving' (1970, 21, 23).

Grams' position reflects the mainstream literature of the 1970s on family life, roles, and parenting, and is in keeping with the work of other recognized family 'experts' at the time, such as Bowlby (1963), Dreikurs (1964), Erikson (1963), and Goode (1964).

The views expressed by Grams and Goode are not very different from those quoted earlier by Penelope Leach (1994).

These views of 'the' family and 'family life' prevalent in the literature of the 1960s and 1970s helped to shape the ideas of professionals, and others who worked with families prior to the 'rediscovery' of child sexual abuse. These views have not disappeared in the 1990s, but are still prevalent in mainstream literature, and continue to dominate practice, especially in the work of psychologists and psychiatrists.

Women are blamed when their children disclose sexual abuse. It appears to be an integral part of the dominant theories in mainstream literature.

The rationale for focusing on the early mainstream literature in this section is to illustrate the sources of influence on professionals engaged in the rediscovery of child sexual abuse, and how that particular 'mindset' impacts mothers.

Alternative Views

As indicated earlier, alternative views include feminist, pro-feminist, and non-sexist views from the literature on the ideology of the family.

Morgan (1985) in his discussion on how the state (defined as government decision-makers) reproduces gender relations, gives an example of how the state enters family relationships not only through decisions of judges and legal experts, but also through the life of each person in the everyday world: 'The gender/state relationship ... is much more than a question of the framing and influencing of legislation; it is also relationships between teachers and pupils in the classrooms, between doctors and patients in consulting rooms, between social workers and clients in home or office and between the police and the public in the street' (72).

It is in these relationships that family members, especially mothers, come up against the state through encounters with various officials and professionals. Moreover, there are really few aspects of state legislation that do not in some way affect families, and at the most basic level, the state is involved in the definition of what constitutes family, marriage, and parenthood (Morgan 1985). The state is also involved in how public morality is maintained (Voysey 1975).

Is it the role of state agencies to construct and maintain public morality? What is the process and how does such a complex and abstract notion become operational?

Feminist scholars remind us how the ideology of the family is embedded in so-called pro-family political movements (such as the 'moral majority,' born-again Christians, and the anti-choice groups), in government policies, and in our cultural ideals.

There are a number of ways to define the family. Rapp (1982) makes the distinction between families and households and suggests we must also examine class level, since 'family' is a very different experience for the poor and lower-class members than for the middle class or rich. Women's subordination is linked to the family as a specific household arrangement and as an ideology (Thorne 1982). In fact, some authors suggest that 'family' is a code word for mother, since women are the core of the family instead of being just one member of the family unit. Most father-child interactions appear to be ignored in the literature (Bridenthal 1982; Spiegel 1982).

Mary O'Brien sees families as having appeared in history and in political theory in a variety of ways that can be considered ideologically charged. She suggests that: '[The family unit] has been perceived as the "basic unit" of political society, as the economic unity of society, as the repository of tradition, custom and morality, as a mode of safely siphoning off the disorderly dangers of sexual passion. It has also been perceived as the most practical mode of rearing children and replacing those lost in battle, or of replacing the labour power ... ' (1983, 11).

As Eichler (1983) points out, 'As soon as we put forward a conception that there is such a thing as "the" family, we are by implication ruling out other similar kinds of groups as non-family' (5). Thorne and Yalom (1982) find the use of 'the' family more than misleading; the authors suggest it is a distorting 'ideological construct,' which assumes all families consist of a breadwinner husband and a full-time wife and mother in the home caring for children (4). This stereotypical nuclear family is no longer viable as the main model for informing government policies and non-government practices, since only 15 per cent of families in Canada still fit this description (Vogel 1997). Women now make up nearly one-half of all employed Canadians (Ghalam 1994).

Feminists over the past decade have not only emphasized the need for a more realistic view of families, including their oppressive or dark side, but also have firmly and consistently (and sometimes outrageously) demanded action for change. Feminists continue to challenge the state and the public to move away from the narrow definition of 'the' family, and also to replace the idealized view of families with a more realistic one that includes the real experiences of women and children.

Feminist literature identifies families as not only psychological, social, and sexual institutions, but also as economic institutions. As Barrett and McIntosh express it: 'It seems almost sacrilegious to intrude economic calculations into the bosom of the family conducted as it is on affectional and not economic principles. Yet if, when we do so, our calculations reveal gross inequities, we can see that like many sacred mysteries, the mystic bonds of family serve to mask mundane exploitation' (1982, 66). Zilloch Eisenstein (1984) explains such economic inequalities as a way for males to counterbalance female sexual superiority in both childbearing and eros.

This type of exploitation is clearly spelled out in the work of Akabas (1995); Armstrong and Armstrong (1981); Baines et al. (1991); DeVault (1991); Dulude (1984); Eichler (1983); Oakley (1974); Reimer (1995); and Smith (1987), where the unpaid labour within families, as performed primarily by women, is the basic foundation upon which a paid labour force outside of the home operates.

An important aspect of families initially singled out by grassroots radical feminists, is the idea that many families are unsafe places for women and children to live (Armstrong 1995; The Canadian Panel 1993; Dobash and Dobash 1979; Dominelli 1986; Levine 1982; Mitchell 1985; Women's Research Centre 1989).

MacLeod's (1987) research found that about one million women in Canada were assaulted each year by males. A more recent study, using a random sample of 420 women, reveals that 51 per cent of women in Canada have been victims of rape or attempted rape and that 27 per cent have experienced a physical assault in an intimate relationship. Fifty-four per cent of girls under age sixteen reported unwanted or intrusive sexual experiences. These findings signify an increase in violence against women. The greatest threats for women come from the men they live with, according to Linda Light (1992).

Over the past two decades, families have been much more politicized, and feminists continue to challenge the prevalent assumptions about the dominance of the father figure in patriarchal family life. There is, however, no universal support in the feminist literature to abolish what we know as conventional families. Within alternative literature, there is much more recognition and awareness of the violence experienced in families by women and children. There also appears to be more openness and recognition of the need to include a broader scope of living arrangements within the definition of families in alternative literature. Such definitions more closely reflect the diversity of current social groups.

A number of studies have examined the concept of blame and the ideology of the family with respect to mothers of sexually abused children. My study, however, makes a unique contribution to the literature, since I use a framework of mainstream and alternative literature to deconstruct and analyse what the authorities (researchers, practitioners, and decision-makers) put forward as the truth about mothers and their behaviour.

Theories of Child Sexual Abuse

I have examined the concepts of motherhood, blame, and the ideology of the family in previous sections of this chapter. I now turn to the fourth major conceptualization in the literature that has an important influence on the direct practice decisions in cases of child sexual abuse. It seems important to address the types of theories that have informed practice with families prior to the late 1980s and the 1990s, since those are the views that continue to dominate practice.

Early research completed on the recognition of child sexual abuse in the UK asked the question 'Should child sexual abuse be included within the child abuse spectrum?' (Mrazek 1985, 49). Child sexual abuse did eventually develop a literature distinct from the literature on other types of child abuse, and theory in this area continues to develop rapidly. As in previous chapters, I divide the literature into two groupings to be discussed separately: mainstream (the traditional clinical) and alternative (feminist and non-sexist). First, a review of mainstream literature.

Mainstream Views

The traditional clinical group provided the early sources of data and

theory that shaped practice on incest and child sexual abuse. Early emphasis was on the 'collusive mother,' the 'seductive child,' the inadequate
male, and the harmless pedophile. Early mainstream theories developed
by Cormier et al. (1962), Henderson (1972; 1983), Lustig, et al. (1966), and
Mohr et al. (1964), contributed to mother-blaming. Some of their views
will be discussed in this chapter.

The definition of child sexual abuse was originally included under the
mantle of 'child abuse' (physical, emotional, sexual, and child neglect)
and treated as a 'family problem.' The dominant abuse theories were used
to explain sexual abuse, as well. Prior to the rediscovery of sexual abuse, a
'medical model' reflecting the influence of pediatricians and other medical professionals was used to explain and treat child sexual abuse
(Giovannoni 1985; Gordon 1988a; Nelson 1984; Pagelow 1984; Parke 1982;
Parton 1985; Schorr 1986).

The first such model appeared in the literature after pediatrician C.
Henry Kempe identified and described 'the battered child syndrome'
(Kempe et al. 1962), a psychological approach that attributed child abuse
to the psychodynamics of individuals. Included under this model is the
'maternal bonding' or attachment theory. It is commonly known as the
'medical model.' According to the basic premise of the medical model,
certain types of adults abuse children and particular types of children
precipitate abuse. The adult abusers and the child-victims can be identified by certain types and combinations of characteristics, such as immaturity, impulsiveness, and dependency. One factor that was thought to
contribute to abusive and neglectful behaviour was the early separation of
mother and infant, at a crucial 'bonding time.'

As research produced more evidence that personality problems on their
own could not explain the causes of child abuse, other social, situational
and environmental factors were integrated into this model (Giovannoni
1985; Pagelow 1984). Some critics of the medical model maintain that it is
still the main intervention model in use today (Nelson 1984; Parke 1982;
Parton 1985; Schorr 1986.

The sociological or socio-cultural approach that attributed child abuse
to dysfunctions of the larger socioeconomic system, and not to dysfunctions within individuals, developed later (Giovannoni 1985; Pagelow 1984).
One of the leaders of the sociological model is researcher Murray Straus.
Critics of Straus et al. (1981) point out that his method of gathering data
(CTS) produces abstract and decontextualized questions, which are in
danger of measuring only general and socially desirable perceptions of
violence (Bograd 1984; Dobash and Dobash 1988). Others point out that
his support for the 'cycle of violence' theory obscures the broader analysis

of violence against women and children (Dobash and Dobash 1988; Pagelow 1984). The work of Straus and his colleagues, however, has formed the basis for the major source of generalizable data on violence (Kelly 1988b), despite the fact that women in his research have been labelled to be equally as violent as men.

The cycle of violence theory is derived from both social learning theory and from psychoanalytic theory; the latter holds that 'the hurt' is held in the unconscious at a pre-verbal level and that parents who have been abused as infants are likely to reproduce the abuse with their own children (Kempe and Kempe 1984).

Many professionals, policy-makers, and practitioners assume the cycle of violence theory to be an unquestionable truth. Its validity, however, has been questioned by a number of researchers (Breines and Gordon 1983; Herman 1992; Pagelow 1984; Wilson 1977; 1983). Although cycle of abuse theories are appealing, Hooper (1992) found them to be too simplistic for explaining complex and emotive issues raised in child sexual abuse.

The ecological model examines life stresses and supports, such as intrapersonal, interpersonal, familial, and environmental. The work of James Garbarino (1995) is associated with the ecological model in the child maltreatment literature.

Child welfare workers still address only individual problems with one case in one family at a time, and do not have the power to change factors, such as poverty, housing, or unemployment, which are the more structural aspects at the basis of some of the problems identified by this model. Ben Carniol (1995) considers the ecological approach more of a mainstream model than an alternative one, despite its focus on societal factors, as it does not reflect a political analysis. I support this view.

Family systems theory continues to be one of the major theories currently used for conceptualizing problems within families, including all forms of child abuse. Studies using this approach tend to focus on women's failure to fulfil their roles as mothers and wives, when defining the problem of child sexual abuse within families. For example, Henderson (1972), Justice and Justice (1979), and Meiselman (1978) illustrate such a focus. The use of this theory continues to influence professionals in their definition of the problem, resulting in mothers being blamed for the child's victimization even when they were not the offenders. Family systems theory also contributed to the placing of blame on the child-victim, as well, since he or she was part of the family system (Freeman 1985; Kirst-Ashman and Hull 1995; Pincus and Minahan 1973; Shulman 1984; Turner 1986; Walsh 1982; Ward 1994; Zastrow 1995).

Indeed, any social work text used in the teaching of social work theory and practice will include family systems theory as a framework for conceptualizing the context of destructive patterns of behaviour in families. For example, the latest text to arrive on my desk, *Social Work Practice: A Canadian Perspective* (1998/99), edited by Frank Turner, has a chapter by Elizabeth Ridgely called 'Family Treatment.' She devotes much of the discussion in her chapter to family systems theory in working with children.

Examples from the traditional clinical literature where mothers are blamed for child sexual abuse include Browning and Boatman's (1977) findings in a study of fourteen incest cases where 'a primary problem ... of sexual withdrawal, passivity and emotional distance in these mothers was reported' (72). Also, Gaddini (1983) reports: 'Incest ... is to be seen as a pathology ... The disorder implies an original disturbance of mother functions in terms of the development of empathy. ...' (357). Cohen (1983) outlines characteristics of mothers involved in incest cases, '... weak and submissive, indifferent, or promiscuous ... passivity ... emotional distance from family ... generally, incompetent behavior as an adult woman' (155). This author goes on to say that 'although many mothers in incestuous families deny knowledge of the incest, current clinical observations are to the contrary' (156).

Henderson (1972) suggests that 'incestuous fathers have usually been rejected recently by their usual sexual partners ... The wives of incestuous men collude with the incestuous liaison by rejecting their husbands sexually and by subtly encouraging their daughters to become the "woman of the home"' (311). Henderson does not discuss the fact that when women are ill or hospitalized, men do not take over their duties, but rather encourage their daughters to be 'little mothers' (Herman and Hirschman 1982).

The diagnosis discussed in mainstream literature such as that of Mrazek (1985) frequently refers to 'incestuous families,' which, of course, assumes pathological family patterns in sexual abuse rather than focusing on male power in the sexual abuse of children. This conceptualization protects men and maintains patriarchal definitions.

This conceptualization protects men because the focus on the family as a whole overlooks the experiences of individuals in the family. If you are informed by theories that look at interaction between individuals to diagnose the problem, and not the behaviour of any one person in particular, such as a father who is sexually abusing a small child, for example, you will need to examine that child's behaviour and ask how she contributed to being sexually abused. This framework falls short when you try to determine what some infant of a few months old has done to contribute to her father sexually abusing her. Heidi Hartmann defines patriarchy as 'a set of social relations which has a material base and in which there are hierarchical relations between men, and solidarity among them, which enable them to control women. Patriarchy is thus a system of male oppression of women' (1992, 103).

Blaming of Children

In addition to mothers being blamed in mainstream literature, many children are also blamed; they are not only held responsible for the sexual abuse, but also, in many instances, are not believed when they do disclose.

Freud's theories are said by feminist scholars to be responsible for having 'blinded' the helping professions to the serious problem of child sexual abuse. Freudian theory holds that the female's wish to be seduced (by her father or other male authority adult figures in her life) finds its fulfilment in fictitious stories and fantasies. Although Freud's earlier writings indicate that he had identified the link between the hysterical symptoms of his female patients and early childhood experiences of sexual abuse that later resulted in an alteration in consciousness referred to as dissociation, he later repudiated that theory because he was unable to obtain support from his peers (Herman 1992; Masson 1984; Rush 1980; Russell 1986).

Henderson (1983) argues that incestuous daughters are generally felt to encourage their fathers' sexual advances or at least to refrain from resisting them. Incestuous behaviour in daughters is at least in part a function of hostile impulses toward the mother and a penis envy ...' (311). This author has considerable influence through his professional psychiatric writings, and in his political role as an elected Member of Parliament in Ontario.

The blaming of children is still very much the current practice from those who hold a conventional point of view. For example, in a November 1989 newspaper article in the *Toronto Star*, regarding a case where a thirty-three-year-old male babysitter admitted to sexually molesting a three-year-old child in September 1988, the judge's decision is telling: 'Citizen's groups are demanding a County Court judge resign or be fired after he blamed a 3-year-old girl for "sexually aggressive" behavior with a babysitter ...' (Kenna, A2). Later, this judge was cleared of any wrong-doing by the Canadian Judicial Council, who reported, 'This was a case of unfortunate choice of words and an unpopular decision, neither of which constitute grounds for formal investigation of a judge' (Vienneau 1990, A13). Although no action was taken by this predominantly male body, public records show the documentation of a large number of individuals (mainly women) who took issue with and publicly condemned such statements about child-victims.

This example is not an isolated incident as too frequently we read in the press about remarks made by judges who blame children or mothers for causing the sexual abuse, and allow the offenders to go free ('Common Sense' 1997), or trivialize the offence by giving light sentences. Such comments were made by a BC Appeal Court justice who dropped a former teacher's sexual assault conviction. The parents have filed a formal complaint with the Chief Justice and the Canadian Judicial Council. Cocker, fifty-two, was convicted of sexually assaulting two students and one former student and sentenced to fourteen months in jail. Cocker appealed the decision to the BC Court of Appeal where the judge stayed proceedings (meaing that he serves no jail time and has no criminal record) of all the offences because of the delay of seventeen months in the trial which evidently had infringed his Charter rights. During the appeal proceedings, Justice Southin said 'What's the matter with parents on Mayne Island to let their children go on a camping trip with only one adult?' (Hall 1997, A3c). The Judge blamed the parents for trusting their children's school teacher to take them on a camping trip. The other insensitive comment that was made in this case was 'Let us keep in mind that these are not severe sexual assaults such as brutal rape or buggery of little boys' (Hall 1997 A3c). This again, indicates that judge's lack of awareness of the psychological effects of sexual abuse on children. A civil suit has been filed against Cocker.

Julia Krane (1990) sums up the situation in her critique of mainstream views: 'Mainstream conceptualizations of child sexual abuse minimize the pervasiveness of male perpetrated abuse of women and children, ignore the hierarchial structure of gender and sexual relations, and obfuscate patriarchal ideology, which glorifies motherhood, idealizes intact nuclear families, and marks power imbalances and male prerogative' (191).

In mainstream literature, medical and psychiatric definitions dominated child abuse theory and practice in the 1950s, 1960s, and 1970s, with a slight shift towards alternative models in the late 1980s. Despite the fact that the etiology of child abuse has been recognized as multi-factored, theory and practice are still heavily influenced by the medical model, which focuses on individuals.

Alternative Views

Before second-wave feminism,[5] acts of violence against women were

conceptualized as violent crimes randomly perpetrated mostly by strangers against innocent victims (Stanko 1988). Although there were attempts
by first wave feminists to focus public attention on crimes of violence
against women and children, those attempts were not successful (Jeffreys
1985).[6]

The second wave of feminism began in the late 1960s and continues to
be a major movement, with growing support at the time of writing (1998).
Second wave feminism is the struggle to liberate women economically,
politically, socially, sexually, and spiritually. It calls for major change in
social structures, institutions and values (Bunch 1986; Eisenstein 1983;
hooks 1989; Tomm 1995). Current efforts represent larger numbers and
more diverse groups of women. Eradicating violence is now high on
the second wave agenda of most Canadian women, although it was not
originally included in the 1970 Report of the Royal Commission on the
Status of Women. The women's movement first took on rape, then wife-
battering, followed by child sexual abuse, and then pornography and,
more recently, sexual harassment – all parts of the same continuum of
violence against women and children (Kelly 1988a). Traditionally, however, child sexual abuse, because it was within the mandate of child welfare
agencies, was guided by a mainstream as opposed to a feminist approach.

The influence of feminists (as well as non-sexist empiricists, such as
David Finkelhor) has contributed to a shift in the handling of child sexual
abuse victims. Recently, more emphasis has been placed on a belief of the
victim's story, support for the victim, responsibility placed on the perpetrator, prosecution for the crime, and the recognition of a need for change in
values, laws, and institutions (Butler 1978; Courtois 1988; Dominelli 1986;
Faller 1988; Finkelhor and Assoc. 1986; Herman 1992; Russell 1986).

How and why has the crime of child sexual abuse been hidden for such
a long period of time? Is the silence around the issue related to the way the
problem was conceptualized? Feminists are primarily responsible for drag-
ging the issue of child sexual abuse out of the closet and into the public
domain (Breines and Gordon 1983; Butler 1978; Herman and Hirschman
1981; Rush 1980; Russell 1986).

There were periods in history where child sexual abuse was part of
religious law and social custom. For example, Florence Rush (1980) documents that according to the Talmud a man who had sexual intercourse
with a female child age three years and one day (and age seven years plus
under Christianity) could consider that child his betrothed, with her
father's permission.

The problem of child sexual abuse surfaced, was acknowledged, but was forced underground again on a number of occasions. For example, in France, according to Masson (1984), Dr Ambroise Tardieu published a book documenting descriptions of thousands of cases of children who were sexually abused between the years 1858–69. Most of these victims were girls between the ages of four and twelve years who had been examined by the doctor himself. But, as Masson mentions, the book was never quoted in the literature, nor was there any public or professional recognition that child sexual abuse was a serious social problem at that particular time in history.

In Britain, between 1884 and 1908, as Jeffreys (1985) documents, early feminists campaigned against the sexual abuse of girls. They lobbied for incest legislation and for women magistrates, police, and doctors so that cases involving the sexual abuse of girls could be more sensitively handled. These efforts, however, brought little response from authorities at the time.

Kinsey et al. (1948, 1953) underplayed the importance of their findings on child sexual abuse. Nine per cent of the female sample (4,441) indicated they had had sexual contact with an adult before the age of fourteen years (Finkelhor 1984, 2). Eighty per cent said it was upsetting, and yet, this was never highlighted by the Kinsey research team (Russell 1986, 7).

Feminist theory on child sexual abuse has continued to progress and, as with the development of theory on rape and battered women, the telling of personal stories by adult incest victims has been central to the development of the theory. Incest survivors such as Armstrong (1978), Danica (1990), Bass and Davis (1988), Fraser (1987), Rush (1980), Turcotte (Studio D, 1987), and Vale Allen (1980) have contributed significantly to both theory and practice by writing about their personal experiences. The victims have become the 'experts' of their own experience; their guidance has informed feminist practice and more recently, that of mainstream helping professions.

The main difference between the types of violence discussed in this section, and the broader definition of child abuse, is the aspect of gender. Whereas men are responsible for the overwhelming majority of rapes, assaults on women, and child sexual abuse, women share as perpetrators in other types of child abuse, such as physical and emotional abuse and neglect. Women probably commit about one-half of the physical child abuse (Breines and Gordon 1983; Pagelow 1984).

Current sociological and feminist theories reflect views on the etiology of violence as more externally oriented than traditional Freudian-inspired explanations. Sociological theories emphasize the importance of stress and learned behaviour, and focus interventions on programs to reduce stress. Feminist theories define the problem as more connected to the social structure and dominant societal values which support inequality. Feminists support interventions focused more on collective action than individual change (Dempster 1992; Gutierre 1987; Krane 1994; McIntyre 1981; Pagelow 1984; Russell 1986). Feminist scholars have developed definitions of child sexual abuse from the rape crises and shelter movements, and in fact, see child sexual abuse as another form of violence against women (Kelly 1988b).

Given a review of alternative theory, it becomes clear that a feminist perspective on child abuse includes the following in its definition and analysis: strongly held views in society that continue to espouse 'motherhood' as the major fulfilling role for females; the sexual division of labour that reinforces women's primary responsibility as caretakers of children, and that discourages men from giving the nurturance of children the same importance as their paid work; existing gender and generational inequities; power relationships that perpetuate male supremacy; the lack of reproductive and sexual freedom of females that works against choice about wanted children; an economic system that operates on the profit motive and ignores the resulting inequities, thus leaving many women and children in poverty; and patterns of child-rearing that socialize male and female children to fit stereotypes that maintain male supremacy (Abramovitz 1995; Breines and Gordon 1983; Butler 1980; Dobash and Dobash 1983, 1986, 1988; Dominelli 1986, 1989; Eichler 1997; Gilgun 1984; Johnson 1992; Krane 1990; Lahey 1984; Russell 1986; Wasburne 1981).

4

The Mothers, the Children, and the Men Who Abused

The mothers interviewed for this study were profoundly affected by the harm caused to their children. Before discussing some of the findings about their children's harm, it is extremely important that the reader is informed of the context in which the sexual abuse disclosure occurred. Therefore, information on experiences in the lives of the twenty-four women interviewed prior to the disclosures made by their own children is provided. The women themselves, then, share in this section what can only be termed a lifetime of violence (sexual, physical, psychological) throughout their lives.

Violence Experienced in Twenty-Four Mothers' Lives

Violence against females is common in our society. According to a national random survey conducted by Statistics Canada among Canadian women eighteen years of age and older, 51 per cent of Canadian women have experienced physical or sexual violence during their lives (Statistics Canada 1993). Only two of twenty-four women in my study were *not* victims sometime in their lives of some form of violence from males. For the purposes of this study, however, my definition is broader than that utilized by Statistics Canada.[1]

More than two-thirds (seventeen) of the twenty-four women interviewed were victims of child sexual abuse themselves. I do not, however, wish to suggest a causal link between mothers who were victims in their childhood, and the victimization of their own children. The participants in my study report an extremely high incidence of sexual abuse in childhood, which is not relfected in other studies. For example, Finkelhor et al. (1997), drawing on U.S. telephone survey in which 1,000 parents were interviewed (both mothers and fathers), stated that approximately one-quarter of the parents reported having been sexually abused themselves as children.

In studies more similar to mine (interview-based), results varied, but still did not appraoch the same levels. Johnson (1992) reported that two out of six women interviewed were victims of child sexual abuse, and Hooper (1992) reported that eight of her fifteen interviewees were survivors. Dempster (1992) reported that fourteen of thirty-four women she interviewed revealed sexual abuse as children. These three studies report rates from one-quarter to one-half of the women who were survivors themselves. Their figures are closer to the Finkelhor findings (1997).

It is difficult to explain the reported degree of childhood sexual abuse against the women in my research. Is it an anomaly or does it reflect the true magnitude of the violence in our society against female children?

The sexual violence reported in The Canadian Panel (1993) indicates a rate of 54 per cent of women who experienced some form of unwanted or intrusive sexual experience before reaching age sixteen. The rate in my study is 66 per cent which, of course, is not a random sample so cannot be generalized. This is higher than any random samples completed in retrospective studies. I do not know why the women who chose to volunteer for my study reflect such a picture, but I would speculate that such a high rate is closer to the rates reported from clinical samples (Dinsmore 1991).

The following seventeen incidents took place before the mother concerned was sixteen years of age:

1. Raped at age eleven (in therapy during interview, experiencing amnesia); thinks offender was a family member
2. Raped at age twelve by male in neighbourhood
3. Gang-raped by four teenaged boys in neighbourhood before age fourteen; also experienced attempted rape by friend of brother
4. Raped before age sixteen (would not say by whom)
5. Fondled by uncle (breasts and genitals) at ages eight and nine
6. Fondled sexually by friend's father at ages ten and eleven
7. Fondled (breasts) at age nine or ten by father and also by her brother-in-law
8. Experienced attempted rape by her brother-in-law before age of sixteen
9. Fondled sexually by step-father from ages five to eight; forced to perform oral sex by teenaged male babysitter
10. Fondled sexually before school age (currently in therapy and experiencing amnesia); thinks offender might have been her grandfather

11. Fondled in genital area and experienced attempted sexual penetration by parents' friends, at age ten or eleven
12. Attempted rape by older known male before age sixteen
13. Fondled sexually by uncle when around ten
14. Fondled sexually in genital area at age four or five by male cousins
15. Fondled (breasts) at puberty by uncle
16. Forced to perform fellatio by older known male before she was fourteen
17. Fondled (breasts) by male music teacher before she reached age fourteen.

Two of the offenders were fathers, nine were other male relatives, one was a male babysitter, one a male music teacher, and four were trusted family friends, two of whom were not specifically named. Four of the mothers were sexually abused by more than one offender.

The women in my study were asked whether their partner (or former partner) had ever harmed them physically, or in a severe psychological manner (interpreted by the women as resulting in lasting effects). Twenty of the twenty-four mothers answered 'yes.' Their responses were as follows:

My husband forced sex on me and hit me all the time. [I was] ... bruised ... Police were called and charges were laid ...

My partner smacked me in the head with his hand and knocked me down ...

My husband hit me only once ... I hit back ... I ended the marriage ... Much psychological abuse ... I had very low self esteem because of how he put me down ...

My first husband chased me with a knife ... He was very abusive ... I was a battered wife ...

My husband hit me three times but my boyfriend used to beat me all the time ...

My former partner raped and battered me ... It was reported to the police and charges were laid ...

My husband raped me and I was also a battered wife ... [I was] beaten many times ... He tried to choke me ... I had to go for medical attention ... Yes, police were called and charges laid ... My husband hit me over the back with a curtain rod when I was pregnant ... the day before [I] went to the hospital ...

I was raped by a male friend who was living with me ... I ended the relationship ...

I considered myself a battered wife ... I fought back but he was stronger ... He was very possessive ...

I was not physically abused by my first husband but psychologically abused ... He had me convinced that our marriage failure was all my fault ... I lost weight and was very unhappy ... He tried to remove our child and physically threatened to hit me when I did not let him take her ...

My husband twisted my fingers and arms and tried to choke me ... He also broke into the house and threatened my mother ...

Not physically but psychologically, my first husband and current husband [used] name calling and throwing things ...

My husband bruised me by grabbing me to throw me out of the house when he was drinking ... a couple of times ... Also, emotionally he puts me down ...

I felt used sexually by both husbands ... My first husband was a mechanic and he brought home a belt off a fan or something from a vehicle to discipline all of us [including two children] ... It hung by the fridge ... The second one treated me like a prostitute ... 'screwing' me as if I were just a body under him ...

My husband forced sex on me and was psychologically abusive ... I felt like a piece of 'poop' when he got through telling me I was no good ...

Early in the marriage I was hit in the face and the threat was there forever ...

Not my current husband but my former boyfriend ... Yes, he gashed my forehead when he smashed my head against a radiator ... Police were not called but I needed medical attention ...

When I was pregnant, my husband physically pushed me down ... Later, he was violent and kicked in the door ... The police were called but no charges were laid ... They took him to the psychiatric hospital ...

Yes ... I considered myself a battered wife ... The police were called a number of times ... but charges were not laid because they said he would get ten or eleven years in jail for throwing a meat cleaver ...

Again, the women in this study reflect a very high degree of violence against them by their partners and husbands. There is also evidence in the research that marital violence is a statistically significant predictor of physical child abuse (Ross 1996, 589). The responses from the women in the three studies similar to mine had the following results with respect to physical and psychological violence from their intimate partners: Johnson (1992), all six; Hooper (1992), nine out of fifteen; and Dempster (1992), eleven out of thirty-four. Although my results are high in this particular area of violence, they are not the highest of the studies similar to mine.

Seven of the twenty-four mothers recalled being physically abused by their own fathers (two by their mothers). Their memories included being punched in the face, being swung off the feet by the hair, and being hit with an army belt as discipline. One mother remembered being called a 'slut' by her father when she was a teenager, and indicated how damaging that was to her own feelings about herself. Two mothers described how their fathers humiliated them. For example, one woman said she had attempted suicide twice before the age of seven because her father always called her a 'stupid blockhead' and made her repeatedly do silly things until she cried.

Five of the women said their husbands abused their own children. One mother recalled her husband spanking their newborn baby for crying. She did not report the abuse to authorities at the time, but subsequently separated from him. This same man, when he was reunited with his daughter eleven years later, sexually abused her and was subsequently criminally charged and incarcerated.

Other forms of violence experienced by these women included: rape or attempted rape by strangers, unwanted sexual advances, exposure of genitals, and sexual harassment.

The mothers were asked whether, at any time, they had had an unwanted sexual experience with a girl or woman. Two mothers answered 'yes' to this question. Both said that although they were not exactly traumatized by the event, they were upset and angry at the time. One woman said a female cousin touched her breasts when they were teenagers; the other woman recalled a strange experience of a woman trying to hold her hand on the bus and following her off the bus and along the street.

Fifteen of the twenty-four women said they had experienced sexual harassment; nine of the fifteen were sexually harassed in the workplace. Only one of the nine women formally reported the harassment to a supervisor. The others said they sort of expected such behaviour from males at work. These women said they did not feel it was worth reporting. Among the remaining six women, three said they were sexually harassed by a lawyer who was hired for divorce proceedings, a dentist during a dental appointment, and a Salvation Army captain after services. Three others were not specifically identified other than being described as older males in positions of authority.

Ten of the twenty-four women interviewed had experienced adult males intentionally exposing their genitals in front of them before they were sixteen. At first, only nine women said they had had this experience. Then, one women phoned me later to say her sister reminded her of an episode in a horse stable when they had witnessed a male exhibitionist together.

When asked whether anyone had ever grabbed, felt, or kissed them in a way that they felt was sexually threatening before they were age sixteen, fourteen of the women interviewed said 'yes.'

Four of the twenty-four women said they had experienced rape or attempted rape by strangers. Women in this study have experienced an incredible amount of violence throughout their lives and yet, according to current research findings, their experiences are not that unusual for women (with the exception of the number who had been sexually abused in childhood). The abuse and violence suffered by women crosses class, race, age, and national boundaries. As suggested by Dominelli (1989), pain, misery and fear form an integral part of the fabric of women's lives, and this study bears out her contention.

It is important to state clearly that this section about the violence perpetrated against these women in no way suggests that this is a total description of who these women are. They are more than the sum of their histories and their experiences of victimization. Indeed, as we move through other chapters, the courage and endurance of these woman will become clear.

Kelly (1988a) uses the term 'continuum' to mean 'a continuous series of elements or events that pass into one another, and are connected by the basic common characteristics that physical, verbal, and sexual coercion and assault are employed by men against women' (115). Using such a framework allows us to more broadly define and name forms of violence that 'more accurately reflect women's experience' (115).

In addition to the various categories of violence defined in this study, women indicated to me that they included their own child's sexual abuse as part of the definition or continuum of violence against them. One mother's words express the feelings of the majority of the women interviewed. When asked: 'What happened to you as a result of your child's disclosure?' she said: 'Basically, you feel like you've been raped.'

Although this study is primarily focused on the mothers of the child-victims, the children's experiences, for the women, are virtually inseparable from their own experiences. In attempting to explain what it is like to have one's own child sexually abused, one mother said, '... it feels like it happened to me.' For this reason, facts about the children, such as what happened to them and how they were affected, are included here, as well as a description of the children and of their offenders. Research reports show that non-offending mothers of sexually abused children experienced greater overall distress, poorer family functioning, and lower satisfaction in their parenting roles than non-offending fathers of sexually abused children (Manion et al. 1996).

The Child-Victims

The thirty-one children in this survey are from twenty-four families in Ontario. The initial intention was to interview mothers whose children were between the ages of four and twelve years when they first disclosed. Because of confusion at referral as to whether the child was between those ages when he or she was abused or when he or she disclosed, there are, in fact, four children who fall outside of that age range (at disclosure). The children, therefore, range in age from one to sixteen years (at disclosure), with the majority (twenty-seven) falling within the four-to-twelve age range.

Twenty-seven children are female, and four are male. No male child was abused by his father, whereas ten of the female children were sexually abused by their biological, step, and/or adoptive fathers.

Based on household income and occupation of the mother and/or father), twelve of the children are from middle-class families and nineteen are from working-class families.

When disclosure first occurred, twenty-one of the thirty-one children were living in two-parent families, while ten of the children were living in one-parent, mother-led families. At the time of interview (six months to three years after disclosure), the number of children living in sole-support, mother-led families had increased from ten to sixteen.

By the time I interviewed the mothers, all of the thirty-one children were attending school. There are no physically or mentally disabled children in this group. One child, however, who was in grade nine, has been diagnosed as a 'slow learner.' All but six of the children were born and raised in Ontario. Twenty-nine of the thirty-one children were born in Canada (one was born in Israel and one in England).

The Nature of the Child Sexual Abuse

The thirty-one children in this study were victims of every type of sexual abuse, from exposure to pornographic material to forced penetration.

The duration of the sexual abuse ranges from a one-time occurrence for four children to five, six, and seven years of abuse for five children. Twenty-two of the children suffered the abuse anywhere from a few times to four years.

There are no particular patterns with respect to the type of abuse perpetrated on a child in relation to the offender. For example, fathers touched, fondled and had sexual intercourse with these children as did relatives, trusted friends, and neighbours. The only exception, as mentioned previously, was that no boy was molested by his father. Since there were only four boys in this study, all types of perpetrators are not represented here.

All of the children in this study were sexually abused within the definition of the *Criminal Code of Canada*, so, in theory, all cases were a violation of the children's bodies, and charges should have been laid. In practice, however, for various reasons to be discussed later, not all offenders were charged with a criminal offence, and some offenders who were charged were found not guilty.

Effects of the Sexual Abuse on the Children

All thirty-one children were negatively affected by the sexual abuse, some more so than others, depending upon their individual experiences. The effects of the abuse on the children were both immediate and ongoing. Furthermore, it is possible that some of the children who do not appear to be seriously affected currently may, in fact, have to deal with the effects of the sexual abuse at a later period in their lives.

The framework used to examine the effects of the sexual abuse on the children in this study is one developed by Finkelhor and Browne (1985). The Traumatic Guide for Behaviour Manifestations divides the types of effects sexually abused children experience into four specific components, which are referred to as traumagenic dynamics. These components are traumatic sexualization, betrayal, stigmatization, and powerlessness. Although these dynamics are not necessarily unique to child sexual abuse, the framework is useful for this study because it can be used in both research and treatment. The authors have acknowledged that the model may be overly simplistic in its classification of children's experiences of sexual abuse, and that there exists a possibility of overlap within the categories.

Unlike physical abuse, child sexual abuse does not, in the majority of cases, produce physical symptoms (only six of the children examined in this study revealed physical symptoms). Therefore, it is important to have some measurement of the psychological injury inflicted by the sexual abuse, in order to provide appropriate treatment for the child. According to Finkelhor and Browne: 'These dynamics alter children's cognitive and emotional orientation to the world and create trauma by distorting children's self-concept, world view, and affective capacities' (1985, 531).

Many of the children in this study had their 'cognitive and emotional orientation to the world' altered and their 'self-concepts' and 'affective capacities' distorted by the trauma caused by the sexual abuse. It would be critical to see each child face to face on a number of occasions before an attempt could be made to clinically assess each child for treatment purposes. It seems reasonable for purposes of this study, however, to use the Finkelhor and Browne framework, along with additional information (provided by the mothers and obtained from agency records) to provide some sense of the effects of the sexual abuse on the thirty-one children.

Only five of the thirty-one children did not appear to fit into one of the four categories of trauma. This is not to say that the experience may not have some future negative effects on their development or their lives, but, given the information currently available on their daily behaviour, these five children have not exhibited behaviours or articulated feelings similar to those of the other twenty-six children. On the other hand, four of the children in this study showed signs of trauma in all four categories. Each of the four dynamics will be briefly outlined and an illustration given of each. The framework is used, then, simply to provide some idea to the reader of the possible harm caused to the child-victims in this study.

'Traumatic sexualization,' the first dynamic, 'refers to a process in which a child's sexuality (including both sexual feelings and sexual attitudes) is shaped in a developmentally inappropriate and interpersonally dysfunctional fashion as a result of sexual abuse' (Finkelhor and Browne 1985, 531). That shaping of the sexuality is not in the service of the child; but for the gratification of the perpetrator. Sexual traumatization may be affected by the developmental level of the child; a younger child may not understand the full implications of the activities engaged in by the perpetrator during the exchange of gifts, affection, and/or attention for sex (531).

Seven children were sexually traumatized by the experience. Six of these seven children experienced either penile or digital penetration or dry intercourse. Five of the seven children were sexually abused over a long-term period (two to seven years). One child was male and six were female. One case illustration might help the reader to understand the type of trauma suffered by the seven children.

Dorothy White said her daughter, Jill, was enticed to participate in

sexual activity with her father by playing games, dancing in scanty cos-
tumes, engaging in deep or 'French' kissing, and acting seductively for his
entertainment. Since the abuse started when she was approximately four
years old and disclosure did not take place until she was past her eleventh
birthday, these activities were well entrenched in her repertoire of behaviours. After disclosure, her mother tried to correct Jill's behaviours. During the interview, she said: 'She has done a few little things that really
stunned me ... It was New Year's and I was down in Ottawa ... She was
playing with my sister's grandchildren ... One child was ten and the other
was six ... They were playing games while we were preparing dinner ...
When I got home I got a call from my sister who said ... her games
[meaning Jill] were kissing [each other's] body ... you start from the top to
the bottom.' Dorothy White said she told Jill 'that was not the proper way
to play,' but having her mother correct these various learned behaviours
and misperceptions about what was appropriate behaviour caused this
child a great deal of upset and confusion, and has resulted in Jill feeling
very unhappy and ashamed to the point where she talked about suicide.
She was still in therapy after two years.

The 'Traumagenic Dynamic of Betrayal,' the second dynamic, is a
child's realization that a trusted person, whom they depended upon, has
harmed them. The child may feel manipulated and misrepresented with
respect to morality issues because their feelings were ignored or disre-
garded. A family member who does not believe the child may also evoke
feelings of betrayal (Finkelhor and Browne 1985, 532).

Sixteen of the children felt betrayed by the offender seriously enough to
be included in this traumatic dynamic category. The majority of these
children (thirteen) were sexually abused by a relative, and the three
remaining children had important relationships with their offender(s).
For example, one male offender was a long-time babysitter and friend of
the family who visited regularly over a period of several years. Another
child lived in the home with the man, who boarded with her family. This
man had taken her on outings, bought her candy, and played games with
her. The third child also had an ongoing relationship with her offender, a
grandfatherly man who lived next door, and the child saw him on a daily
basis; her family knew and respected him until the disclosure.

It became apparent after disclosure that all of these children had made
some attempt, however feeble, before the actual disclosure, to engage the
attention of a family member concerning their victimization, but nobody
understood their messages at the time.

Some of the behaviours exhibited by these sixteen children, as de-

scribed by their mothers, included extreme clinging to parents (especially
to mothers), isolation and withdrawal from peers, aversion to intimate
relationships, distrust of men, anti-social behaviour in school, and anger
and hostility directed at those around them. An illustration of one child
who manifested some of these behaviours is Gertrude Davis' child, Barbara,
who was sexually abused by her biological father over a period of six years.
The abuse escalated over the last two years, from the time Barbara was nine
until she disclosed at age eleven, when her father attempted vaginal
penetration. Ms Davis describes her child as follows:

She's a smart little girl ... Before this happened she used to get honours ... now she
just scrapes by ... I had been going to the school and saying ... what's wrong at
school ... Her marks are dropping, she's acting out [and] she's acting crazy ... and
they kept saying to me ... it's got to be at home ... He started abusing her on
Monday night ... when I was still up and had the girls [club] there ... She'd come
down and stand by my chair and be really obnoxious and say ... 'I'm not going to
bed ... If you can sit with the girls, [then] I'm sitting with the girls ... I'm not doing
anything you say ...'

Later, Gertrude Davis said that she realized Barbara was trying to tell her
something, but she had not understood at that time what it was. Now what
Ms Davis says about Barbara is that 'she's developed into what I call a kid
without a conscience concerning the family.'

'Stigmatization,' the third dynamic, describes the bad feelings that are
communicated to the child during the sexual abuse and which the child
incorporates into her or his own self image. Such feelings of shame and
guilt can also occur or be reinforced through secrecy or, after disclosure,
depending upon the way people in the child's environment respond to her
or him and to the sexual abuse. Some children, because they feel stigmatized, will isolate themselves, or may join other stigmatized groups in society,
such as those involved in drugs, criminal activity, and/or prostitution. If
negative characteristics are attributed to the child, such as 'damaged goods,'
this will increase the child's sense of stigmatization. On the other hand, if a
child is told that the sexual abuse was not her fault, her feelings of stigmatization could be assuaged (Finkelhor and Browne 1985, 532–3).

Six of the children have been stigmatized by the sexual abuse. All but
one of these children experienced either penetration or attempted penetration by their offenders. Four of these girls were abused by their fathers.
One girl was abused by her grandfather, and one boy was molested by an
adolescent male.

Mary Fletcher's daughter, Hope, was one of the children who was stigmatized. Ms Fletcher described Hope in the following way:

Well, [she] is very very aggressive ... very defiant, and has very low self esteem ... I found out that my daughter is sleeping with guys ... actively having sexual inter-course with them ... has been involved with dope ... is skipping school ... goes into rages ... flounces out ... disobeys all rules ... [has] no regard for her times to come in ... she smokes [and] she was at the point where [her new friends] were pressuring her to sell dope.

Hope later became suicidal and, according to her mother, was 'on the street,' despite every effort she and her husband made to help their daughter, and despite all of the helping agencies involved with Hope at the time.

'Powerlessness' is the last dynamic of the four. Powerlessness refers to 'the process in which the child's will, desires, and sense of efficacy are continually contravened' (Finkelhor and Browne 1985, 532) by the offender during the sexual abuse. The child's territory and body space are constantly invaded against her or his wishes and the child is rendered powerless. Powerlessness may deepen as the child is unable to obtain the understanding of significant adults (536).

Twenty-six of the thirty-one children felt some form of powerlessness as a result of the sexual abuse. For fifteen of the children, however, the disempowerment was so severe that it affected their emotional stability. Of these fifteen children, five were subjected to the use of force and threats. The remaining ten were in situations where they felt trapped, and this also increased their sense of powerlessness. Olga Kadishun describes her daughter, Ida's personality before and after the abuse:

[B]efore all this started ... she was very outgoing [and had] no sense of fear ... She had all sorts of stitches from falling ... like a tomboy and then ... later ... the teacher said ... she was threatening to put her back in grade one class because she couldn't control her behaviour ... I said this does not even sound like my daughter ... It must be someone else's kid ... She started having nightmares, a lot of nightmares ... For a year I had to put blankets on the windows ... she would get up crying and say 'I hear somebody out there.'

Ms Kadishun said she realized (post disclosure) the level of fear that had been instilled in her daughter by the offender when, on a particular outing, Ida thought she saw him. This is how Ms Kadishun described Ida's behaviour: 'And all of a sudden ... it was like two seconds ... she was up on my lap ... She was shaking so bad ... and she said, "I'm gonna be sick ..." I said, "What's the matter ..." She said, "That man" ... "and when I looked I thought it was him, too."' Ida was placed in a support group, but still needed individual therapy for more than three years after disclosure.

All of the mothers of these children were devastated by the trauma their children suffered as a result of the sexual abuse. Each child's injury became her mother's injury. But in addition, the mothers were forced to deal with a number of other problems besides their children's pain (to be discussed in the following chapter). As one key informant put it, 'I don't know which is worse, being the sexually abused child or being the mother ... because where is this going to fall? On the mother ... of course' (Key Informant 'E-D').

The Twenty-Eight Men Who Were Responsible for the Sexual Abuse

There is no typical list of characteristics of an offender; they are as diverse as the victims. The men in this study who sexually abused children ranged in age from fifteen to seventy-eight. Although one small boy of nine was reported to be molesting a five-year-old boy, when this was investigated, it was found that the nine-year-old child was the victim of teenaged boys himself, and was repeating with other small children what had been done to him.

Eight of the twenty-eight offenders were below the age of twenty-five and two were in their seventies, but the majority of the men were in their thirties and forties. Although occupations were not known for some of the offenders, where this information was available, it was apparent that their occupations were also quite varied, ranging from unskilled and student to businessman, engineer, and county clerk.

Seven of the twenty-eight offenders were said to have used pornographic pictures or films with the child-victims in this study. Some of the women revealed the pornographic content used with their children during the interviews.

The use of alcohol/drugs was mentioned by seven mothers as part of the abuse situation.

Six mothers said they knew the offenders had been victims of child sexual abuse themselves. Since this question was not specifically asked during every interview, information was not available on all offenders with respect to their own victimization; only where it was spontaneously volunteered by the women interviewed. Although not all men who were sexually abused as children become offenders, research findings indicate that parents who were sexually abused themselves have high rates of sexually abused children (Finkelhor et al. 1997).

Mothers were asked if they knew or experienced any other violence perpetrated by the offenders in cases where they were partners or relatives. Of the twenty-eight offenders in this study, twenty-one were known to have committed other violent acts (but had not necessarily been criminally charged or convicted of these acts); for seven offenders, this information was unknown.

Seventy different children were said to have been molested by the twenty-eight offenders in this study (thirty-one from this study and thirty-nine additional children). In six cases, this information was unknown, so the information shared here is a conservative observation.

An important question that each mother was asked was how the offender got the child to keep the secret. Did he use threats and/or bribery? If so, what exactly did he say to the child? The following responses give some indication of how offenders managed to keep the sexual abuse a secret:

- seven threatened to kill the child if she or he told
- two threatened to hit the child if she or he told
- two threatened to harm someone else in the family
- two warned the child that he, the offender, would go to jail if she or he told
- three warned that nobody would believe him or her
- three used bribery to keep the child from telling (candy, gum, money, and clothes)
- two warned the child not to tell her or his mother or she would be mad with him (the offender)
- three did not warn the child not to tell by using bribery or threat, but simply said, 'It will be our secret'

Two fathers used other persuasive tactics to molest their children by telling them the behaviour represented their love and caring affection. For example, one father told his four-year-old daughter, 'Daddy needs to do this because this is how Daddy loves you.'

5

How the Mothers Responded to Disclosure Events

An important issue that must be addressed by intervening professionals when they are investigating a child sexual abuse report is whether or not the child's mother was aware that the sexual abuse was occurring prior to disclosure. Other related questions which are central to the intervention process are: To whom did the child first disclose? Did the mother believe her child? What action followed? What was the mother's response to the disclosure? Who called the child welfare authorities and reported the sexual abuse? Each of these issues is addressed in this chapter.

Sgroi (1982) discusses two types of disclosures: accidental and purposeful. Accidental disclosure usually refers to those cases where the victim or offender did not tell the secret but it became known through: (1) a third party; (2) an unplanned physical injury to the child; (3) a sexually transmitted disease or pregnancy; or (4) because of precocious sexual activity of a young child. Three accidental disclosures were reported in the interviews in this study. The remaining twenty-eight children disclosed purposefully – they told the secret to someone.

Since many of the current theories explaining child sexual abuse still focus on the culpability and collusion of mothers and victims, it seems important to describe what mothers in this study said and did after disclosure. This section deals with some of the issues mentioned earlier as they relate to mothers. Each of these cases is documented in the agency records and it is my impression after interviewing the participants in this study that the women minimized the events of the sexual abuse, and did not, as popular media and father's rights groups might suggest, exaggerate them.

The responses of the twenty-four mothers can be grouped into the following three types for discussion purposes: (1) mothers who knew; (2) mothers who were suspicious; and; (3) mothers who did not know.

The number of mothers in each of the three groups, with a description of the circumstances, follows.

Group 1: The Mothers Who Said They Knew (four mothers)

The mothers who knew their children were being sexually abused covers two categories: (1) those mothers who chose not to make a formal report immediately because they felt they could not, for various reasons, deal with the situation at that particular time; (2) those mothers who had already brought that information to the attention of child welfare authorities previously, but the abuse had not been validated after investigation (it was, however, validated upon subsequent disclosure).

Group 2: The Mothers Who Were Suspicious (three mothers)

This group covers the mothers who were becoming 'suspicious' that their children might possibly be victims of sexual abuse and were beginning to take steps before the sexual abuse was actually validated by their own children or by mandated professionals.

Group 3: The Mothers Who Did Not Know (seventeen mothers)

The category of mothers who did not know of their children's sexual abuse until disclosure covers three types of situations: (1) those who did not notice any changes in their children's behaviour prior to disclosure; (2) those who were quite aware of a number of dramatic changes in their children's behaviour and were attempting to determine the cause through assessments and other means; and (3) those whose children disclosed almost immediately after the sexual abuse occurred.

Issues of Awareness, Action, and Belief

More than two-thirds (seventeen) of the twenty-four mothers in this study did not know that their children were being sexually abused. Of the seven remaining mothers, three were becoming suspicious and were taking some form of action, and four mothers said they knew their children were being sexually abused but felt they were unable to do anything for reasons that are discussed later in this chapter.

Two mothers who did know of the abuse situation and immediately reported it to child welfare authorities and the police were unable to have their cases validated on the first report. The reasons for the lack of validation, in both cases, were threefold: both offenders denied, each child recanted her story, and there was no medical evidence of the sexual abuse. Both mothers believed the children had told the truth the first time, but were unable to do anything but continue to encourage the children to tell them if it happened again. In one case, the child's father was the offender and the abuse went on for a three-year period before the child disclosed to her mother the second time. The police were called immediately and criminal charges were laid. In the other case, the offender was a friend of the extended family. Both of these children (from the same family) had been threatened with death if they told their mother.

Twenty-three of the twenty-four mothers took some kind of immediate action once they were told of the abuse. The results of this study are consistent with those of Dempster (1992), where all thirty-four mothers took some form of action toward ending the sexual abuse and protecting their children. Not all of the mothers in my study were successful in protecting their children. One was badly advised by the person in whom she confided and cautioned about a possible law suit. Another was intimidated by her husband who vehemently denied the child's story. Like many women who feel responsible for holding their families together, this woman was apprehensive about pursuing action in light of the possible negative effects it might have on the family. She did report later, however.

Twenty-three of the thirty-one children who were victims of sexual abuse told their mothers first. Of the remaining eight, three children from one family told their father first; one child told her small friend, who immediately told her mother (the child's babysitter); two other children told their best friends, who persuaded them to talk to their mothers about it; one child told her therapist first; and one child told her school principal first.

Circumstances prevented some of the children from telling their mothers first. For example, three children in one family disclosed to their father first because their mother was still sleeping, and their father was the first one they saw in the morning after the abuse. One child told her best friend after they had seen a play at their school performed by a professional acting troupe aimed at prompting children to tell someone right away if they are being sexually abused. Another child was with her babysitter when she disclosed. The child became alarmed while playing with dolls and another child removed the doll's clothing. When her little friend asked what was wrong and why she looked so frightened, she described what had been done to her. One child was taken to her mother's therapist in hopes that she would tell whatever it was that was causing her to act so 'out of character.' Her mother was sitting in the waiting room, and was called in immediately when the child disclosed. Another child developed a pain in her stomach at school and was sent to the principal's office, where she disclosed what an older boy had done to her on the school grounds after school hours. The principal called her mother immediately. The last child in this group was on vacation when she disclosed. While the victim's mother was out shopping, the child disclosed to the daughter of her mother's friend. Within hours of telling her friend, she disclosed to her own mother.

It seems clear that mothers, because they are generally the caregivers of children, are told first when their children have been harmed. The delays in the children disclosing in this study might be explained by the threats, bribes, and warnings given to the children by the offenders. As indicated earlier, a number of children were told they would be killed; that someone in their families would be harmed; that nobody would believe them; and that they could go to jail if they told anyone about the sexual abuse.

Mainstream literature suggests that children do not disclose to their mothers because of poor relationships between mothers and their children. This may well be the case in circumstances where fathers are not the offenders, but the mothers in this study indicated that relationships with their children were constantly being undermined in every way possible by the fathers prior to disclosure. For example, the mothers stated in the interviews that prior to disclosure they noted how their husbands, the children's fathers, allowed these particular children special privileges. Fathers interfered with routine discipline, and permitted these children to do things that were not within the normal range of accepted behaviours in their homes. Specific examples are discussed later in this chapter.

Twenty-four of the thirty-one children who were victimized in this study were believed by their mothers when they first disclosed, and those mothers never wavered in their belief in the veracity of their children's stories. For seven other children, mothers had different reactions. Four children were between the ages of two and four years at the time and their mothers were uncertain initially because of the children's ages and levels of understanding, but these mothers eventually believed their children. Two mothers believed their children initially, but later were doubtful after they discussed the disclosures with other family members. These two mothers were persuaded that it was entirely possible that their children (the victims) had lied and/or exaggerated to get attention, as these children had a history of such behaviour. This behaviour is now recognized as being caused by the trauma of abuse (so it is possible that the lying was attributable to earlier victimization). These were the only two children of the thirty-one who were placed outside of the home after the sexual abuse disclosures (one in a foster home, and one with relatives).

The mothers of these two children became ambivalent about their children's disclosures for a short while but eventually did believe them and were reunited with them.

The behaviour of the family members (mainly sisters and mothers) in suggesting the victims were lying was perhaps an attempt to protect the men in the family who might otherwise face possible incarceration for the offences. Family members were possibly protecting the family unit and family ideology by discrediting the children's stories. According to Baker Miller (1977): 'Women are taught that their main goal in life is to serve others – first men and later children ... [S]ince women have had to live by trying to please men, they have been conditioned to prevent men from feeling even uncomfortable' (57, 61).

In addition to not wanting to make the men in their families feel uncomfortable, the loss of economic support of the men must be considered as an important disincentive to women sharing the information with outside authorities.

One mother just could not believe her child at first so the child went to school and told her school counsellor, who immediately called the CAS and reported the abuse. Later, a second child in the same family disclosed, and this mother believed her second child immediately so that both children were eventually believed.

Of the seven children whose mothers were slightly ambivalent at first, four were children of mothers who had been victims of sexual abuse in their own childhood and had not been able, for various reasons, to deal with the trauma caused by their own abuse. The literature on adult survivors suggests that amnesia can take place that makes it impossible for victims to retrieve their own memories of molestation (Williams 1994). 'If a survivor hasn't remembered her abuse or acknowledged its effects, she may not be able to recognize signs that her children are in danger ...' (Bass and Davis 1988, 279). As well, 'being a victim of child sexual abuse could compromise parents' ability to supervise or care for children in a way that makes them more vulnerable' (Finkelhor et al. 1997, 6). It is important to recognize, however, that coping mechanisms such as memory loss are the body's creative method of allowing the victimized child to continue to function in her daily life after the trauma.

I think it highly unlikely that a mother would have volunteered for this study if she had not believed her child's disclosure. I did not seek out mothers to interview who did not believe their children. There are indeed mothers who are unable to believe their children's disclosures, and who do not reconsider their position within a short period of time. Twelve of the fifteen key informants I interviewed discussed such mothers. Also, through my own professional experience in child welfare work, I have encountered a few such mothers, but found them to be in the minority. The statistics in child welfare agencies do not support the claims often heard in professional discourse that most mothers do not believe their children, as such children are usually placed in the care of the Society. Of 184 children who attended crisis support groups in one Ontario program, only 20 were in foster homes at the time of referral (within four weeks of disclosure) (Metropolitan Toronto Special Committee 1988, 2). Sometimes, however, the children are placed with relatives initially. In such cases, they might not show up in the statistics as having been removed from their homes.

A group of mothers who did not believe their children's stories over the long-term would constitute an interesting, but different study. What is being examined here is the impact of various friends, family members, neighbours, and social and judicial systems upon non-offending mothers as part of mothers' experiences after disclosure. If a child were placed under long-term care, the child's mother would have a very different experience within the system.

More than three-quarters of the mothers in this study stood solidly with their children from the first disclosure, and all mothers believed their children within a six-month period after disclosure.

Each mother had a different response to her child's disclosure. The following examples help to illustrate the various types of responses in the three groups mentioned earlier.

Group 1: Four Mothers Who Said They Knew of the Sexual Abuse

Shelly Brown said her three-year-old daughter, Ina, told her of the abuse by asking the question 'Mommy, why does Daddy always stick his finger in my bum?' This mother confronted her husband at the first opportunity and she said, '[He] was hurt, scared and outraged ... His affect was right on ... and he said, "Let's call the authorities and get it investigated."' Her response was, '[W]hy bother if it is not true.' Later, Ms Brown discussed the child's disclosure with a life-long friend, who felt it should be addressed further. At this point, she felt that she knew it was true, but that there was no way she could deal with it. Her husband was running for political office at the time. They did not speak of the allegation again until approximately six weeks later, after Ms Brown shared the disclosure with her therapist, who subsequently advised her to go home and ask her daughter more about the sexual abuse and to treat it as an important and serious complaint. Ms Brown spoke with Ina about the abuse and this time her daughter shared more details with her, and seemed very relieved to be able to discuss it. Shelly Brown confronted her husband for a second time, this time at his place of work, and she said, '[H]e looked me straight in the eye and said, "I didn't do it."' She left after making it clear to him that she believed their daughter, and felt that he had been lying to her. After driving around and around the block in her car to try to come to grips with the situation, she decided to call the Society and report the sexual abuse. She ended the relationship with her husband, the victim's father, and subsequently divorced him.

Ms Brown's response in immediately confronting her husband was an appropriate response. His denial left her unable to act further at the time; although she says she did believe her daughter, she really did not know what to do. Her ambivalent feelings about the situation led her to seek out first a friend, and then a therapist. Both gave a clear message about the importance of listening to her child, and taking action. It was later learned that not only had the sexual abuse taken place when the child was at home with her mother, but also later, when her father had supervised, court-ordered visits at the paternal grandmother's home, while the offender's mother was in charge of the visits.

Shelly Brown had received support from others to pursue the matter further despite her husband's outraged denials. The following mother did not have that kind of support. Her circumstances were somewhat different, since the offender had been a trusted friend next door and not her husband.

Anita Marshall believed her child, Janet, when she told her that a neighbour had touched her vagina. Two years previously, at age five, her child had reported that the same neighbour had exposed himself and had masturbated in front of her. On the first occasion, Anita Marshall went immediately to a friend's home to share the disclosure with her. She described her friend as a 'very level-headed, methodical, and organized person.' Anita Marshall said, 'As soon as she opened the door, I started to cry ... I was so upset ...' After her friend was told about the disclosure, she asked her, 'Are you sure? You have to have dates, times ... You can't make accusations ... you have to have proof.' Since she did not have the proof, she decided to keep her eyes and ears open until she had more information. Two years later, her child disclosed again. Anita Marshall called the child welfare authorities anonymously and asked a few 'what if' questions. When she was told by the Society intake worker that it was her responsibility as a mother to make a formal report, she did so immediately.

This mother said she was intimidated by the prestige and status of her neighbour, the offender, who was respected in the community and seen as a grandfatherly figure to the small children in the neighbourhood. The advice she received from her trusted friend was to be very cautious and to make sure she had all the facts before she made a formal complaint against this man. Anita Marshall chose not to tell her family, Janet's school teacher, or her babysitter. Neither did she tell anyone at work. Her husband was told about the disclosure, but he did not want to talk about it. He suggested they try to forget the matter and not dwell on it. When asked why she told only one friend and her husband of the disclosure, she said she did not trust people with the information, as they might gossip.

Given that scenario, and the outcome of the case, (where the offender received only thirty days house arrest because of his advanced age), it is suggested here that Anita Marshall might not have wanted anybody to know about the sexual abuse because she somehow felt responsible and guilty that this had happened to her child and this could possibly reflect negatively on her mothering. Perhaps, if either of the two people she had told, her husband (the child's father) or her friend, had encouraged her to report to authorities the first time her daughter disclosed instead of cautioning her not to act, she might have done so. Or, if she had shared the disclosure with a few others, like the school teacher or the babysitter, she might have received support from them to report the first disclosure.

Dorothy White was told by her adopted daughter: 'Daddy was touching my pee pee.' She took her daughter, Jill, to her family doctor immediately for an examination. Since there was no physical evidence of abuse, the doctor advised her not to call child welfare or the police department. This mother did believe the abuse had occurred however, and shared this information with women friends, one of whom called the Society and reported the abuse for her. The child was interviewed with the use of the anatomically explicit dolls at which time she admitted the abuse, but later she recanted her story. The police officer and the child welfare worker felt there was insufficient evidence of sexual abuse and declared the incident invalid.

Dorothy White believed something had happened and tried to keep a closer watch on her adopted daughter, although she was working outside the home at the time. Her husband, on the other hand, was retired and therefore at home on a regular basis with Jill. Three years later, when Jill disclosed a second time, Ms White immediately called the police and the Society. Her husband, the child's step-father, denied any responsibility for the abuse and called the child a liar. He later admitted to the offence and was criminally charged, found guilty, and incarcerated for six months. Dorothy White later divorced her husband because of the sexual abuse.

In spite of her doctor's advice not to report the first disclosure to authorities, this mother did report. When professionally trained social workers and police were unable to obtain sufficient evidence to validate the case, Dorothy White still believed her daughter's original story. It is not unusual to have a child recant her story when threats are used against her, and in this instance Jill was told she would be killed if she told her mother. The child continued for three years to keep the secret. Meanwhile, Ms White's husband, the child's step-father, continued to try to undermine the relationship between mother and daughter by giving Jill special favours, such as candy and money. He also allowed her a number of other inappropriate privileges for her age (pre-teen), such as wearing lipstick. Jill finally decided to tell her mother when she was eleven because she said she was afraid of getting pregnant by her step-father. She risked telling, despite the threats, and despite the deteriorating relationship with her mother.

This mother was seen by the child welfare authorities as not having been protective enough of her daughter and she was ordered into a crisis support group for mothers as part of the conditions made in a supervision order through the child welfare court. Ms White attended the group because she was afraid her daughter would be removed from her care if she did not comply with the agency's wishes and the court order. Here, we see a mother being held responsible for the abuse her daughter suffered at the hands of her adoptive father. Dorothy White was expected to protect her child from her husband.

The following mother experienced a similar situation, when her child disclosed, then recanted, but three years later disclosed again. Ingrid Hogg knew of her child's sexual abuse, because her daughter had disclosed when she was four years old. Later, however, her daughter denied the sexual abuse during an interview by the Society's intake worker. No further intervention was possible at the time, but this mother said she knew that the denial was a lie, and she encouraged her daughter to tell her if it happened again. She noted a change in her daughter after access visits to her biological father's apartment. She thought her former husband, the child's father, might have been the offender but, without proof, she was obliged to send the child for access visits on a regular basis.

Finally, approximately five years later, despite numerous warnings by the perpetrators that they would kill the child if she told anyone, Fiona did tell her mother that the offenders were two men who knew her father.

Ingrid Hogg immediately called the police, who came along with the intake worker and took the child's statement. It was later learned that other small children were involved as well. One alleged offender had his case dismissed because of a technicality, and the other was charged; both men were at large in the community when these interviews were conducted. Ingrid Hogg's response to her daughter's early disclosure was immediate and appropriate. She said she knew Fiona was telling the truth the first time and did not believe her when she recanted. This child had numerous problems urinating, which were being treated by her doctor, but no hospital or medical expert at the time made the connection or became suspicious that the child's problems might have been caused by sexual abuse.

This case is of particular interest, since many of those who had been told about the abuse blamed the child's mother for not providing better supervision or protecting her daughter. It was later determined that the episodes of sadistic abuse to Fiona happened during her regular access visits to her biological father's home. He was considered the caregiver of the child on those particular weekends. There was no mention by professionals as to why the father let this happen to Fiona. It brings home again the point that mothers are held responsible for the protection and safety of their children no matter what, even when the children are in their father's care. There was no removal of access from this father; no child welfare court order mandating him into a support group where he would learn how to better protect his child; or even a referral to a support group to get him through this tragedy.

Group 2: Three Mothers Who Said They Were Suspicious

The three mothers in Group 2 did not know for certain that their children were victims of sexual abuse because their children had not verbalized it to them. They were becoming more and more suspicious, however, that their children might be victims of sexual abuse.

Rachel Cohen was aware of the overly attentive behaviour of an older male friend towards her son, Ben, and she tried to discourage the relationship. Finally, about six months before disclosure, she called the friend's wife and said, 'I don't want my son seeing your husband any more ... He has to have his own friends.' Her friend did not take her wish seriously. Both scoffed at her suggestion and the offender continued to be involved in her son's life. Rachel Cohen's worst fears were confirmed when the police arrived at her door one weekend and advised her that they were watching a particular perpetrator with four young boys, and they suspected her son, Ben, was one of the boys. Ben was called in and questioned by the police, but he immediately denied there was any sexual involvement with the alleged perpetrator.

Ms Cohen continued to question her son and eventually he did admit that this neighbour, who was a friend of the family, had been sexually abusing him. Ben had been told by the perpetrator not to tell his mother.

The police were called by Rachel Cohen and charges were laid against the perpetrator. Two years after the date of disclosure, he pleaded guilty and was sentenced to forty-five days in jail on weekends. This perpetrator was free to carry on with his life at work and at home, although he was not permitted to be around small children or visit parks. For the most part, the offender was able to enjoy his freedom while the mothers and children involved were living in torment because their lives had been on 'hold' until the court proceeded with the case. Delays in court, according to Rachel Cohen, were in the interests of the offender and not in 'the best interests of the children' or their mothers, who had to go through the pain of the delays on a day-to-day basis.

In Ben's case, the offender was the babysitter for the boy from the time he was four or five years of age. The child received a great deal of attention from the offender, a professional in the community with children of his own. He helped Ben with school projects, took him on outings such as skating and swimming, bought him special gifts, and gave him money to spend. The child's biological father had legal access through the courts, but was uninvolved with his son.

The offender's wife was also a friend of the family, and visited the Cohen home frequently. Rachel Cohen said that she, too, received gifts from the offender, who was very generous when she was short of cash.

It seems clear that Ben liked the attention from an adult male, the trips, and the extra money given to him. It is also clear, however, that he did not like the sexual abuse that went along with it. He said he wanted it to stop and he told the offender this, but it did not stop. The attention was a manipulation in order for the perpetrator to continue to have access to this boy to satisfy his own sexual needs. This is a recognized pattern of pedophilic behaviour (Araji and Finkelhor 1986; Gondolf 1987; Sgroi 1982; Groth and Birnbaum 1981).

Ben did not tell his mother because the offender told him that he, the offender, would go to jail if the boy told. Ben did not want this to happen to his friend at first, but, later when the man would not stop fondling him, he decided that the only way he could get the abuse to stop was to tell his mother, which he did after the police had discovered the offence. Ms Cohen blames herself for not taking more decisive action at the time. It is important to mention here that there has been no discussion whatsoever from any professional or from any family member about the lack of interest Ben's father had shown in him.

Michele Richard was also a mother who was suspicious. She said initially she noticed nothing in the way of behavioural change with her seven-year-old daughter, Margot, but admitted, 'I was a mess personally myself ... so I wasn't paying as close attention as I might have ...' After several months, when her life started to come together, she said she noticed, each time her daughter returned from visiting her biological father, that she was more distraught. Since her ex-husband had sexually abused her young cousin, she did not trust him, so she said to her daughter one night when she was putting her to bed, 'You know, if anybody ever touched you in a way that made you feel bad ... it's okay ... you can tell me ... because it happened to me when I was young, too ...,' and her daughter disclosed that same night. She said that her father had sexually touched her while she was visiting him.

This particular mother did not trust the local Society, so she called her family doctor, who advised her to see her lawyer immediately. Her lawyer called the local Society while she was in his office and made a formal report on her behalf. Michele Richard blamed herself for not noticing her child's distress earlier. It is not unusual for women to blame themselves, since they receive the message that society expects that they will not allow any harm to come to their children, even when they are not present.

The third and last mother in Group 2, Catharine Burns, was also a 'suspicious mother.' She took her child to two different doctors with anal bleeding and the child was treated for constipation and given mineral oil, which did not stop the bleeding. Finally, this mother got very suspicious when she noted dry blood in the perineum area while examining her child. She said, 'I think at that moment I knew ... My blood ran cold ... I just felt everything through me was a horror ...' Her daughter, Virginia, was only four years of age at the time, and had not told her mother what was causing the bleeding, because her father told her not to tell their secret to her mother, his wife, or she would be mad at him. She immediately took the child to trusted relatives and shared the information with them and they supported her suspicions and encouraged her to seek help. Ms Burns called child welfare authorities to report the abuse. The intake worker who answered the telephone discouraged her from making a formal report of the sexual abuse. This response will be discussed later. Nonetheless,

Catharine Burns took her daughter to the hospital, and her suspicions were confirmed. This is considered an accidental disclosure, since the child was injured but did not tell until after the diagnosis had been made by a doctor. The doctor indicated he would have to report to the local Society, which he did, and the weekend duty worker arrived the following morning and interviewed Virginia. Ms Burns was told later that her husband was contacted by police officers. He left the family home immediately at the suggestion of the police officers involved. All charges were dismissed, however, because the child was unable to testify in court when her father spoke to her and made eye contact with her in the courtroom.

Ms Burns had never been a victim of sexual abuse herself, but was brought up in what she described as a very loving upper-middle-class home. It was very difficult for her to comprehend that she could have married a man who would commit such a painful and cruel act to their child. Even after she struggled through her own disbelief, with no suggestions or suspicions from three different doctors as to what could be causing the rectal bleeding in her child, and after she received positive support from relatives to make a formal report to the appropriate authorities, this mother was aware she was being persuaded not to make a formal complaint from the very agency mandated to receive such complaints. This was an unexpected response from a child welfare intake worker mandated to protect children, and will be discussed later in Chapter Six.

Group 3: Seventeen Mothers Who Said They Did Not Know

Five mothers said they did not recall their children exhibiting any dramatically different behaviour during the period of abuse, although, in retrospect, some mothers recalled certain behaviour that they couldn't explain at the time, and subsequently attributed such behaviour to the effects of the sexual abuse. Although each mother's experience is unique and separate from any other mother's experience in child abuse situations, I have tried to select one mother from these five to illustrate some of the issues involved for the mothers who did not know of the sexual abuse before disclosure and whose children did not exhibit any particular behavioural changes that might have alerted their mothers that something was troubling them.

Elizabeth Sutton said her daughter, Penny, had been watching an episode of the television program 'Golden Girls,' which dealt with sexual orientation. When it was over, Penny said to her mother, 'I have something to tell you ... I hope you will not be mad at me ...' Her daughter then proceeded to tell her that she was being sexually abused by her uncle. Ms Sutton said: 'My reaction was a combination of disbelief and sadness ... I felt sorry for her ... I didn't tell her I didn't believe her. I just didn't want to think that this had actually happened.' Later, Elizabeth Sutton found out that her daughter was prompted to disclose the abuse after she had seen a play in school that day about children reporting sexual abuse.

Ms Sutton had been divorced but later remarried to a man whom she described as a wonderful partner, and the best relationship she had ever experienced. When her daughter, Penny, disclosed that her uncle, her mother's brother, had been sexually abusing her, Ms Sutton wanted to go to her parents' home where her brother lived and confront him. She requested that her husband accompany her for emotional support, but he hesitated and she said 'he didn't feel it was his place,' which Ms Sutton said 'put me through another set of confusing emotions ... so I asked my sister because I really felt I needed moral support.' She and her sister went to their parents' home to discuss her child's disclosure but she said 'my father ... reacted in anger and proceeded to throw me out of the house ...' Her brother denied the allegation until he failed a lie detector test; he then admitted his responsibility for sexually abusing her daughter, his niece. He was seventeen years of age at the time of disclosure. No criminal charges were laid in this particular case because Elizabeth Sutton requested that the police not proceed with charges against her brother.

Eight of the seventeen mothers in Group 3 did not know of the sexual abuse, but the behaviour of their children was indicative that something was wrong. For example, one previously well-behaved child punched her teacher; two other children began hitting other children for no reason at all; two cried at the least little correction by their mothers; two were bed-wetting; and three were having persistent nightmares. All of these children were much more difficult to manage at home and a number were taken for various behavioural assessments. Most of these children were experiencing difficulties in school as well as at home.

Gertrude Davis could not understand what was causing her daughter Barbara's unusual behaviour. She visited the school and the teachers were equally confused as to why a child who had been an 'A' student had begun to do so poorly in her school work. Psychological assessments were completed, but nothing was clarified about the situation. Finally, one evening, her daughter Barbara, clad in only her nightdress, ran to the next-door neighbour's house, where her mother was visiting, to tell her mother that her father had just approached her sexually that evening. After Ms Davis recovered somewhat from the shock, she went home and confronted her husband, who admitted the abuse. She then packed her two children into the car and spent the night with relatives until she could decide what to do. It then became clear to Ms Davis why her daughter's behaviour had been so difficult for several months.

Four children in Group 3 disclosed almost immediately after the abuse took place. For example, three disclosed within twenty-four hours, and one child disclosed after the second time the abuse had occurred, which was within a few months. It is interesting to note that in no instance of the four disclosures in this category was the perpetrator the child's father. Telling one's mother immediately seems to be much easier for children if the offender is not the child's father. There were ten children sexually abused by their fathers, but the majority of these children took a very long time to disclose the abuse.

The types of action taken by the mothers from groups 1, 2, and 3 has been described in detail. It might have appeared to the child-victim or to others involved that a number of these mothers did nothing; however, the evidence from this study shows that in all but one of the twenty-four cases, the mothers took some form of action immediately following the children's disclosures. And the one mother acted within the next two days. This action was not necessarily calling child welfare authorities, but it frequently included some form of follow-up, such as confronting the offender, telling a friend, or perhaps taking the child to a doctor. I now turn to the reporting of the sexual abuse to the mandated agencies.

Who Reported

Twenty-six reports were made to the child welfare authorities with respect to thirty of the thirty-one children in this study (one was not reported because the victim had reached sixteen years before she disclosed) and two families had more than one offence. Eighteen of the twenty-six reports were made by mothers of child victims. The remaining eight reports were made by others, including: two reports made to child welfare by hospital social workers; two made by family doctors; two made by police; and one each made by a school counsellor and a babysitter. Nearly three-quarters of the reports to authorities, then, were made by the children's mothers, which speaks to their need to protect their children, even though the economic and emotional costs of reporting were considerable in terms of their own lives, especially when the offenders were their partners or members of their families.

Mothers responded supportively to their children's disclosures in spite of the stress when the offender was either a partner or someone closely connected with the family. Who, then, supported mothers themselves during their crisis situations?

Support for the Mothers

This section might be easier to understand if the responses are divided into two separate groupings: (1) those who were married or had live-in partners; and (2) those who were sole-support mothers. At the time of disclosure, seventeen of the mothers were either married or had hetero-sexual live-in partners, while seven were sole-support mothers living on their own with their children, although some of these women had male friends whom they were seeing on a regular basis. At the time of the interviews, the situation was somewhat different: exactly one-half (twelve) of the mothers were either married or had live-in partners, and one-half were sole-support mothers. Some of the latter twelve mothers had male friends whom they were seeing on a regular basis.

Of the seventeen mothers who were married or had live-in partners at disclosure, only three named their husbands or male partners as the most emotionally supportive person for them at the time. Five mothers eventually left their husbands, who were, in fact, the offenders. One mother was left by her live-in partner, whom she said could not handle the crisis in the home created by the child's disclosure (although he was not the offender himself).

Those named most frequently in a supportive role by mothers (with partners) were their sisters. Others who were named the most supportive, more frequently than husbands or partners, were female friends and female neighbours.

Ingrid Hogg was divorced from her child's biological father and had had a live-in partner for approximately four years. When her daughter Fiona disclosed sexual abuse by friends of her father, the situation in the home became very tense, with visits from the police department and child welfare authorities. In addition, there were court dates, doctor's appointments, missed work, and, of course, the pain that both child and mother were experiencing as a result of the abuse. Ms Hogg said she went through periods of uncontrolled crying. Her live-in partner couldn't handle it. She said, 'If you wanted someone to come over and give you a hug and just say ... it's okay, we'll get through this ... I wasn't getting that.' Her partner moved out and ended the relationship with her because of the disclosure. This is not an unusual situation, since research shows that men are not often emotionally supportive and, in fact, they turn to women rather than other men for emotional support for themselves (Baker 1984; Rubin 1976). Johnson (1992) found that the mothers in her study found it easier to follow through with protective action if they received emotional support from significant others. Hooper (1992) found that only two of the fifteen mothers she interviewed had what they called a confiding relationship with their partners/husbands.

Elizabeth Sutton was a woman who looked for support from her husband at the time of her child disclosure. As discussed earlier in this chapter, he refused to accompany her to her parents' home in order for her to confront her brother. Her sister eventually went along for moral support.

With the exception of the three partners who supported these mothers (Carolyn O'Brien, Mary Fletcher, Rose Foote), the majority of men – brothers, fathers, husbands, and friends – did not provide emotional support to the women in these particular crisis situations. Bridget Hesse gave a very insightful explanation of why she told only her close women friends but not their husbands: 'Most men don't handle this type of thing very well.'

Of the seven sole-support mothers, none named her current boyfriend or any male friend as the most emotionally supportive to her at the time of the crisis. Three named a female friend, two named their mothers, one named her sister, and one said she did not get much support from anyone (friends or family).

Although a few of the mothers' mothers were supportive, some were clearly not. For example, Nina Kew said her mother was not very supportive when she told her about her granddaughter's disclosure. She said, 'It's your fault, you married the guy.' Ms Kew said, 'That made me feel really guilty ...' Other sole-support mothers indicated that their families were split in terms of loyalty to a relative who was the abuser. The results of this study with respect to the lack of family support is similar to the results reported by Hooper (1992) and Dempster (1992).

6

The Mothers' Experiences with Child Welfare Intervention

Before describing the child welfare system's response to the mothers and their individual experiences of intervention from that system, which in this study is the Children's Aid Society (as the province of Ontario designates societies to carry out its mandate to protect children) I would like to provide the reader with background information on how the Ontario system operates, and what some of the major influences were in the development of legislation and policy.[1]

Federal and Provincial Laws Regarding Child Sexual Abuse

There are three relevant types of laws that address the problem of child sexual abuse in Canada: (1) through the power of *parens patriae*, child welfare workers, as agents of the state, are mandated to intervene in families to investigate a suspected case of child sexual abuse; (2) through civil laws, citizens are legally responsible for the reporting of suspected child sexual abuse to child welfare agencies, with special responsibility placed upon professionals (in Ontario); and (3) through criminal laws, perpetrators can be charged on any one of a number of offences applicable to sexual abuse under the *Criminal Code of Canada* (Bala 1991; Lane 1982; Giovannoni 1985).

It might be assumed that these laws are designed to guarantee the protection of children from sexual abuse, but they are not always effective. Not all children tell someone that they have been sexually abused, nor do all citizens or professionals report known cases of child sexual abuse to the mandated authorities. Despite the fact that, according to Robertshaw (1981) in all the provinces of Canada, mothers, professionals, and citizens are legally obligated to report suspected child abuse to a mandated agency.

Not all those who commit such offences against children are criminally charged, for various reasons that are discussed later.

Brief History and Background of Child Protection in Ontario:
Policies, Practices, Laws and Standards

In the province of Ontario, where my research was conducted, the Children's Aid Societies provide the mandated child welfare services for the protection of children. The child welfare institution is referred to here as the Society and/or the Agency. The entry point of the Society happens at the most critical stage of crisis in a family, usually just after the disclosure of the sexual abuse, but before other professionals become involved, although some women do seek help from their family doctors first.

Until child abuse was included in *The Child Welfare Act*, 1965, child welfare services in Ontario were mainly concerned with delinquency and complex family issues, such as the lack of basic needs (housing, food, and clothing), problems with alcoholism, and unemployment. There was no special focus on 'child abuse,' as such (Carter 1987a).

When a special focus on child sexual abuse was incorporated into agency policies and programs in 1965, however, it created tensions in child welfare that have yet to be resolved (Parton 1985; Schorr 1986). A spokesperson for the Societies suggested that 'the total protection and prevention work of societies is being distorted by the single focus of abuse' (Caldwell 1983, 4).

In the early stages of this special focus, under the heading of child abuse, ministry regulations directed all Societies in Ontario to report to the director of the Children's Services Bureau 'all incidents of alleged physical abuse, all alleged physical neglect, all alleged malnutrition of children and those incidents of sexual molesting of children in which (a) a pre-puberty child is involved and (b) charges have been laid. A pre-puberty child is defined as a child of up to and including age 11 years ...' (Ontario Ministry 1974, 1.03).

Initially, then, there was a qualifier on reporting the 'sexually' abused child to the ministry. Only those children eleven years of age or younger in which criminal charges were laid were considered reportable to the ministry at the time. A child of tender years (under age fourteen) was permitted to testify in court only at the discretion of the judge. As might be expected, few children ever appeared in criminal court as witnesses prior to the early 1980s. Given the narrow age definition, the restriction on the child as a witness in the courts, and the directive that criminal charges had to be laid before the sexual abuse was considered a valid case, it was understandable that very few cases were documented in Societies at that particular time (Carter 1987a).

This is not to say that sexual abuse of children was not found within Society caseloads at the time. According to the research of Linda Gordon (1988b) completed on child welfare records in Boston from 1880 to 1960, child sexual abuse cases were redefined by professionals; that is, child sexual abuse was called something else. Females who were child-victims were frequently considered 'delinquent' before the 'rediscovery' of child sexual abuse. Gordon suggests that this redefinition served to remove scrutiny from families.

The use of the term 'rediscovery' refers to the fact that child sexual abuse is not a new phenomenon, but was identified throughout various stages of history. It did not, however, get placed on the political agenda until after the beginning of the women's liberation movement (Gordon 1988b; Jeffreys 1985; Rush 1980). As a result of feminist critiques since the 1970s, child sexual abuse has been recognized as a major social problem and a crime against society.

In an attempt to determine how cases of child sexual abuse were being handled in Toronto by child welfare authorities, a review was undertaken of how fifty children under age twelve were treated for sexual assault at the Toronto Hospital for Sick Children between January 1972 and January 1976. Lane (1982) found 'little or no reference in the [child welfare] records to the sexual assault of the children nor any indication of the psychological or other trauma experienced by the child. The families were multi-problem families with so many other problems in the family of higher priority ... that the case workers did not have time to spend with the children and the families coping with the sexual assaults' (19).

There was little or no focus on the sexual abuse of the victim as a priority. The Garber Report (Ontario Ministry 1978a) recommended that the Ontario Ministry of Social Services develop standards of service for all Societies. Other recommendations focused on measures to establish protection service on a twenty-four-hour basis throughout the province, provided by qualified social workers with specialized training who would be assisted in decision making by multidisciplinary child abuse teams.

In 1978, sexual abuse was specifically included in the *Child Welfare Act*, Province of Ontario. When the newly disclosed cases of child sexual abuse began flooding into agencies in the early 1980s, workers quickly became aware of the inadequacy of the physical abuse treatment model to appropriately deal with sexual abuse cases. The overwhelming majority of abusers now appeared to be males; however, most agency child abuse programs were designed for the caregivers, who were primarily mothers (Carter and Zanutto 1984).

The dynamic of sexual abuse was different from that found in physical abuse cases (Finkelhor 1984; Russell 1986). Medically, little physical evidence is typically found during the examination of sexually abused children (Ellerstein and Canavan 1980; Finkel 1983). Also, sexual abuse cases require different intervention techniques and treatment modalities, as well as a re-examination of existing values. Other types of abuse are not as gender specific – that is, almost exclusively a male crime. Child welfare authorities and the Ministry of Social Services initially defined child sexual abuse as a 'family problem,' rather than a crime against the child and against society. This approach favoured keeping the family 'intact.' Intact families were ones that were considered complete or undamaged, having mother, father, and children living together in the same home. Training materials stressed that 'family involvement is the treatment of choice. Failing this, police involvement is to be considered' (Ontario Ministry 1979, 31).

The 1980s

On 18 January 1979, a memorandum was issued by the solicitor general following the Garber Task Force Recommendations (Ontario Ministry 1978a), urging police forces and child welfare agencies in the province to follow a written set of guidelines for collaboration on child abuse cases. Although this was an important step in beginning the collaborative process, it was not until 1983 that the first formal indication of regular and routine police involvement in investigative work with child welfare was visible. A protocol was implemented, outlining procedures for the Society and the police to coordinate their investigations and assessments of all reports of child sexual abuse (Metropolitan Toronto 1983, 2).

Nearly one-half of the fifty communities surveyed throughout the province had developed written protocols to direct such collaborative procedures regarding child abuse cases by the mid 1980s (Hagens et al. 1986). It became part of routine procedures that police officers and child welfare workers carry out joint investigations in these cases. This resulted in an increase in the number of criminal charges laid in comparison to previous years. For example, in one early study (1977–8) of 918 cases, which combined all types of child abuse in Ontario, approximately 10 per cent of the cases were categorized as sexual abuse cases. In only 16 per cent of the 918 cases were criminal charges laid (Ontario Ministry 1978b, 22). Badgley et al. (1984) reported that 34.3 per cent of offences in a child welfare sample of 1,438 children in 1981–2 had criminal charges laid. The laying of criminal charges has increased significantly since the adoption of protocols throughout Ontario.

During the 1980s, programs for crisis and support groups developed and referrals for treatment were made. A special priority was assigned to child sexual abuse cases that was absent before that time. Now, the child was believed, supported, and in many cases provided with treatment (Carter 1987a).

The ministry's *Standards and Guidelines for Management of Child Abuse Cases* were developed specifying the procedures to be followed in the management of child sexual abuse cases. They specified the criteria against which the performance of workers and agencies were to be measured, providing the basis for holding agencies accountable for the protection of children (Ontario Ministry 1986, 9).

The *Standards and Guidelines* suggest that consultation from specialists in the fields of social work, medicine, law, psychiatry, psychology, and education should be available for use in selected cases.[2]

As indicated earlier, the *Child and Family Services Act* 1984, Province of Ontario defines sexual abuse in relatively broad terms, addressing sexual abuse in Sections 37 (2) (c) and (d), which state that a child is in need of protection where:

the child has been sexually molested or sexually exploited, by the person having charge of the child or by another person where the person having charge of the child knows or should know of the possibility of sexual molestation or sexual exploitation and fails to protect the child [or] there is a substantial risk that the child will be sexually molested or sexually exploited as described in clause (c) and in Section 75 of *CFSA*, where abuse is defined as 'a state or condition of being physically harmed, sexually molested or sexually exploited,' Sub. Sec. (1).

The *Criminal Code of Canada* introduced new legislation concerning assault and sexual offences in 1983. Further changes were brought about in 1988, when Bill C-15 was proclaimed by the federal government as a response to a number of the fifty-two recommendations made in the Badgley et al. Report (1984). The new legislation created new laws concerning offences in relation to child sexual abuse, refined the existing offences, and, created new provisions in the giving of evidence. In addition, gender issues were addressed by the use of more specific language

(Stewart 1987). There are now seventeen offences in the *Criminal Code* that could apply to child sexual abuse (Wells 1990).

The reforms which began in 1983 were enacted as the *Criminal Law Reform Act, 1984* and covered eleven sections. The main changes involved repealing previous sections of the Act and replacing them, and also adding new sections. Briefly, some of these changes covered (sec. 35) situations where a female person would no longer be convicted of offences if she were under restraint, duress, or fear of the person with whom she had sexual intercourse; (sec. 665) restitution allowances for offenders convicted of an offence; (sec. 668.3) dangerous offenders section for those who were sentenced to imprisonment for ten years or more and had caused serious personal injury to others, as well as other changes (Badgley et al. 1984, 1311–14).

Criminal charges with respect to child sexual abuse are brought under the *Criminal Code of Canada*. The police are responsible for the enforcement of 'the Code' and the prosecution of offences. In some areas of Ontario, specially trained police and Crown attorneys are designated to investigate the sexual abuse and bring the charges to criminal court.

Child welfare is administered in the province of Ontario by fifty-four Societies who were serving the more than 2.2 million children in Ontario at the time of my research. A few First Nations Societies provide services to native children and families exclusively (Ontario Association 1989).

The Societies in Ontario were staffed by approximately 2,000 social workers and social-work supervisors, as well as approximately 2,000 other staff. Seventy-five per cent of the social work supervisors held degrees in social work, while 64 per cent of workers who were engaged in front-line service held degrees in social work (Ontario Association 1989).

How the Mothers in This Study Experienced Society Intervention

It is important to recognize that when a Society is called to investigate child sexual abuse, the visit to the home creates an automatic crisis situation for family members, especially for mothers.

According to Aguilera and Messick (1982), when any individual is faced with a problem that she or he cannot solve, tension and anxiety increase, thus normal functioning ceases; such a state is considered to be a crisis state. Sgroi (1982) argues that 'interveners do not really have a choice about precipitating crisis at the time of disclosure; a crisis will occur regardless' (88). All twenty-four mothers interviewed described themselves as being in a 'crisis state' at disclosure or shortly thereafter.

Twenty-three of the twenty-four mothers had a Society worker involved with their families as a result of the disclosure. One mother was not involved with the Society because her daughter was over sixteen when she disclosed, and, as discussed earlier, the Society mandate in Ontario includes only those cases where the child is under the age of sixteen years. For the majority of mothers (thirteen), this was the first contact they had ever had with a Society. Seven of the twenty-four mothers interviewed already had an open protection file when their children disclosed. An additional three mothers had had some previous contact with the Society (two through earlier investigations for sexual abuse, and one who had adopted two children), but the files of these three women were closed until the current disclosure. When I interviewed the women, (six months to three years post-disclosure), only five of the twenty-three protection files were closed; eighteen files were still open at their respective child welfare offices.

All of the mothers said they felt helpless and overwhelmed by the time the Society worker appeared on the scene. The outcome of their crisis seemed to depend partly on the way the Society worker handled the situation, and partly on the emotional support and understanding these mothers received from others in their immediate environment. This was also a major finding of Johnson (1992).

For some mothers, child welfare intervention meant that they did not have to handle the crisis alone and it became a turning point in their lives. For others, the Society's intervention appeared to exacerbate the crisis and increase the pain, guilt, and fear. For example, in an early U.S. study, 87 per cent of protection workers believed that mothers gave their unconscious consent to incest (Dietz and Croft 1980).

A number of issues developed directly as a result of the disclosure itself, and the subsequent involvement of the Society tended to compound problems for some of the women, creating additional stress and anxiety. Some of the main issues are briefly discussed and examples are given to illustrate the mothers' experiences with the Societies.

Images of child welfare agencies persist in some communities that are passed on from one woman to another, and in some cases from one generation to another. Such images are not always considered positive. The images originate from the feelings that arise out of experiences other women have had and shared with the respondents, from their own experiences with child welfare, and from what they have read or seen in the media (which may or may not have been accurate). The data from these interviews indicate that one-third (eight) of the twenty-four mothers had a lack of trust in child welfare agencies before they had even become involved with them, which proved to be a definite impediment to the helping process. For some mothers, that initial impression of the Society was reinforced, for others, it was changed.

Lack of Trust in Child Welfare Societies

Ingrid Hogg had a general lack of faith in the professionals mandated to protect children from sexual abuse. Her own experience as a child-victim contributed to that impression: 'The people involved in this whole thing ... don't know what they are talking about ... or what they are doing ... not a clue because if they did this stuff wouldn't be happening and offenders [wouldn't be] getting away with it ... It is still happening.'

During the interview, Ms Hogg remembered how she had wanted the Society or somebody in authority to help her when she was a child-victim, but nothing was done and now her own child is a victim and she feels overwhelmed and frustrated with the system and feels little has changed to protect children.

Bridget Hesse said she could not really trust the Society so the family engaged three lawyers, one for her, one for her husband, and one for her daughter. She said she felt it was highly unlikely that mothers in her situation would share their own real feelings of anger towards their children with the Society because of the fear of having one's child removed. The anger between children and mothers was expressed by most of the mothers interviewed. Some women stated that the anger was caused by their feelings that the children withheld the information from them. On the other hand, the children were angry at their mothers because they felt their mothers did not understand the messages they had tried to communicate. When asked how she felt the Society had handled her case, Bridget Hesse said:

Well ... I think there has to be a better way to do these types of things ... I guess ... from day one I felt very intimidated by them ... because I thought they were going to control me and they were going to destroy my life ... I told them ... the intake worker and the caseworker ...' I don't like what you are doing ... I don't trust you people ... I have yet to hear anything good about you.' I warned them to back off and they did ... but only after we brought out the heavy artillery ... They try intimidation.

When asked to explain what the 'heavy artillery' was, Ms Hesse indicated the lawyers she had engaged.

Gertrude Davis experienced a series of events with the Society that left her very bitter about their handling of her case. For example, after the report had been made to the Society, Gertrude Davis was afraid of losing her children: 'I took my children over to my girlfriend's house next door and said to her, "Please keep the kids in your house and please don't let them out ... these people [the Society] are coming ... and they're not touching my kids or taking my children away from me ... so you keep them."'

The Society workers arrived and wanted to know where her children were, at which point this mother said she became panic-stricken:

I don't know now if I remember things the way they really were or if it was so coloured by fear ... At the time I felt ... if I don't produce my kids ... they'd find out where they really were and take them away ... so I did produce my daughter ... the Caseworker took her down to the rec. room and interviewed her and I had a hard time agreeing to that because I didn't want to put [Barbara] through it ... but they threatened to remove her from home.

The interviews continued at the home of this mother with both male and female workers from the Society. Ms Davis described the conversation: 'It was: "Mrs [Davis] ... what's your sex life like with your husband ..." and I really couldn't see that one had anything to do with the other ... If I never let him touch me that's no excuse to hurt the child ... no excuse at all ... [There was] a lot of: "What kind of mother are you?"; "How did you find out about this?"; "What did you do when you found out?"'

According to this mother, the Society workers went back to talk to their 'head people,' and it took them about a week, at which time they decided they would have to interview the members of the family again. This time, they met along with other professionals from the community, including a doctor and a therapist, in a meeting room at the Society's offices. A police officer attended the meeting, as well. Again, Gertrude Davis was the one who was questioned, rather than her husband, the offender. She said, 'I'm asked all kinds of personal questions about my sexual relationship and my family background ...' The various agency representatives later met together: 'At about five o'clock at night, about the time the Society would close, I phoned them and I said: "I know you had a meeting about 10 AM, why haven't I been informed ... I'm throwing up ... Tell me ... what the hell is going to happen to our lives ... You can't do this to us."'

The Society representative informed her that there would be criminal charges laid against her husband, the offender, even though she had been previously advised by other professionals involved in the case that charges would not be laid. Gertrude Davis said, 'It was like ... they continually lied to you so you wouldn't be afraid to tell them [things].'

Despite the fears of losing their children expressed by many of the mothers during the interviews, only two out of thirty-one children in this study were actually placed by the Society outside of their own homes as the result of the sexual abuse and the events that followed. As noted earlier, in both cases, the mothers believed their children at first, but became ambivalent after discussing the disclosure with other family members. Although there were indications in the data of considerable emotional upset at the time of separation, both mothers supported their children's placement, and eventually both daughters were returned to their own homes after a short period of time.

Mothers are legally required to call and report to child welfare officials when they learn of the sexual abuse of their children. The agency that is supposed to help them also has the power to work in ways seen as punitive and unreasonable by the women, however. The pervasiveness of the ideology about the institution of motherhood is so strong that most women experience a sense of failure if they are separated from their children or even if that threat is made. Women also experience a sense of real loss when their children are removed from their homes.

Overt and Covert Methods of Mother-Blaming

The mandate of the Societies is clearly to protect children from abuse, whereas the police mandate involves the laying of criminal charges against offenders. The Society works through the framework of child welfare legislation to protect children. The social workers in the Societies do not make these laws, but are responsible for implementing them. Most of the workers in front-line work are women.

Bridget Hesse was very concerned when she received her copy of the Child and Family Services Protection Application, served on her by the caseworker prior to her child welfare hearing, which stated 'where the person having charge of the child *knows or should know* of the possibility of sexual molestation' (emphasis added). Bridget Hesse said she became very upset and was crying when she read it and said to her worker:

'You are accusing me of something I didn't do ... how dare you!' and he said: 'well ... that's just standard' ... and I said: well, then the standard should get changed [because] that's not right ... you are implying that every mother that walks in here who has a child who is sexually assaulted is in all likelihood guilty herself ... just by association ... and that's not right.' You know that protection application just floored me ... We are supposed to be mind-readers ... or fortune tellers or something.

Bridget Hesse's husband, the offender, was also upset at the implications in the protection application, and subsequently made a statement in the court assessment that only he and the victim knew of the sexual molestation but that his wife could not have known about it before his step-daughter disclosed.

The actual wording from the *Child Welfare Act* was reproduced on the protection application, and appropriate boxes were checked as reasons for the need for protection of the child. In Bridget Hesse's case, box 'c' was checked, indicating 'sexual molestation or sexual exploitation.' Copies of the protection application were served along with a Notice of Hearing to all appropriate parties who might have an interest in attending the child welfare court hearing with respect to the child in question.

The key informants involved in this area of the work were asked during my interviews with them about their views with respect to the particular wording of the legislation. The comments below reflect the views of the majority of key informants interviewed, although there were strong opposing views expressed, as well.

I think that is a valid concern to raise to the extent that the definition is used to ascribe knowledge to people who have no reason to have it ... It ought to read that there would be clear evidence that would have pointed her in that direction and she would have been willfully blind or reckless about whether it exists ... while one ought to be teaching parents how to develop a relationship with one's child ... so the child will tell you, it clearly ought not to be found seriously wanting as a parent if, in fact, you don't develop that, or the child doesn't tell you ... and you have no way of finding out (Key Informant 'K-C').

Nina Kew took her daughter, Joy, to her family doctor first and was told he would have to report the abuse to child welfare authorities. She felt very threatened that her child would be removed, but her doctor explained to her that it was not her fault that her husband, the child's father, had abused their daughter.

Ms Kew was referred to a support group by her Society worker which she attended, and Joy was referred to play therapy. At the end of the group program (fifteen weeks), however, the worker said she felt that Ms Kew needed more help because she was still so angry (at her ex-husband and at men in general), so Ms Kew repeated the group treatment, but said, 'I felt that I had failed or something was wrong with me ... because I didn't know any other mothers who were told they had to repeat the group.' Ms Kew did, however, feel obliged to do what was suggested by the Society because she said she was afraid of losing her daughter if she did not comply.

Both the police officers and the child welfare workers appeared to focus their attention on the women. This is due in part to the fact that women bear the major responsibility for the caring and rearing of children in our society. On the other hand, both agencies are informed by notions that the activities of the caring for and the rearing of children are 'natural' to women. Legitimating ideologies, as well as institutions such as the media, police departments, child welfare agencies, and families, reinforce the notion that women, as mothers, perform such tasks out of some 'maternal instinct' or biological nature. Considerable cross-cultural evidence, however, ties women to primary parenting because of their lactation and pregnancy functions and not because of instinctual nurturance beyond these functions (Bleier 1984; Chodorow 1978; DeVault 1991; Rosaldo and Lamphere 1974; Sanday 1986). The caring and rearing tasks, then, are socially defined roles rather than biologically based urges or instincts.

Two Mothers Face Dilemmas

Ten of the offenders in this study molested their own children. In four of the ten cases, the abuse occurred during access visits as the women were already separated and/or divorced from the children's fathers. Three of the women left their marriages immediately after disclosure and the remaining three stayed in their relationships. Two of the three who stayed, however, separated within a year of the disclosures, leaving only one mother of the ten who chose to remain in the relationship with the offender. This is what it was like for two of the three mothers who attempted to keep their marriages together after the disclosures.

Bridget Hesse is from a very traditional and religious background where 'family life' is important. She said she decided to give her marriage every possible chance of survival because she still loved her husband, and he felt remorseful for having molested his step-daughter.

Bridget Hesse's husband had been a very good provider, not only for their own immediate family, but also for Ms Hesse's extended family. Bridget Hesse had become disabled and was unable to work outside the home. One assessment on file indicated that Bridget Hesse 'leans toward economic dependence on her husband' and because of this situation, the child welfare worker assessed Bridget as a victim herself. In choosing to remain with her husband, Ms Hesse had alienated herself from her mother, sister, and daughter, although her daughter did eventually agree to have her step-father return to the home.

Gertrude Davis was very clear in the interview about why she chose to remain with her husband after the disclosure. She told the court her reasons, as well. She said she had no special training that would permit her to work outside of the home in order to financially support her children, whereas her husband was making in the area of $80,000 annually. She and the children could not have survived financially, in her estimation, unless they stayed with her husband and he remained at work.

The situation in this particular case provides a classic example of mother-blaming. In the presentence report, it was learned by Gertrude Davis that if her husband, the offender, should feel rejection, either real or imagined, for any reason, there was a good chance that he would 'reoffend.' So Gertrude Davis asked the Society: 'If you leave me policing the situation ... and something goes wrong when I turn my back for one minute ... and he touches that child ... what's gonna happen? I would be charged with gross neglect ... Oh ... I was just shoved up against the wall ... all the time.'

The dilemma was not an easy one and this mother's health suffered to the point where she finally chose a lower standard of living for herself and her children because she could not stand the pressure of being held responsible for her husband's behaviour. Within a year, she and her children had separated from him. Later, he committed suicide.

Shirley Cooke remained with her husband because she said she was unable to make a decision to leave. Her husband's earnings were significantly higher than her own and she decided she had to prepare herself to leave when she was more financially secure. Also, her daughter was over sixteen years of age and did not want her mother to go to the authorities or to break up the family because of the disclosure. Ms Cooke's husband actually moved out of the house within a year. She was able to secure a comfortable income for herself and sufficient funds to cover the education of her daughter (the offender's step-daughter) through the assistance of her legal counsel.

A Mother Reports her Husband for Sexual Abuse

Catharine Burns, in an attempt to get information, called the Society and explained her dilemma to the intake worker about her four-year-old child, whom she thought was being sexually abused by her husband, the child's father. The intake worker, in providing general information to this mother, gave the following advice: '"You should really think about this before you get involved in it ... It is ... no light matter" ... And then he told me he couldn't help me because I wasn't the correct religion, but he said: "Your daughter will have to see a doctor ... *if you are going to go ahead with this*" (emphasis added).

A mixed message such as this from a front-line worker on call to a mother in a crisis situation could only contribute to further confusion for her. The fact that she did not identify herself suggests that such advice would be given to any such mother who called with a similar problem. A less courageous mother than Catharine Burns might well have ended any proposed action to protect her child at that point. This response from the intake worker was a violation of his social work responsibilities, since his mandate is clearly to protect children.

Ms Burns then took her daughter to the hospital for examination and when the diagnosis was confirmed by a specialist, she was told that the hospital would report to the Society. Like other mothers in this study, this mother had heard negative things about the Society and did not know what to expect. She indicated that she very much wanted to speak with a mature woman in her 'vulnerable state,' and was hoping for a female worker. Her hopes were dashed when two males appeared, 'a social worker and a big burly policeman,' arrived as the investigating team. They interviewed both Ms Burns and her daughter, Virginia. Before the Society duty worker left, however, he said: 'Well, Mrs [Burns], on behalf of your daughter I want to thank you for your courage in coming forward.' Catharine Burns was extremely pleased and relieved to hear this.

That meant a lot to me ... That was really great ... I'll always remember that feeling ... because it was so hard ... and I felt like I'd done wrong on all sides ... I betrayed Virginia ... I betrayed my husband ... I'd hurt other people by exposing [the sexual abuse] ... You know, it made sense to me ... because kids can't do it for themselves ... So anyway ... that was very helpful ... to close the interview with ... He was good ... so I felt bad about my first impressions.

Who Is the Focus of Child Welfare Intervention?

The interviews in this study revealed that although some mothers felt fearful and intruded upon by the Society's intervention, other mothers clearly wanted to draw on the expertise of social workers in handling the situation. Six mothers actually sought out that kind of help from the Societies. The following two examples will illustrate the similarity of these mothers' experiences.

Kellie Curren, when asked what her experience with the Society's involvement was like, said: 'Good, after I did some hollering.' Only once after disclosure did she see a worker from the Society. She and her daughter, Karen, were both referred to support groups, where she heard the other mothers talking about the help they were receiving from their workers. Kellie Curren called the Society, and asked for help and was told by the intake worker who had visited her on that one occasion at disclosure: 'Some people come across as really being together ... and I thought you knew exactly what you were doing and where you were going and didn't need our help.' The intake worker apologized for not recognizing her need for help and subsequently provided her with a caseworker. From that point on, she apparently had a positive experience with the Society.

Pamela Hill, like Kellie Curren, obviously impressed the intake worker that she could handle things on her own after her son's disclosure of sexual abuse by his older cousin. Ms Hill did not even have the support of other mothers in a crisis support group situation, as Kellie Curren had experienced. After a long period of anxiety about what she should or should not be doing, Pamela Hill called the Society to ask for help and learned that her file had been closed. She told the intake worker that she felt they had left her 'hanging,' and that she had no direction, but was left on her own to make decisions about her son Paul's behaviour, and also to cope with all the problems the disclosure created within their extended family. The Society worker's response was: 'We will reopen your file.' Since that time, she said, 'everything has been great.'

These experiences raise questions about the different levels of involvement of child welfare workers with the mothers and suggest that the criteria for intervention and ongoing contact may need to be reviewed, since current practices offer service to families on the basis of the intake worker's discretion alone without consulting with the women themselves.

Contradictions Experienced by the Mothers

Dorothy White had reported to the Society three years earlier that she suspected child sexual abuse because her daughter said her father had touched her 'pee pee.' An investigation with the anatomically explicit dolls revealed no indication that the child had been abused. This child's mother felt that the authorities did not believe her at the time and said, 'I guess because I had been going for psychiatric treatment they think I'm crazy or something.'

Later, however, when the child disclosed a second time, the sexual abuse was validated by the Society worker. Ms White was ordered into child welfare court and a supervision order was obtained for the child's protection despite the fact that the offender was no longer in the home, but had been incarcerated. The conditions of the order included that the mother co-operate with the Society, that the mother attend a group for non-offending mothers, and that there be no direct or indirect contact between the victim and her father, Ms White's husband. Unlike Bridget Hesse, Dorothy White did not have her own legal counsel in child welfare court to represent her rights and to challenge the order mandating her into a treatment group, even though she was a non-offending mother: 'I went to all the sessions ... They said I had to cooperate ... so I said gee ... I better shut my mouth ... I thought maybe they will take this child away from me ... I had not protected her as I should ... I brought her into a home where a man was abusive to her and why didn't I know, and why didn't I see it?'

The ideology of motherhood trapped Ms White into seeing herself as totally responsible for anything that happened to her step-daughter. This raises the question whether a married woman should be expected to be constantly suspicious about her husband's behaviour around their children.

Shelly Brown found herself in an impossible situation, since the court ordered 'supervised access' of her two children. This access took place in the paternal grandparents' home, where, according to Shelly Brown, both children were being re-abused by their father.

The worker said if I allowed supervised access, they would take the kids ... So I went to my parents and stayed in 'the bush' [in the northern part of the province] for three months, and my dad said, 'If anybody comes on my property I will protect my rights ...' so there was no access for three months ... I just said, "if you want to put me in jail go ahead ... I'm not allowing anybody to touch my kids ...' The kids were fine, they never asked for their dad.

Russell (1988) talks about a women's underground movement developing in the United States that makes it possible for some mothers to protect their children when court orders give legal access to fathers who have sexually abused their children. An example of this is the well-publicized court battle concerning the case of *Morgan v. Foretich.* Dr Elizabeth Morgan served two years in prison for refusing to disclose her daughter's whereabouts after the court gave her ex-husband, Dr Eric Foretich, access to their child, despite the disclosure of sexual abuse made by their daughter, Hilary, and despite allegations of sexual abuse made by another daughter from a previous marriage ("Morgan vs Foretich" 1989). Similar cases have come to the public attention in Canada as well. For example, Gail Bezaire's trial in Toronto in 1987 was the first where a Canadian woman was ordered into court for the abduction of her own children because she felt they were at risk for revictimization (Crean 1988).

Judges and professional agencies are not held legally responsible for the revictimization or the future safety of a child in the same way that mothers are. These practices are rooted in an ideology of motherhood where the notion of mothers as sole caretakers of children is maintained and reinforced (Caplan 1989; Chesler 1987; Chodorow 1978; Crean 1988; Levine 1982; O'Brien 1983).

Paradoxically, the state uses these notions to shape interventions, while these ideas work against implementing or realizing interventions. For example, sufficient resources are not made available for basic child care needs (food, housing, child care, and protection from harm). Gordon (1988b) suggests that when caseworkers lack the resources to help clients materially, they may focus on psychological problems. Also, greater numbers of women in the United States and Canada now are unable to protect their children because of access and custody orders favouring fathers who have sexually abused their children (Chesler 1987; Crean 1988).

The Child Abuse Register

In Ontario, as in some other provinces in Canada, child welfare workers are required to report to the Child Abuse Register the names of abused children and abusers, once that abuse has been investigated and verified. The Societies must also complete a follow-up report after a four-month period, and yearly thereafter, until the case is closed. The legislation under which 'the Register' is governed is the *Child and Family Services Act, 1984* (Sections 68, 71, 72). Policies and guidelines to operationalize 'the Register' are set out for the use of the *Societies in Guidelines for Reporting to the Register* (Ontario Ministry 1981) and *The Child Abuse Register: Guidelines for Expunctions* (Ontario Ministry 1982).

The burden of proof for registering the name of the abuser on the Register differs from that expected in either criminal or civil actions. The Society must have 'credible evidence' only, under the present legislation, not 'proof beyond a reasonable doubt,' as is the case in criminal standards, or even 'on the balance of probabilities,' as in civil standards (Thompson 1987).

The Child Abuse Register report identifies the abuser, the abused child, and the parents of the child, and provides information concerning the abuse and action taken. A name will remain on the Register for twenty-five years unless it is removed through an Expunction Hearing (Bala 1987).

The Register's functions are to assist in the identification of child abuse cases, to facilitate research and case management, and to act as a deterrent against further abuse. A review of the Ontario Register, however, revealed that it had limited utility for identification of child abuse cases, it is not used for research purposes, and the deterrent effect is questionable (Bala 1987).

During the interview process, mothers were asked if they knew whether their worker had placed the name of the offender on the Child Abuse Register. Thirteen of the twenty mothers said they did not know or were not aware of the Register; six of the mothers said yes, that the worker had said the offender would receive a registered letter informing him that his name was placed on the Register, and one mother said she was informed that her husband's name would not be registered.

Using the present standards and guidelines, all but four names should have been registered, since each had 'credible evidence' available. Of the four cases not eligible to be registered, one was disclosed and investigated outside of the province, one had not gone through the Society (child was over sixteen), and in two cases the abusers were not 'caretakers' in keeping with the definition set out in the legislation.

Thirteen of the mothers knew nothing of the Register. It is difficult to know whether the women had not been informed of this process or if they were told by their caseworkers of the reports to be filed but did not retain the information because there was so much else going on in these women's lives at the time.

Agency records revealed that twelve of the twenty names eligible for the Register were in fact filed, while the remaining six were not filed, and two reports were pending. Of the twelve reports filed, four were returned because of unknown addresses. Of the six reports not filed with the Register, but eligible for filing, it was recommended by the workers that these be registered, but this was delayed in the agency bureaucracy for unknown reasons and registration did not take place.

Records also show that one very young child was denied treatment at an agency on the basis that the abuser's name had not been registered on the Child Abuse Register by the Society. This practice of penalizing a child because of an agency's policies was noted in only one instance, but even that one instance points out how a lack of interagency co-ordination and co-operation can affect the attempt of mothers to obtain needed resources for their children.

There are plans under way in Ontario to abolish the controversial Child Abuse Register and instead to use a system of police checks for all those whose work will involve them with children, such as teachers, coaches, foster parents, and so on (Coutis 1994).

The idea of screening through the Canadian Police Information Centre to detect potential child abusers instead of using a Child Abuse Register is a good one in the writer's opinion. Such an arrangement does not address the issue of families, however, where the majority of child sexual abuse occurs. For this reason, I believe that some type of Register should be maintained but one which meets its established goals more effectively.

Child welfare services can help mothers of sexually abused children, and mothers do need that help. Societies occupy a critical position in the social agency network, one that can either facilitate or encumber the successful resolution of the crisis faced by non-offending mothers of sexually victimized children. That potential to help seems dependent upon at least five factors: the particular ideology that drives agency services; the particular ideology subscribed to and promoted both consciously and unconsciously by workers in direct contact with mothers; the framework of laws governing the actions of child welfare workers; whether or not sufficient resources are allocated to provide services for the needs of both children and mothers; and whether the workers dealing with mothers are appropriately trained and sensitive to women's needs and rights.

My findings are not unlike those of Julia Krane (1994). Based on in-depth interviews with mothers of children who disclosed sexual abuse and their female social workers from an Ontario child welfare agency, Krane argues that child protection work is a very complex process; many of the activities involved are taken for granted, hidden, and gendered.

7

The Impact of Other Institutions

The previous chapter discussed the agencies with the legal mandate to intervene in child sexual abuse cases (Children's Aid Societies). This chapter examines six other agencies, organizations, or institutions that were involved with the mothers in this study: medical personnel, police, schools, courts, workplaces, and crisis and support counselling groups.

Medical Responses

The range of medical responses to child sexual abuse includes hospital personnel, family physicians, medical specialists, nurses, and others who are in any way involved with assessing, referring, examining and/or treating the child-victims, the child's mother, or other family members as a result of sexual abuse disclosure.

According to the Standards and Guidelines for Management of Child Abuse Cases (Ontario Ministry 1986), the investigation of child sexual abuse should include, where appropriate, medical examination of child-victims, diagnosis, and treatment. As well, there is to be immediate documentation by medical doctors of any physical evidence found as a result of the abuse. The evidence must be documented within forty-eight hours of the last molestation for criminal court purposes.

The medical examinations of child-victims is a controversial issue. Some professionals feel that unless it is absolutely warranted, the medical examination can be like a second assault to a child. Other professionals emphasize the importance of the medical examination for a number of reasons. Some children worry about having been physically harmed by the abuse (the expression 'damaged goods' is seen frequently in the literature). Therefore, a physical examination seems important to reassure the child there was no physical damage caused, or if there were signs of physical injury, then the child could be assured that whatever difficulties were found would be treated by the doctor (Heger 1996; Porter et al. 1982; Badgley et al. 1984). Badgley et al. (1984) emphasize the importance of the medical examination for the child-victim in order to ascertain whether they may have contracted a sexually transmitted disease, such as AIDS (Acquired Immune Deficiency Syndrome). Also, it is important to determine if a pregnancy has occurred as a result of the sexual abuse.

Although most children are more comfortable seeing their own family physicians when they experience a personal, medical, or emotional crisis, it is now generally recognized that medical examinations in cases of child sexual abuse are becoming a highly skilled specialty, and that specialists are frequently designated in hospitals where such referrals are made. Unless pediatricians are skilled in giving routine anal and vaginal examinations to children, the abuse may not be detected.

Research indicates that in the majority of cases of child sexual abuse, a medical examination does not produce physical evidence that can be used in the criminal court system (Badgley et al. 1984; Finkel 1983; Krugman 1986), since the majority of cases do not involve penetration, but rather sexual fondling of the child. A lack of evidence, however, does not necessarily mean the child has not been sexually abused or even penetrated. Pediatricians Herman-Giddens and Frothingham (1987), who have had considerable experience in examining children for sexual abuse, conclude the following about female victims: 'The hymen, contrary to common notion, is often a slack, thick, folded stretchable tissue which may persist after digital or penile penetration. Findings secondary to sexual abuse are often subtle. Acute tears or bruising are rare because force is seldom a part of the sexual acts committed against a child' (203).

Of the thirty-one child-victims from this study, fewer than half (fourteen) were given medical examinations post-disclosure. Only five of the fourteen medical examinations produced physical evidence that could be used for criminal proceedings against the perpetrator.

One child was unable to have her examination completed because of fear, and in two cases the results of the medical examination were termed 'uncertain.' The remaining six examinations yielded no evidence whatsoever.

In addition to medically examining and referring child-victims, family physicians, because they are generally trusted by mothers, are sometimes very influential with respect to events after disclosure of the sexual abuse. Many doctors advise mothers what to do next and help them to sort out their confusion about disclosure events.

The following selected case examples illustrate the nature of the medical response to the sexually abused children. Three mothers discuss situations where there was positive physical evidence of their child's sexual abuse; one mother discusses a situation where no physical evidence was available after the medical examination; two mothers explain 'uncertain' medical outcomes; and one mother discusses other aspects of her experience with her family physician.

Medical Examination Yielding Physical Evidence of Sexual Abuse

Betsy Hamilton indicated during the interview that it took three tries before she got her daughter, Gillian, and son, Allan, in for examinations by medical specialists after disclosure. There had been two cancellations and about a six- to eight-week waiting period. After the examination, both children indicated they were very uncomfortable with the examination and would have preferred a female physician. Although the medical examination revealed no physical evidence that her son had been sexually abused, there was evidence that her daughter had been vaginally penetrated. This evidence was documented by medical specialists and presented to the criminal court during the trial.

Joan MacDonald had her child, Fran, examined by a specialist at the hospital within the forty-eight hours suggested in the ministry guidelines. The four-year-old girl would not allow a male doctor near her, however. This mother was very pleased that the hospital was flexible enough to switch her child to a female physician immediately. The results of this medical examination revealed positive physical evidence of sexual interference. The evidence was documented and presented by the examining physician in a criminal court trial. The offender was found guilty and incarcerated, but, more importantly, Fran was protected from further abuse by this particular individual. Despite a brutal molestation, the examining doctor emphasized how important it was that her daughter had not experienced penile penetration.

Catherine Burns took her child, Virginia, to four different doctors before the sexual abuse was diagnosed. Her family doctor referred her to a specialist for rectal bleeding, a pediatrician for blood work, and then, finally, to a pediatric specialist in child sexual abuse. The child was first diagnosed as having constipation and given mineral oil. The mineral oil was administered but the rectal bleeding continued. Blood tests were done and the clotting times were normal. Finally, when Ms Burns could see external signs of trauma and blood in the anal region, she herself became suspicious and took the child to the hospital with a suggestion of what the diagnosis might be. She was correct.

Catherine Burns was initially horrified to see a waiting room full of parents and children when she arrived at the hospital. She felt anxious, fearful, and embarrassed about what would happen to them in the crowded waiting room. Later, she said she was much relieved when the hospital receptionist quietly wrote 'suspected sexual abuse' on her card, and did not add to her upset by engaging her in a loud discussion about the reason for the visit in front of the others in the waiting room.

It did seem inappropriate to Ms Burns, however, when the nurse who was taking them to the examining room asked her (while they were still walking in the hall) who she thought the perpetrator was. This mother said, 'That was a hard line to say ... I choked a bit on it ..., and said [Virginia's father] and then the nurse said, "well, you've done the right thing coming here." That was really good for me to hear at that time when I was so confused.'

Catharine Burns had a two-hour wait before her child was medically examined. According to her, 'the examining doctor was nice, but he was upset by it, you could tell ... and he said, "well frankly ... I can't see that it could be anything but [sexual abuse]. I'm gonna have to phone child welfare."' Despite very good physical evidence, the perpetrator was never criminally charged with the offence. Details of this case are discussed later in this chapter (in the section on court experiences).

Medical Examinations That Did Not Yield Physical Evidence

Carolyn O'Brien expected her child, Ruthie, to be medically examined the same day she disclosed, since the Society worker mentioned an examination should be done. Ruthie was not examined until six months after disclosure, however; the reason for this delay is not known 'I was not pleased with the examination when it did occur,' Ms O'Brien said. Her daughter said she was very uncomfortable with the examination and 'sore down below ...' afterwards. As might be expected, no physical evidence of the sexual abuse was found, and, indeed, it is difficult to understand why the agency proceeded with this type of intrusive examination of the child six months after the report.

Medical Examinations Where Results Were Termed 'Uncertain'

Shelly Brown indicated that there was a delay of two weeks in getting her daughter, Ina, medically examined. The examination yielded no definitive evidence, although there was some separation of the hymen, which was said by the doctor to not necessarily have been caused by sexual abuse. The results were termed 'uncertain' for court purposes.

Nina Kew went to see her family physician directly after her child disclosed. She was referred by him to a specialist at the hospital and a call was made to the Society. Nina Kew said she became very upset because she feared she would lose her daughter, Joy, as a result of the abuse. Although her daughter was found to have a bump on her hymen, there was no clear evidence that the bump was caused by the alleged sexual abuse. Criminal charges were not laid because Joy was considered too young to testify in Criminal Court. Unsupervised access was terminated for Nina Kew's former husband, Joy's father, however, as a result of the disclosure.

Unhelpful Advice from Family Physician

Although Pamela Hill felt there was no need for her child, Paul, to have a medical examination after disclosure, she did visit her family physician for advice on what to do. Pamela said her doctor suggested she call a child psychiatrist. When Ms Hill indicated to him that she was thinking of reporting the sexual abuse to the Society, he said, 'Well, ... you know sometimes these things are really blown out of proportion.' Despite her doctor's advice, Pamela Hill called the Society and reported the abuse. She said as it turned out that she was glad that she had done so because her own child would be safer from the offender, her nephew. She had hoped that he would be forced to get treatment.

In the end, only four out of thirteen mothers made positive statements about the way their children were handled by medical professionals. Although there were differences in the responses of the women interviewed depending upon their geographic locations, in most areas in this study there were considerable delays in examining children, and long waiting periods when they did arrive for the arranged medical appointment. Small children and female children appeared to be more comfortable being examined by female doctors. Some doctors in this study did not obey their legal duty to report child sexual abuse to the Society. In two cases, doctors appeared to place considerable emphasis on whether or not penetration of the vagina had occurred even when the child was brutally interfered with and severely traumatized by the sexual molestation. It is not always possible to determine digital, penile, or object penetration in children by conducting a medical examination, but the child-victim can be reassured by a sensitive and skilled physician.

Some medical students are now being trained to diagnose sexual abuse and, progressive doctors place the highest importance on taking a history from the child, since most sexual abuse cases have few or no medical findings (Heger 1996).

Police Responses

The police were involved in twenty-three of the twenty-four cases of sexual abuse in this study. One case was not reported to police officials as the victim was over sixteen years old when disclosure took place and she made the decision not to report to the police. Selected case examples are presented in this section regarding particular issues related to police intervention.

Some Favourable Comments

Pamela Hill commented favourably on both the handling of the case generally, and the approach taken by the police with respect to her son, Paul. Five-year-old Paul was given the choice of whether or not to have two male police officers sitting in while he was being interviewed by a female intake worker from the local Society (with his mother present). Paul chose the two women alone and, according to Ms Hill, the police officers 'just sat behind the one-way mirror ... and when it was finished ... they told him what a good job he did and gave him candy.'

Jackie Wall also indicated she liked both the interview process the police officers used and the way they interviewed her daughter, Lori. She also spoke positively about their method of handling alleged offenders: 'They just handcuffed him [the offender] and said, "You are under arrest" ... and started reading him his rights ... They were great!' Ms Wall showed unusual courage and ingenuity by managing to get the nineteen-year-old alleged offender into her car on the pretext of going somewhere else, then she drove him directly to the police station herself. When the car stopped in the police station parking lot, the offender jumped out and ran, but Ms Wall got two nearby police officers to chase him. The offender did not know that the child had disclosed to her mother before the car trip.

Police Reluctance to Lay Criminal Charges

Initially, when Dorothy White called the police late at night after her daughter, Jill, disclosed the abuse, she said, 'Two giant policemen in uniform' came to her home. She was instructed to wake her husband, the alleged offender, who was in bed, asleep. One officer took her husband outside to the police car for questioning, while the other officer interviewed Jill in their home. Dorothy White was asked by one of the officers, 'Do you have a place to go for the night?' She called a friend to check out a possible arrangement. Her friend replied, 'Well surely you can ... but why?' Dorothy White said, 'I was in shock and didn't think straight until she said this to me because ... [the police officers] just told me if I don't leave they would take the child to the Society and remove her from home and I told them ... nobody was removing her from home ... he [her husband, the offender] was to be removed.'

After disclosure, Dorothy White said, 'I was really upset because the police officer would not lay charges.' Ms White pursued the matter with those she thought might help her. She was able to get a letter of support from the director of an advocacy group for parents of sexually abused children, addressed to the senior Crown attorney, indicating the police position on her case. The letter indicated how the police were concerned about her husband's age (seventy-three) and not concerned about her child's age (eleven at disclosure). This letter and a follow-up visit to the senior Crown's office appeared to change the decision of the police and they proceeded with charges. The offender was subsequently charged, found guilty, and incarcerated.

Another mother, Nina Kew, said that after her daughter, Joy, disclosed and the police investigation was completed, the police officer phoned her and said that since her daughter was only four years old, 'her evidence wouldn't stand up in court.' This mother said she learned later from a Crown attorney who spoke at her crisis support group that the police do take cases to court with children younger than four years of age. The police officer involved also indicated to this mother that 'they didn't charge him because he didn't admit it.' Nina Kew said, 'That's stupid to admit it ... like ... if he robbed a bank he wouldn't admit it ... so I said, "Of course he's gonna deny it ... He'd be stupid if he admitted it."'

Child Molesters at Large in the Community

Ingrid Hogg was not able to allow her child out by herself because the offender was still in their neighbourhood. He continued to make telephone calls in which he threatened to kill Jill if she told anyone what he had done to her. When this mother contacted the police, they suggested to her that she get an unlisted number. They indicated they were unable to give her any further help with the problem of protection for her child to and from school.

Ingrid Hogg felt this man should never have been acquitted of the criminal charges. When the police Sargeant showed Ms Hogg's nine-year-old daughter fifteen photographs of different men and asked her to identify her offender, she was unable to do so. Her mother asked for a line-up of men or for them to place the alleged offender in a crowd for identifying purposes as she thought her daughter would be able to identify him in person, but the police Sargeant said that would be difficult for them to do under the circumstances. She said, 'They know he's guilty ... There's proof on paper ... There's even medical proof ...' She questioned that such a dangerous child molester should be allowed to remain in the community unhampered, to molest other children. Ms Hogg's daughter was one of five female children sexually molested by two men. The other offender was charged and sentenced to nine months in jail for sexually assaulting two nine-year-old girls. This sentence was followed by two years of probation.

What is the status of an unconvicted molester? According to an expert key informant in the justice system: 'If there is no conviction ... it has no importance in our society ... If a person is found not guilty or charges are not proceeded with ... it is deemed he was not guilty ... and that he did not do it ... in law' (Key Informant 'B-C').

In practice, however, we cannot dismiss the situation quite as easily. The *Criminal Code of Canada* is imperfect in protecting children from sexual abuse because of the standard of evidence required in the courts (this is discussed in more detail later in this chapter). The very fact that known child molesters are at large in the community makes it unsafe for children and creates a nightmare for mothers such as Ingrid Hogg, who work outside the home, are on a limited budget, and are unable to have their children escorted to and from school every day for protection.

A case in point is the Ontario trial of Joseph Fredericks who sexually raped and then killed eleven-year-old Christopher Stephenson on 18 June 1988. Fredericks, who lived less than a kilometre from the boy's home, was found guilty of first-degree murder in Christopher's sex slaying, but he had sexually molested eight other children before he attacked Christopher. He was not charged criminally until he had molested his seventh victim, at which time he was sentenced to twenty-two months for that offence, served his time, and was released (Hudson 1989).

The ways in which the legal and social service systems are operating currently do not protect children from sexual molestation. Dominelli (1989) poses the following important question for society, 'Why should children's rights to an unmolested existence be valued less than the protection of a man from false accusations?' (294). It cannot, in fact, be the conclusion of any thinking person responsible for the safety of children that 'it has no importance to society if the person is not found guilty or charges are not proceeded with.' When a known child molester is set free in a community with little or no monitoring of his behaviour it is tantamount to giving him permission to molest other children.

Police Failure to Act in Breach of Probation

Anita Marshall's daughter, Janet, was sexually abused by a local businessman. Approximately one week after the offender was convicted, he appeared next door (which was a violation of the conditions of his probation). When Ms Marshall called the police to report the offender, the police would not send a car (while the offender was there) because 'they said they were too busy ... that they had other priorities ... so they [the police] said I was to file a complaint ... which I did do.'

Ms Marshall then indicated that she received a phone call from a detective the following day telling her to call the next time he broke his probation. She said, 'No, he has already broken his probation.' She was told that the police had contacted the Crown and had been advised to proceed that way. When this mother said, 'Would you repeat that?' the detective said, 'Do you have a hearing problem?' and hung up.

When asked her opinion why the police handled the complaint the way they had, Anita Marshall replied: 'He [the offender] is a well-established man and I am almost beginning to think it is either too much paperwork for [the police] to process ... or justice may be blind but she can sure feel the weight of money ... I am Mrs Nobody ... I am away down here ... and he comes down with his lawyer and his financial pull and well-established place in society and I don't have any of that.' Ms Marshall said she really wondered whether the police were there to protect her child's rights or maintain the offender's comfort.

Although a few of the mothers interviewed for this study found police intervention to be a positive experience for them and their children, the overwhelming majority complained bitterly about the manner in which police officers handled their investigations of child sexual abuse.

Some of the women interviewed for this study were neutral concerning their comments about police investigations and follow-up of the sexual abuse, and remarked generally that they could have done a better job without giving specific suggestions. A few of the women highly praised the work of the police officers with whom they were involved, however. For example, two different mothers indicated they appreciated the encouragement and support they received from the police in both family and criminal court. Police are usually required to give their testimony in court concerning the evidence gathered, so they would be able to speak with the women and their children before and after court proceedings. Because police officers are in and out of court frequently as their job requires, they are undoubtedly much more comfortable in court surroundings, whereas all of the women in this study indicated they were very intimidated by having to appear in court. It is understandable how grateful these women would be to have a familiar face and a few supportive words in the court environment.

One mother expressed her appreciation of the rapid response the police made in determining the need to arrest her daughter's suspected offender immediately. Within a few miniutes of her complaint, he was read his rights, handcuffed, and arrested. This same mother was pleased that the police officer kept her informed of what was happening as the case proceeded.

Two mothers expressed positive feelings about the sensitivity of the police officers in interviewing their children. In both these cases the children were pre-school age and video and audio tapes were used to obtain the children's account of the sexual abuse. Both these officers had special training in interviewing children.

The types of complaints that mothers of the sexually abused children made concerning their dealings with police intervention included: lack of enforcement of court orders (i.e., breach of bail conditions and various other violations of probation); not laying criminal charges when it was indicated; lack of special police training in the area of child sexual abuse; advising a mother to leave her own home and threatening to have the Society remove her child; lack of action when there is fear of having a molester in the community who may reabuse; lack of sufficient female police officers; delay in confronting alleged offenders; low priority given to the safety of children and women; more interest in protecting the comfort of offenders than in protecting the rights of the child-victims; taking small children to the police station for interviews; and, in one case, concern for the advanced age of male offenders that appeared to take a priority over young children.

Each province has its own guidelines for police investigations of child sexual abuse. Ontario was one of the first provinces in Canada to develop joint investigations between child protection social workers and police officers. In the early 1980s, Children's Aid Societies, the police department, and the Crown Attorney's Office designated specific personnel to become child sexual abuse specialists in the Metropolitan Toronto area (Metropolitan Toronto 1992).

Police conduct an investigation to determine whether there are reasonable and probable grounds to believe that a criminal offence related to child sexual abuse has been committed. The police officer must gather evidence in order to establish the facts and determine if criminal proceedings are appropriate. This includes:

• preserving the crime scene
• obtaining the child's account of events
• obtaining a statement from the alleged offender
• obtaining statements from other witnesses
• arranging to obtain and preserve any physical evidence
• obtaining medical and other expert opinions
• determining the need to arrest a suspect
• submitting a report to Crown counsel if criminal charges are recommended (Ministry of Attorney General et al. 1998, 36).

Although police are responsible for criminal investigations, the court case is presented by the Crown attorney. There are sometimes disagreements between police officers, Crown attorneys and child protection agencies regarding the handling of cases and whether or not there should be criminal charges laid (Raycroft 1991). Training for police officers is dependent upon the financial resources available in each province and/or municipality. In some areas, there are police specialists in child sexual abuse, in other areas cases are handled in a more general manner.

Research shows that police interventions improve when the police officers have had special training in the area of child sexual abuse investigations, when clearly designed protocols are implemented, and when traditional attitudes toward women do not inform the officers' intervention process.

Workplace Responses

This section examines the work patterns of those women interviewed; whether or not they shared the disclosure in their workplace; the kinds of responses experienced when they shared at work; and what it was like for those women who made the decision not to discuss their child's sexual abuse with their employer or others on the job.

Work Patterns of the Mothers

The majority of mothers (fourteen out of twenty-four) interviewed were not working outside the home at the time their children first disclosed the sexual abuse; ten were in the paid workforce. Eight of the ten women were working outside the home on a full-time basis while the remaining two worked part-time.

There is a core group of sixteen women who did not change their work patterns during or after disclosure. Eight women continued to work full-time outside the home, and eight women remained at home full-time. Of the remaining eight women who did shift patterns, two moved from part-time to no work outside the home, two women changed from no work outside the home to part-time paid work, and four women changed from no work outside their homes to full-time paid positions, as they separated from their offending partners.

The Decision to Share Disclosure at Work

Six of the ten women who were in the paid workforce during disclosure shared the disclosure at work with their supervisors, friends, and coworkers. Also, three of the eight women who joined the paid work force post-disclosure said they shared the disclosure at work. A total of nine women, then, chose to share the sexual abuse of their children with others at work. The majority found negative responses. Two of the women who chose not to tell their bosses or coworkers had an equally upsetting experience, as illustrated below.

Anita Marshall indicated that she chose not to tell anybody at work, but one coworker heard about the disclosure elsewhere, and she approached Ms Marshall at work, who said, 'I felt a little uncomfortable about it ... She wanted the information ... She did not have a genuine concern so ... I kept it quiet.' Ms Marshall paid a heavy emotional price for not sharing at work, as she found it difficult to sever her personal life from her job situation.

Although Shirley Cooke did not tell her coworkers or supervisor that her daughter, Marilyn, had been sexually abused by her husband, she did share with them when she subsequently separated from him, as he was an important official in the community.

To illustrate the responses received by the women who chose to share their experiences at work, three of the six mothers tell what it was like for them.

Ingrid Hogg decided to share the disclosure with her manager at work because she said she recognized what terrible emotional shape she was in, and she was also concerned about the amount of time she had to take off work for various court sessions and other meetings and arrangements with respect to the disclosure: 'I didn't even care if they fired me or I quit. I was at that point ... I said if you can't believe me ... you can deduct me a day's pay ... When I first told my manager he sort of blamed me ... He said, "You should be watching your kids." I said, "Listen, wait a minute ... you gotta listen to the story first" ... But as I got talking ... he was agitated ... and analysing it and blamed me.'

Eventually, Ms Hogg's manager came to understand that the sexual abuse was not her fault, and he became very supportive during the subsequent calls she received at the office.

Betsy Hamilton's experience was the opposite: 'I took my supervisor aside ... because suddenly I was getting a lot of calls from the police and the Society and ... said my children have disclosed that they were abused ... and I will have to take some time off periodically for court and I wanted her to be aware that this was going on ... I did not want to be penalized ... I didn't want to lie and say I want a day off because I'm sick.'

Ms Hamilton's supervisor was very sympathetic initially. Later, however, when the stress had begun to manifest itself at work, Betsy Hamilton asked for some time off and she found that the situation had changed (within about two weeks). Her supervisor became emotionally distant. After about six months, Ms Hamilton was called into her supervisor's office and told that coworkers had complained about her attitude. The supervisor went on to say that perhaps the pressure on the job was too much for Ms Hamilton and that this was not the right business for her. Betsy Hamilton said she gave the following response to her supervisor: '"The pressure on the job is not what's bothering me ... I've explained what's going on ... that's what's bothering me" ... and that was basically how it was left ... She said, "Think about what you want to do," and I thought about it and gave her my resignation the next morning.'

Betsy Hamilton quit her job, but was unable to collect unemployment insurance. When she applied to UIC, she realized that bureaucratic rules did not allow for her type of situation: 'They, of course, said, "Why did you quit your job?" I said, "Well, it was personal ..." and they passed me on to another counsellor, who said "I have to put something down," and I said again ... "It is too personal" and she said, "If you tell me I won't put it down ..." I just burst into tears ... and said my kids have been abused and I can't think about all this.'

When asked if there was anything she thought the UIC counsellor could have done for her, Ms Hamilton suggested that maybe it was true that she could not qualify because of her emotional condition, but she suggested that maybe she could have been put on sick benefits by the counsellor.

Elizabeth Sutton said it was very bad at work for her during the crisis period after her daughter disclosed. Ms Sutton said, 'It was so bad ... that my boss called me in and said, "are you having problems at home?"' When asked how he responded after being told, Ms Sutton said: 'Everybody you tell who hasn't been involved in this reacts differently ... Some with disgust, some with shock ... some with anger ... I got the impression [my supervisor] acted with disgust ... like "Well, my God ... what is your family like?"'

This type of response added pressure to an already emotionally burdened mother trying to do her job to the best of her ability without disrupting the workplace.

Post-Disclosure Workforce Response

The eight women who joined the workforce after disclosure, continued to experience some emotional difficulties as a result of their children's disclosure. Three of the eight made the decision to share the information about their children's victimization with those at work. Of the three who told, one felt she was given excellent support, one had a mixed response, and one felt she received a negative response. The latter is illustrated below.

Olga Kadishun joined the workforce one year after disclosure in a temporary secretarial position. Her daughter, Ida, however, was still in therapy and experiencing a great deal of emotional trauma at the time. She therefore quit her secretarial job (without telling anyone about the sexual abuse) and took a job as a waitress from ten P.M. until two A.M. in order to be available for Ida's therapy. Despite her executive secretarial skills, she took a lower paying job in order to get her child to therapy. Later, Ms Kadishun took a full-time position as an executive secretary. On this new job, she decided to tell her employer:

I had to leave a few times and I did not want him to feel I was being negligent ... After all, I have to work with this man ... I think he should know ... and the reaction ... like they don't know how to react ... It's like ... now what do I say ... now what do I do ... and it's just ... you know ... you don't tell anybody this has happened to a child ... Why not? You know society *should* know about it ... but it it is hush, hush ... all the time.

Later, Ms Kadishun told others at work and found much the same response: 'I found they said, "Well ... that's awful and I'm sorry it happened," but then ... "Let's not talk about it."'

The majority of mothers who decided to share the disclosure at work had a negative response from coworkers and supervisors and, in some cases, sharing at work even exacerbated their problems.

Crisis Support Groups/Counselling

Two-thirds (sixteen) of the mothers interviewed said they had attended a crisis support group after their children disclosed. Most of the women enjoyed the participation and got a great deal from the groups. Of the eight mothers who did not attend support groups, five were offered groups, but declined; one mother said that although she was not offered a group, she was not interested in attending even had one been available to her. The other two women said they would have been interested in attending a group, but none was available to them.

Reasons mentioned by the women for not attending the group programs offered to them were: The group was not appropriate (e.g., it was for the non-offending partners); they did not want to publicize the abuse; their husband was not supportive of group attendance; and they had a general dislike of group involvement.

Description of the Groups Attended by Mothers

Since the women interviewed live in different geographical areas, the groups they attended differed in a number of ways. The group programs lasted anywhere from six weeks to six months, with the average length being twelve weeks. The size of the group ranged from five to thirty participants at any one time, with an average size of eight to twelve participants. A number of mothers repeated the program on their own, while two mothers were advised to repeat the program by their Society workers. Three mothers were ordered into the support groups by court orders.

One of the major differences in the structure of the groups was the open or closed group concept. The advantage of the open concept is that there are no waiting lists and therefore all women are able to enter the group immediately, at the peak of their crisis. The disadvantages of the open group concept mentioned by the mothers were: the group became overcrowded, with as many as thirty women in attendance during some sessions; there was little opportunity to build trust with other women, since there were new people continuously joining the group; because new participants always got priority to speak first, women whose only support was the group were unable to count on dealing with a particularly stressful issue in the group on any given night.

In some areas, the groups for the child-victims were held the same evening as the mothers' group, and therefore mothers and children travelled together. Some programs offered separate offenders' groups, as well.

The goals of one of the largest group programs as documented in their materials are as follows:

- to increase the number of children who could be maintained at home with non-offending family following disclosure of sexual abuse;
- to reduce the pressure which causes children to recant their stories;
- to supplement and reinforce the ability of mothers (as non-offending caregivers) to support the child-victim through the crisis and
- to recreate a safe, healthy environment for her child(ren); and,
- to reduce the likelihood of re-abuse by heightening awareness and self-esteem.

Attendance of Groups by Other Family Members

All but two of the thirty-one children attended crisis support groups. Of the two who did not attend, one had no group available to her, and one chose not to attend a group. According to the women, the majority of the children said they enjoyed attending the groups and looked forward to them. Most mothers felt their children benefited from attending the groups.

It is interesting to note that although two-thirds of the mothers and all but two of the children attended crisis support groups, the situation was very different for fathers. Only one of the offenders in this study attended an offenders' group, and no non-offending father attended a crisis support group.

This finding is not peculiar to my study but appears to be the norm in situations of child sexual abuse cases in the Metropolitan Toronto area. When the key informant with expertise in crisis support groups was interviewed, she indicated that although initially there were twenty non-offending fathers interested in attending an eight-week group specifically for non-offending fathers, only six attended the first week and only one non-offending father in the entire Metropolitan Toronto area completed the course. The group was disbanded owing to a lack of referrals. Although four men expressed interest in attending a support group at a later date, after outreach work was done to encourage and involve men, none of them showed up on the date the group was to begin.

When the key informant was asked why she thought there was such a difference in interest and attendance between men and women, her response was: 'I guess it's role stuff ... let mother handle it ... I don't have the time ... I need to make the money ... and the specific things I heard from them '[the non-offending fathers] were: 'I don't need to come ... everything is fine ... my wife and child went through the program and enjoyed it a lot ... They put all the responsibility for holding it together on her ... that's her job ... that was the flavour of it.' (Key informant O-A)

This study suggests that the non-offending father sees himself – and is seen by others – as slightly removed from the painful experiences of the child and the mother after disclosure. Fathers do not give any indication that they feel responsible for providing emotional support to other family members, whereas the women are both identified by others and identify themselves as central to the children's recovery from the traumatic experience and also central to keeping family relationships in place. Fathers in this study were not highly involved in the emotional life of their families in emotionally supportive ways.

Treatment Issues of Groups

In the descriptive materials of one of the group programs, the following list of treatment issues for mothers is outlined for the group leader's focus:

- Inability to trust
- Impaired self-image
- Denial
- Unreasonable expectations
- Failure to establish and enforce limits
- Anger
- Impaired communication
- Assertiveness
- Impaired socialization
- Concrete environmental help

As outlined in the literature provided for group leaders under each of the categories listed above, several assumptions provide a profile of non-offending mothers. These mothers: have experienced a lack of nurturance in their own backgrounds; have low self-esteem; feel unattractive as women;

deny the sexual abuse of their children; have a tendency to place unreasonable expectations on their husbands and on their children; fantasize the 'perfect marriage'; experience blurring of roles; have much pent-up anger; tend to deny their own responsibility in the sexual abuse; have poor communication skills; tend to be passive; have limited social skills; are isolated; and need help to access concrete services.

The above profile of non-offending mothers fits with the descriptions discussed in previous chapters of mothers in the mainstream literature; it does not apply to the women interviewed in my study, nor those in studies similar to mine (Dempster 1992; Hooper 1992; Johnson 1992; Krane 1994). Each mother interviewed had her own unique personality and strengths. My findings do not support all of the above assumptions about non-offending mothers. Moreover, many are demeaning and disrespectful to women, in my opinion.

All of these mothers were overwhelmed by the experience of their children disclosing sexual abuse, and desperately needed emotional support, direction, information, and some assurance of future economic stability for themselves and their children. The one assumption in the above list that was accurate was the need for help to access concrete services.

Comments about the Groups

One of the complaints about the groups attended by some mothers was the lack of focus on themselves. There appeared to be a certain resentment that group members always talked about the child-victims and how better to protect their children. For example, this quote from the interview with Jackie Wall illustrates the point: 'It really bothers me that I can go to these groups and not talk about my own self ... The focus is always on the kids.'

This particular mother was later reassured that towards the end of the group sessions, the leaders would focus on the mothers and make individual referrals for follow-up counselling, if necessary. Other mothers also expressed their disappointment that they were discouraged from dealing with their anger and rage in the groups.

Most of the women did, however, benefit greatly from attending the groups. For example, Rachel Cohen was very positive about her experience in the group and describes one of the special times: 'Yeah ... one of the best things that happened to me was the party during Christmas. Every single child and every single mother got a gift and it was hey, you are no different just because you were abused and hey moms ... you've been through a tough time, too, and this is your treat, and it's like I almost had tears in my eyes. Really, it meant so much to me that they would do this for everybody ... It was so nice.'

The chemistry in the groups varied, though. Some of the women made friends with other women at the groups, and these friendships continued after the groups ended. Other women spoke of their discomfort with women in their group and described how they felt they had little in common with them. A few women became volunteer group leaders themselves after their own group experience. Those interviewed also spoke however, of women who sat in the group for fifteen weeks and never said a word.

School Responses

I was able to obtain comments from all twenty-four mothers about their experiences within the school system, since all thirty-one children were attending school at the time I interviewed their mothers (six months to three years post-disclosure). The children's school experience ranged all the way from kindergarten to high school.

The definition for children's 'school experience' for this study includes teachers, principals and vice principals, school counsellors and guidance counsellors, school board representatives, and other school personnel who may have come in contact with either child-victims or their mothers with respect to the sexual abuse.

Of the twenty-four mothers interviewed, twenty shared some information with the school system about their children's disclosures. Those mothers who chose not to share this information with their children's schools gave the following reasons for not doing so: one child was over sixteen when she disclosed and did not want to tell others about the abuse; in one family, two children were sexually fondled before school age; three children in one family had only one incident with a male person in their home whom they would not see again, so their mother did not feel it was necessary to share the information with the school; and one mother lived in a small community and did not want the school or neighbours to know of the sexual abuse.

Selected comments of the twenty mothers who did discuss the disclosure with the school system are presented in order to illustrate the typical degree of sensitivity and/or support given to the women or to their children by school authorities.

There were two children sexually abused in the Hamilton family. Both parents had a meeting with the teachers of both their children to share the necessary information about the disclosure. Betsy Hamilton said they found the teachers very responsive, indicating they would be of any assistance they could. The teachers assured the parents that the information shared would be held in strict confidence, and go no further within the school system, which the Hamiltons appreciated. Betsy Hamilton was particularly pleased with the support her daughter, Gillian, received from her physical education teacher, who had been a victim herself.

Gertrude Davis described one teacher as being very kind and supportive about her daughter's disclosure, even to the point of sending her a letter. Ms Davis described the school principal as 'just a saint,' but one teacher with whom she had previously gotten along very well began to act in an unfriendly manner towards her after disclosure. According to Ms Davis, when she confronted this teacher about her behaviour, the teacher responded: 'I can't believe you did not know this was going on ... How could a child be hurt in her own home without the mother knowing ... Did you allow this to happen? I'm so mad at you ... What kind of a mother are you?'

This mother was devastated by the teacher's accusations. The position taken by this teacher is not unlike that held by other professionals. For example, some key informants who were interviewed for this study believed it impossible for mothers not to know of the sexual abuse. Suzanne Sgroi, author of the *Handbook of Clinical Intervention in Child Sexual Abuse* (1982) writes: 'Mothers can perhaps be most generally described as failing to protect the child victim ... Most mothers of incest victims are aware, consciously or unconsciously, that the incest exists' (28–9).

Sgroi was one of the first professionals in the field to publish a handbook with clear instructions on case management of sexual abuse. In this book, however, she maintains and perpetuates many of the suppositions about mothers from mainstream clinical literature.

Dorothy White's daughter, Jill, wrote the following graffiti on the wall at school: 'Fuck off ... I'll kill you, you bastard.' The mother and Jill's therapist interpreted this behaviour as anger towards her father for molesting her over a number of years. The principal's response to the graffiti was to threaten to charge Jill under the Young Offenders Act, and also to transfer her to another school, 'if she didn't toe the mark.' Ms White explained to her daughter's school teacher and principal that her daughter was in therapy after suffering child abuse. She insisted the principal come to her home and apologize to Jill, and tell her he wanted her to return to his school. The principal did as she suggested, and Jill did return.

Olga Kadishun indicated that her youngest daughter, Ida, 'suffered drastically through the school.' She said that instead of the teachers being supportive and encouraging her daughter in school, 'she'd be punished ... I put it to [the teachers'] ignorance ... not knowing what to do.' This particular school insisted on receiving information directly from the child psychologist who was treating Ida, but Olga Kadishun refused to give it to them, as she was concerned it would stay on Ida's school record and would be used against her. Ida failed that school year, even though she had been doing well in school prior to the molestation.

Kellie Curren found the school principal and two of the teachers 'not very sympathetic at all' with her daughter. The principal, according to Ms Curren, was so negative that she felt she had to contact her local school board and report him. Ms Curren indicated that this same principal was initially against having a special play on sexual abuse presented to the children and parents within his school. He also refused to distribute any literature on child sexual abuse to the children in his school.

The teachers made no allowances for her daughter, Karen, at all. In fact, Ms Curren suggested there was a real lack of sensitivity in the way Karen was handled in the classroom after the teachers were told about the sexual abuse. Ms Curren, who later helped other non-offending mothers in situations of child sexual abuse, said there was little understanding on the part of the teachers in that particular school about the experiences/ feelings of sexually abused children. She felt the teachers needed training in the area, not just on how to report, but also in being more supportive of the child-victims and their mothers.

Mary Fletcher's seven-year-old son, Brian, was molested at age five, and began acting very disruptively in school over that two-year period before disclosure. At first, his mother thought it might be a personality conflict with his teacher, but later she said, 'He was so bad in school that he was referred to a psychiatrist.' The recommendations of the psychiatrist were that Brian would go to school only half days. The other half day, he would stay at home with his mother and receive special educational instructions from her (as planned by the school).

Ms Fletcher was enrolled at university herself and also had a part-time job. She felt the school was putting the problem back on her, since they were unable to manage her son in the school system for full days. This mother was obliged to disrupt her university and employment arrangements in order to provide the necessary educational instruction and home care for her youngest child. There was an assumption made by school officials that Brian's mother could rearrange her life to accommodate their planning, which included an understanding that this mother would be at home five afternoons per week. Mr Fletcher had full-time employment, so Mary Fletcher was able to stay home when necessary to carry out the plan, but the expectations placed on her were clearly onerous.

The Effect of Victimization on School Work

When mothers were asked if they thought their children's school work was affected by the sexual abuse and subsequent disclosure, nineteen mothers said 'yes,' and five mothers said 'no.' Although five mothers said no, four out of the five indicated they were worried about their children's inability to deal with the problem of their sexual abuse more openly. For example, those mothers who said 'no,' expressed the following opinions about their child's behaviour with respect to their achievements at school:

I think she separated herself from [the sexual abuse] ... like ... this is what happened ... and then she shut the door on it ...

She does everything right ... She has excelled, but she has never been quite satisfied with herself and she isolates herself.

Well, she seems okay but it all seems to be a front.

[The school] said they hadn't noticed anything ... but ... if anything came up they would let me know about it ... but she was cranky and moody and seemed to revert back a few years and become very babyish ... and she did not want to discuss [the sexual abuse].

It does seem that some children are able to keep their school work at the achievement level established before the sexual abuse and control their behaviour in school despite the experiences they have been through. Research and practice, however, show that there is a price to pay, as this particular type of coping mechanism used by children to get through the abuse and to get on with their lives may well present problems later in life. For example, if children cut off their feelings and deny their experiences, this may prevent them from 'tuning in' and being aware of their own feelings later (Bass and Davis 1988; Berliner and Stevens 1982; Herman 1992).

The nineteen mothers who felt their children's school work suffered because of the sexual abuse and the subsequent disclosure indicated four major ways in which this manifested itself: behavioural problems, isolating themselves from peers, school work deterioration/lower grades and various exhibited and verbalized fears.

Behavioural Problems at School

The types of behaviour problems that mothers discussed concerning their children in the school setting included: urinating on other children; exposing their genitals to other children; beating other children; running away from school; hitting the teacher; writing obscene language on school property; kicking other children; and making rude and sexual comments to others.

Such behaviours are described as typical in the treatment literature of sexually abused children (Faller 1988; Finkelhor and Brown 1985; Herman 1992).

School Work Deterioration

Four children failed their whole year at school and mothers attributed this failure directly to their victimization. Other children were just not able to maintain their previous high standards of achievement in their school work.

Isolation

Many of the children in this study were described by their mothers as wanting to isolate themselves from peers, family members, and friends after the disclosure. This seemed to be related to their own lowered self-esteem, likely a result of the sexual abuse. The child-victims argued more often with their friends and, in some cases, lost their best friends through such arguments. Their mothers said they noted the children were staying in their bedrooms for longer periods of time, and acting in a distancing way with others in the household.

Fears

A large number of children were fearful. One of the reasons stated for this fear in some of the children was related to seeing the offender on the school grounds or on their way to or from school. Another was based on being within the same household as the offender, which brought the possibility of revictimization. Some children, because they could no longer concentrate on school work or keep up their good study habits, were slipping behind in their marks, and these children had the additional fear of failing their school year. These fears are not uncommon with children who have been sexually abused (Gil 1993; Johnson 1993; Terr 1991).

School was also seen by mothers as an important stabilizing factor in their children's lives, however. It is therefore even more important for school systems to be knowledgeable and sensitive to the issues of child-victims.

On balance, there were more positive than negative comments made by mothers about their experiences with school systems. I have chosen to emphasize areas where change is needed to reduce the trauma on both mothers and children involved with school officials, however, and therefore have articulated more areas of negative experiences in this section.

Court Experiences

In the Province of Ontario, where this research was conducted, there are essentially three ways in which a report of child sexual abuse could reach the court system: through the criminal justice system; through child welfare or family court (child protection); and through a custody and access dispute (civil).

Some mothers in this study experienced all three court systems. Only one mother was not involved in any court system as a result of the disclosure. Although six mothers were involved in child welfare or family court and six mothers were involved in the civil court through custody and access issues, this section will address only the criminal court system, as this was most frequently discussed by the mothers interviewed.

Criminal Justice System

Twenty-eight offenders were involved with the twenty-four families of this study. Twenty-two offenders were initially charged with a criminal offence. In six cases, no criminal charges were laid for various reasons: one case (of the sixteen-year-old victim) was never reported to the police; in another the child was thought to be too young (four years) to testify; one male teen was only warned by the police, but not charged; one alleged offender could not be located in Canada; one offender was too young to be charged (nine years old); and in one case the police believed there to be insufficient evidence to proceed with charges.

Of the twenty-two offenders charged: nine offenders were convicted and sentenced to thirty days to two years less a day; two offenders were convicted and given suspended sentences (three years each); in four cases charges were dismissed after the preliminary hearing; one alleged offender was found not guilty of the offence; and six cases were still pending in the criminal court system when the interviews were conducted.

The comments of the twenty-two mothers involved with the criminal justice system include their responses with respect to Crown attorneys, judges, sentences, lawyers, and general experiences within the system itself.

Crown Attorneys

Catharine Burns said she was told who her Crown attorney would be and she called him to seek direction. He told her to meet him an hour before court. She and her daughter, Virginia, went for the appointment, but her assigned assistant Crown was sick that day, and another assistant Crown met with her just to postpone the meeting for another day. Ms Burns found this very annoying, so she phoned her Crown attorney and said, 'We are not going to be a piece of paper on your desk, and we are not going to meet an hour before court.' Ms Burns said he replied, 'Well, why don't you come down ... and we'll meet.' After they met, the Crown attorney became interested in the case and spoke with the hospital and the doctors in preparation for court. Ms Burns said, 'I just got fed up and angry ... and he responded well to it.' Later, she was able to engage her own lawyer.

Even though it is generally accepted that Crown attorneys are overworked, it appears that some can and do make time for court preparation with mothers of victimized children if mothers themselves take the initiative to ask for appropriate attention and time. If eligible, it is advantageous for women to retain their own legal counsel and advocate. This is not always possible, however, as some women cannot afford it. Consequently, they generally accept the sometimes hurried case put together by the busy Crown, who may choose to see the mother and her child only an hour before court, as happened to a number of women in this study.

When Jackie Wall was asked if she had spoken to her Crown yet, she laughed and said 'Yeah ... I've spoken to quite a few ... Every time you go to court you end up with a new one.' Lack of continuity and follow-up was a problem this mother felt strongly about, as her small daughter had to retell her story to a number of different Crowns.

One key informant who was considered an expert in this area was asked during the interview whether a Crown assigned a case sticks with it, or if Crowns change [cases] part way through. He replied, 'It's unusual, but always a possibility to have another Crown take over ... as a result of a scheduling problem ... but there would be another Crown assigned ... who would meet with the young victim ... well in advance of court ...' This key informant's description of the process does not seem to reflect the experiences of the mothers in this study. And most of the women interviewed had their cases assigned to the same court system (geographically) described by this key informant.

Carolyn O'Brien said she found her Crown to be 'a very nice person,' but there was a certain disadvantage in having the Crown present her case (in comparison with having legal counsel of her own, as in the offender's case). The offender was able to get together with his lawyer and discuss whatever he wanted, whenever he wanted, whereas Ms O'Brien could only see the Crown when she had time to give her. She said the Crown would always ask her if she had any questions, but she said, 'when I got home I would think of things I should have said ... but then couldn't reach her.' Ms O'Brien said, 'I think I didn't tell her about enough things for evidence ...' The alleged offender was found 'not guilty' in this particular case.

There appears to be a disadvantage with respect to sufficient time for a thorough case preparation when the Crown presents a case of child victimization to the court. Society loses out when an offender who is guilty is not convicted, because that individual then has the freedom and opportunity to return to the community and molest other children. Research shows that without treatment, the likelihood of the offender committing further offences is strong. Even with treatment, recidivism rates for this type of crime are high (Badgley et al. 1984; Groth et al. 1982).

Anita Marshall's daughter, Janet, did not have to testify in court, as the offender pleaded guilty. Neither Anita Marshall nor Janet ever saw the Crown who presented their case, but Ms Marshall did send him a letter outlining the situation. She was unhappy about the outcome of the case, and the lack of evidence that was placed before the court with respect to other children who had been molested over a number of years by this same man. The offender was not incarcerated, but rather given a suspended sentence because of his advanced age. He was back in the community within a few days, with very limited monitoring by probation officers, creating fear for the victim and her mother. Insufficient evidence was placed before the court to allow the judge to know what a risk this man would be to other children in the community.

It is interesting to note that in the twenty-four cases in this study, age became an important factor in one-third (eight) of the cases. But it was always the age of the offender, not the age of the victim, that was brought up for discussion and decision-making concerning charges (with the exception of those instances where the authorities felt some victims were too young to testify and charges were therefore not proceeded with). The male offenders were said to be either: too old to charge (in two cases); too old to be given the regular sentence (in two cases) for this offence; too young to charge (in three cases); or too young to be given a regular sentence for the crime committed (in one case).

Olga Kadishun's daughter, Ida, was very seriously traumatized by the sexual abuse perpetrated by the father of one of her friends in the neighborhood. When Ms Kadishun heard the sentence given to him by the judge, she was very upset and said to the Crown: 'Do something about this.' She said in his response he implied that her child had not been beaten and was at least still alive. Ms Kadishun felt the Crown clearly tried to trivialize what had happened to the four children victimized by this offender. There was no appeal to a higher court.

In this particular case, the offender was sentenced to two years less a day and he served eighteen months. Two years after his release, he was charged again on three counts of sexual assault to a minor, and was incarcerated early in 1989 for another two years. He served approximately eighteen months of this sentence again, and was released into the community the following summer. Since the offender was diagnosed as a pedophile, and since the prognosis for curing pedophilia is not considered hopeful, there is a strong likelihood that he will again molest other children. How will mothers of future victims know of the potential harm this man could be to their children when he moves into their neighborhood? This should be the responsibility of our criminal justice system, who already know of this man's potential harm to small children.

The careful monitoring of offenders released and alerting communities of the potential dangers are important methods that should be the responsibility of the state. Olga Kadishun's response to the second criminal court hearing for this offender was one of confusion:

He had the same lawyer ... What I don't understand is how he is so well protected ... if [the court system] had done something when [Ida] and the other children went through ... he would not be able to harm these other children. I believe these men are potential child killers ... I think they can get into a panic ... I honestly believe that one day we will read of this little man killing a child.

The information collected in this study shows that the criminal justice system did not protect a number of children from being revictimized by known child molesters.

Judges

There were six mothers who made comments about the judges in criminal courts, based on their own personal experiences. Three of the six mothers illustrate their views below.

Catharine Burns felt that her daughter's case should have gone to trial from preliminary hearing because there was sufficient evidence without putting her daughter on the witness stand (medical evidence and the father's confession in a personal letter to his wife). The judge dismissed the charges, however, because the child was unable to give evidence due to her distress in the courtroom on seeing her father, the offender. Ms Burns responded:

> My feeling is ... that the judge looked at it ... like ... this is incest ... you don't want to see this guy go to jail for incest ... His opinions about incest ... well ... he thought this belongs in family court ... They just don't want to bother ... Keep it in family court ... he's not gonna go out on the streets and hurt anyone else ... the judge figures in his own silly mind ... So as long as we keep the kid away from him ... everything will be fine and you know ... it's not fair ... because it's not true.

This mother went on to say that, in her opinion, judges needed special training in the area of child sexual abuse.

This case, in fact, does point out the potential for harm to other children and to other women when for some reason an offender is not charged for the offences he committed. In this particular instance, Catharine Burns' ex-husband, the offender, is now living with another young woman who is expecting his baby. How will his new partner know that the likelihood is strong that this man will commit this crime again against another child, possibly her child? Will she be blamed if her child is molested by her new partner? The findings from this study and similar studies (Dempster 1992; Hooper 1992; Johnson 1992; Krane 1994) suggest that this new mother will be held responsible for her partner's offence if he should molest their child as well.

Carolyn O'Brien's nine-year-old daughter, Ruthie, gave what her case worker described as 'very good evidence' in court. Her uncle denied molesting her. The judge found the defendant 'not guilty' of the offence.

Ms O'Brien and Ruthie were both very upset about the judge's decision. Ms O'Brien said:

I was told that one of the reasons why we lost was that Ruthie wasn't psychologically damaged enough ... like, she was pretty well normal ... when she gave her testimony ... She should have been more emotionally upset ... The judge could not believe anything happened to her. It makes you think you perhaps should keep your child away from counselling so that she would be so miserable ... that it would convince the judge ... that something awful happened to her.

Given the nature of the evidence required for the criminal court, there was no such 'hard' evidence presented in this case. But three things worked against providing the best evidence possible: the actual case took two years to come to trial and the child's memory for detail was not (nor should it be expected to be) accurate; the mother, in this case, did not feel she had sufficient access to the Crown who was presenting the case on a continuing basis in order for her to provide the best evidence possible; and that there was a delay of six months in the medical examination of the child. Although such examinations are unlikely to yield any medical results, if there had been evidence, it would have been lost. This case, in the final analysis, came down to the offender's word against the child's word before a judge, and the offender's word was more impressive to this particular judge.

Anne Bartlette was asked what the most upsetting part of the whole situation of the abuse had been for her. She said, 'When the judge said my kids were lying.' Although she said he did not say that in so many words, charges were dropped and the judge advised the alleged offender to 'get away from this family because ... your ex-wife was just doing this for spite.' Her partner's defence was that she told the children to say that they had been sexually abused by him, so he could not have access to his daughter. This is ironic, because Ms Bartlette was one of the mothers who did not believe her daughter when she first disclosed. Her child reported the abuse to her school counsellor, who subsequently sent the Society and police officers to their home.

This particular man had allegedly abused other children in the past. The evidence, however, had not been substantial enough to convict him in criminal court. The offender went back to the community, a free man. There was absolutely no monitoring of his behaviour, with the exception of supervised access to his children. Fortunately, Ms Bartlette had the support of her local child welfare worker, who would not allow him unsupervised access, because they believed the children's stories despite the criminal court decision. This is one instance where child welfare did provide support for the mother in the court system with respect to keeping her children.

The Process

The majority of women found the entire experience in criminal court an extremely upsetting process. As one mother stated, 'Nobody ever told me ... take somebody to court with you.' The need for moral support from another individual becomes very important to anyone forced to appear in a criminal court proceeding, especially with respect to child sexual abuse.

A number of important issues about the court process were discussed during the interviews. For example, the majority of mothers were very concerned about the length of time it took to get the case to court, and then, once it was scheduled, the number of delays that the offenders' lawyers were able to arrange to slow down the entire process. This was very hard on the children who had to testify, as the longer it was drawn out, the greater the chance that younger children would become confused with dates, times, and events.

Carolyn O'Brien's daughter, Ruthie, was molested for a six-month period when she was between seven and eight years old. She was cross-examined by the offender's lawyer two years later, when she was nearly ten, at which time she was expected to remember all the details about the seven times her uncle had molested her.

This mother provided me with a copy of the court transcript on the case and I was therefore able to note the types of questions this child was asked by the defence lawyer. Included were the following questions:

What furniture was in the room at the time? Where exactly was the furniture located? Who else was in or out of the house that particular day? What day of the week was it? What were the weather conditions? What particular clothes were you wearing? What type of clothing was the offender wearing? Where had he touched you? What had he said? What had you said?

The molestation took place in her uncle's home, from which she had moved the day of disclosure. This child had not returned to or lived in that particular house for two years. The child's mother felt that the two-year delay in getting it to trial placed an unfair burden on her child to remember such details from when she was seven.

The criminal court process was not designed for hearing and appropriately dealing with cases of child sexual abuse. It is a truism that, if you want to commit a crime for which you are most unlikely to get caught, molest a very small child – the smaller the better – because the child cannot present evidence the court will accept and you are unlikely to have a witness to the crime. New laws that have dispensed with the need for corroborative evidence do not seem to have changed the situation greatly.

Rachel Cohen said she was very angry at the criminal justice system because of what happened to her son. She said, with reference to the man who sexually abused her son: 'He was in jail one night and out the next day ... We kept going back to court to get a preliminary hearing date ... and he kept being able to delay ... which is not right for the children they have to get on with their lives ... They say that child sexual abuse is a priority ... The disclosure was last August and here it is June of this year ... and we still are not in court ... What kind of priority is that?'

Most of the mothers interviewed were not satisfied with the light sentences given the offenders. In some instances, the length of sentences given seemed to trivialize the crimes committed. For example, Kellie Curren's child was molested by her male cousin from the age of five until she was ten, at which time she disclosed. Her sexual abuse included vaginal penetration. The offender, because of his age (seventeen), was sentenced to thirty days in jail, to be served on weekends. This child told her mother she felt cheated because she was unable to tell her story in court, since the offender pleaded guilty. There was no order for him to report to a probation officer, or even to seek treatment. This mother had information that he had also molested other children. These details were not brought before the court. The young offender's father was able to hire a very expensive lawyer to represent his son, and apparently to keep important evidence out of the court system.

Although the maximum sentence for sexual abuse of a child is ten years, no offender in this study received more than two years in jail. This speaks to the seriousness of the crime in the judges' and in society's estimation. Those who commit property offences, according to one key informant, are taken more seriously when it comes to sentencing.

Although I would argue for longer sentences for offenders, this is only because there are no viable alternatives to jail at the present time. Until there are other methods for dealing with offenders, it is important to keep child molesters off the streets in order to protect children. Offenders do not necessarily receive treatment in jail, as programs may not be available or, if they are, offenders may reject them.

There are a variety of treatment methods used with offenders; the most common approach is psychotherapy, based on the assumption that offenders sexually abuse children because of internal emotional conflict. This is thought to be relieved by helping the offenders to become more self-aware and better able to understand their underlying issues, and through such introspection, control their undesirable behaviour. This method covers one-to-one therapy, group therapy, family and marital therapy, milieu therapy, and self-help group therapy (Groth et al. 1981). In Ontario, paroled sex offenders received specialized treatment at clinics and through individual psychiatrists and psychologists (Makin 1990). Other approaches include the psychoeducational method of treatment, which addresses life-management problems such as alcohol- or drug-dependency, vocational and educational rehabilitation, and strategies to cope with anxiety and frustration. Behaviour modification approaches use aversive conditioning whereby the offenders' inappropriate sexual responses (an example might be an erection on viewing themes of violence) is paired with noxious events (such as electric shocks) in order to eliminate the behaviour. Chemotherapy is also used with some offenders. Depo-Provera is injected into the muscles weekly. This lowers the offenders' testosterone level and subsequently diminishes his sexual arousal. This technique releases the offender's compulsive urge to commit sexual offences (Groth et al. 1981).

Unfortunately, prison treatment programs lack the financial resources to treat all sexual offenders. For example, of the 161 sex offenders serving less than two years in the British Columbia system in 1995, only 60 were able to receive treatment while in prison. Professionals working in the correctional system are constantly lobbying governments to address prevention issues, upgrade programs, and increase supervision of sex offenders released from jail and/or on probation (Yeager 1995).

Lena Dominelli (1989) has suggested an interesting alternative to jail on the basis that offenders only have their patterns of 'might is right' reinforced when they are incarcerated. Her proposed plan includes a special rehabilitation centre where convicted offenders are to be sent to work on their attitudes and behaviours, to be released only when their victims (women and children) felt that they had reached better standards of behaviour and respect for others.

June Ronan's father molested her daughter, Alice. He had also molested June when she was a child, as well as one of her siblings. Through 'plea bargaining,' the offender, who had at first denied the offence, was later talked into pleading guilty to a lesser charge (common assault). The child's grandfather, June Ronan's father, was sentenced to eighteen months probation, with no jail sentence to be served.

Plea bargaining is used extensively in cases of child sexual abuse. Police officers and Crown attorneys argue that the harmful effects of having small children testify in court must be weighed against allowing the offender to plead guilty to a lesser charge. If the offender denies the charges, and he will agree to plead guilty so the child does not have to be put through the trauma of the witness stand and questioning from the defence lawyer, than it does seem like a useful strategy. By the same token, however, it also adds to the trivialization of the offence by reducing the charges, and therefore the length of the sentence.

A number of mothers mentioned the stress that was caused by the criminal court system's acceptance of what could only be described as 'bullying the child-victims' when they were on the stand giving testimony. For example, Betsy Hamilton was very upset about what happened to her children at court. Her daughter, Gillian, fainted in court because the offender, through his lawyer, claimed she and her brother were lying. She said, 'The lawyers tried to trick them ... It was pretty awful what was happening.' Eventually, the offender pleaded guilty to a lesser charge and was incarcerated.

The criminal court process, judges, Crowns, lawyers, and the laws have all created serious difficulties for women whose children have been sexually victimized. Catharine MacKinnon (1987), a noted legal scholar, would expect such an outcome for women caught in the legal system. She argues that we do not have laws that reflect the experience and aspirations of women and, in fact, 'We are not allowed to be women on our terms.' She argues that 'the definition of women in law and in life is not ours.' We either 'have to meet the male standard for women: femininity ... or the male standard for males ... In these spheres we do not find women from women's point of view' (71).

Another legal expert who feels women do not receive equality within the legal system is Madame Justice Bertha Wilson of the Supreme Court of Canada. In a 1990 memorial lecture at Osgoode Hall Law School entitled 'Will Women Judges Really Make a Difference?' she said, 'A distinctly male perspective is clearly discernible and has resulted in legal principles that are not fundamentally sound ...' She went on to say, 'Some aspects of the criminal law in particular cry out for change, since they are based on presuppositions about the nature of women and women's sexuality that in this day and age are little short of ludicrous' (1990, 13). Justice Wilson concluded that female judges will probably make a difference once more of them are appointed.

In this chapter we have heard in women's own words what it was like to be involved with the various institutions after their children disclosed. These women experienced institutionalized sexism almost everywhere they turned but especially within the legal and judicial systems. The mothers in this study experiened a lack of priority in hospitals, with police, with child welfare systems, and in the education and court systems. The women were blamed by social workers and counsellors, ignored by police officers, and their children's victimization was frequently trivialized by the court system. They experienced professionals who lacked adequate training, were unsupportive, and in some cases gave unhelpful and misleading advice.

The overwhelming majority of women described devastating experiences with the various institutions, and they cried out for change in the current system that would provide more sensitive and respectful attitudes toward women and children and more enlightened and less sexist policies and laws.

8

Key Informants' Attitudes and Views

The fifteen key informants interviewed for this study were selected on the basis of the following criteria: their ability to articulate the 'official position' of child welfare in Ontario; their influence in formulating previous or current legislation and policies; their experience in implementing child welfare and criminal justice policies on a day-to-day basis through intervention in families or with offenders; and their special knowledge and experience in dealing with women and women's issues. I selected ten key informants on the basis of my knowledge and experience in the area; the remaining five were chosen by their respective agencies/organizations for interviews. The group selected is not totally inclusive of all those involved in the child sexual abuse area; based on my experience, however, it covers the major players with respect to issues of practice, policy, and research. The fifteen can be divided into the following five categories: Direct Intervention (medical doctor, police officer, child welfare representative, crisis group worker); Legislation/Policy/Programs (legal advisor, policy analyst, agency director); Court (senior civil servant, Crown attorney); Academic (sociologist/researcher, social work professor, women's studies professor); Social Activism (feminist activist, legal counsel/women's advocate, media consultant/women's and children's advocate).

Although no detailed information was gathered from key informants on their background, age, income, or other demographic data, such as was collected from mothers interviewed, a general description can be given in order to provide a sense of those who made up the key informant group. Each member was given a code letter ("A" through "O") to protect his or her identity. Following this identity code letter is an additional letter ('A' through 'E') designating which of the five categories with which each key informant is associated. For example, all key informants involved in direct intervention have an 'A' after their identity letter; legislative/policy/ programs, 'B'; court, 'C'; academic, 'D'; and social activism, 'E'.

The gender breakdown of seven females and eight males provided the opportunity to capture the differing views of both sexes on the various issues discussed. The majority of key informants are parents, with four of the seven women being mothers themselves. Key informants represent a very wide age range, from the late twenties to the late sixties. All key informants were white. As might be expected of a group of experts, the key informants are a highly educated group. All but two hold university degrees. Seven are either medical doctors or hold PhD degrees.

Only female members of the key informant group indicated that they or their children were survivors of child sexual abuse. In each of the three cases, the offenders were the biological fathers. The fact that three out of seven female key informants had the same experience is another indication of the pervasiveness of the crime. No male key informant indicated that he or his child(ren) had been child-victims, and no key informant said he or she had ever sexually abused a child (nor were they asked the question).

During the interviewing process, each key informant was asked about her/his own feelings, thoughts, and views with respect to the notion of 'mother's role' within families. Probing questions were used in an effort to determine the underlying assumptions and values held by the key informant about women, children, and family life, and specifically about cases of child sexual abuse and related issues. Key informants were asked: Can children be believed or do they lie about their victimization? Are children responsible for their victimization? Does sexual abuse really cause harm to the children involved? Should mothers be held responsible or partly responsible for their child's victimization? Do mothers contribute to the abuse of their children by being passive?

The following selected quotes will illustrate some of the views of the key informants from the social activism category.

During one interview, the issue of a mother's responsibility for the sexual abuse of her child was being discussed, and I asked the key informant, the following question: Some people suggest that mothers are always responsible for their children even at a passive level, so that in effect, there are no so-called 'non-offending' mothers. What do you think?

Well ... sure ... because I could just take that one step further ... broaden that one more step ... there's no such thing as a non-offending community. Where are you going to draw the line? I mean ... why do we draw the line at mothers? Is that to defocus our own responsibility as a community ... as a culture? Is that our way of getting off the hook? Say it's Mom's fault so that we do not have to look at our own unsupportive, uncaring, and unresponsive action? (Key Informant 'M-E')

Another key informant from this group was asked to comment on whether or not there were large numbers of women who commit the crime of child sexual abuse, and the reply was: 'I guess I will be much more shocked if I find this is true ... I will be much more disappointed, ... no, I don't think that we will find that it is true in the area of sexual abuse (Key Informant 'D-E'). When asked why she felt this was the case, the key informant indicated that, in her opinion, women care more than men do about others, and added: 'The relationships that I see where women are with women, women are with children, and women are with men ... they are much better relationships than men have with men, men have with children, or men have with women. It clearly has to do with the way we have been socialized' (Key Informant 'D-E').

Two key informants from the occupational category of legislation, policy, and programs provide the reader with some of their views on specific questions I posed in the interviews.

One key informant was asked to discuss the terms 'offender' and 'non-offending' mothers as they relate to child welfare legislation, and a child in need of protection. The following quote is part of that discussion:

It is not so much the parent who doesn't protect a child against degradation in the neighbourhood, but someone who thinks that if *usually she* is too tough with visitors in the home, perhaps *her* visitors, then she will lose companionship, economic support and therefore she is not too fastidious ... and if it means that children in the family ... particularly daughters are not viciously violated ... but if they are abused or if they are involved inappropriately in sexual talk and provocation, then she'll let it happen because it suits her purpose ... so the expression was used that ... a child is in need of protection where the parent causes or permits abuse [emphases added]. (Key Informant 'G-B').

This quote is indicative of this key informant's views. Throughout the interview, it became clear that the conventional ideology of 'the' family dominated this key informant's thinking about the child and his/her family. Mothers were blamed for the sexual abuse of their children even when they were 'non-offending' mothers.

Other comments made by GB idicated that he believed that a child's safety might have to be sacrificed in an effort to keep the family unit together, in cases where the child's father was the offender. For this key informant, the long-term best interests of the child were to keep his or her family 'intact' (meaning together/not damaged).

Another key informant, from this occupational category was asked: 'What's frightening about the child sexual abuse disclosure for the mother?' The response was: 'The disgrace, the loss she faces in terms of her marriage, but also the sense that she wasn't sexually adequate ... it calls into question her capacity to be the woman of his life ... "I wasn't enough"' (Key Informant 'J-B').

This key informant demonstrates not only misinformation in the area of why offenders offend, since offenders are known to have sexual relations with their partners, other women, and also children simultaneously (Burgess et al. 1985; Groth et al. 1981), but also a very narrow description of a woman's role, and her importance in a marriage relationship. This quote exemplifies the thinking and comments found in the entire interview data with this particular key informant, who appeared to express a much greater depth of understanding and empathy for adult male offenders than for women or child-victims.

In another question posed to the same key informant I asked: 'Any ideas about causal factors? What do you think causes men to sexually abuse small children?' The response:

I guess what has impressed me most is that it is not sexual ... I mean ... it's usually a sense of gentle, loving, affection(ate) relationships where they feel comfortable in this kind of a situation ... a sense of ... like children and yet the person's an adult ... one boy who was in ... computers ... the guy has become ... an expert in computers out of that relationship and now that is his career ... Things are not just black and white ... How much was there real caring? For some children it's the most significant relationship they've ever had, the attention, what they've always wanted from adults, but sometimes it's just mostly abusive. (Key Informant 'J-B').

The following quotes reflect the views of key informants in the occupational categories of direct intervention, court systems, and academia, respectively.

I asked one key informant: 'Do you think mothers' know what is going on?' The response was: 'Maybe on an unconscious level, you know when the disclosure is made there is always a guilt feeling for the Mom, let's say she was spending too much time at work, or whether she did know about it and let it go on. I think that on some level they feel responsible for creating that environment and I guess because of those feelings I tend to think they could have done something about it' (Key Informant 'I-A'). This illustrates a mother-blaming attitude by the professional interviewed.

The context of the next response was a key informant discussing cases of sexual abuse from a professional experience, and including personal views and beliefs about one case.

I had a case involving two young fellows. I guess they were ten and eleven at the time, the grandfather sexually molested them ... He would take them up to his cottage ... The police said they had been buggered by the grandfather ... Nobody believed the kids ... The young kids didn't hate their grandfather, he was their grandfather and they loved him, and I really don't think that at the time when this was going on, they thought it was that bad. They must have thought well he's my grandfather, if he's doing this it might be right. I think that it was only after the agencies got involved and said he did *this* to you! They got them in counselling and said to them this is terrible! (Key Informant 'B-C').

Another key informant was sharing views and experiences about clinical work in the past:

'I was aware of incest cases ... after the Second World War ... where Daddy was in a sense a stranger and a hero ... After the war we had a whole raft of these cases ... The taboo hadn't worked for them ... There did not seem to be much damage done (Key Informant 'A-D').

All three of the above key informants expressed similar attitudes about the criminal behaviour of child sexual abuse; that is, mothers could do more to protect their children, and the sexual abuse may not really harm children, anyway.

Another key informant from the Academic group expresses a different point of view – one based on research findings about mothers of sexually abused children. I asked the question: 'Do you have any sense of how mothers are involved in this problem of child sexual abuse?' The response was:

We found three main groups of mothers [in research study] (1) a very small group who ... may have been active participants or were actively involved in the abuse of the child; (2) a second group who, it would appear may have known about the ongoing abuse of her children but believed, for many reasons, often to hold the whole family together or perhaps just deep disbelief that abuse is occurring chose to remain silent until it became otherwise known; (3) and the largest group would be those mothers who were really unaware what was occurring (Key Informant 'F-D').

Age, gender, and occupation all appear to be important factors in examining the attitudes of individuals with respect to sensitivity regarding women's and children's rights and needs. For example, those younger, female and in occupations categorized as being related to social activism demonstrated the most sensitivity during the interviews, whereas those older, male, and in the occupations or disciplines related to legislation, policies, and programs tended to show the least sensitivity to women's and children's rights and needs.

Given the responses of those key informants in positions of decision-making over the lives of women and children, it becomes obvious that the services received very much reflect the values and attitudes held by these key informants (mainly men). The fact that the majority of the mothers interviewed felt blamed by the existing legislation, policies, programs, and workers delivering the services, is therefore not surprising, given this small snap-shot of the views and attitudes of those in decision-making positions over the lives of women and children.

Female Key Informant's Views on Child Sexual Abuse

Seven of the fifteen key informants interviewed were women. Their theories for explaining why children are sexually abused did not differ substantially from those given by the mothers interviewed. These responses can be divided into three categories: gender and power; family systems model; and cycle of violence.

Five of the seven female key informants' ideas fit under theories of gender and/or power with respect to why children are sexually abused. For example, one key informant ('M-E') said, 'Well ... initially, I think it's power and then it becomes a sexual addiction.' She went on to explain that like any other addiction, it is almost impossible to change once it has taken hold of the individual. She stressed the importance of early intervention to stop the behaviour before the addiction stage, when the offender is still an adolescent.

Another key informant expressed the view that she felt the problem was a power issue with men when they sexually abused small children, but that offenders needed treatment to correct these attitudes.

When asked: 'Why do you think adult men sexually abuse small children?' two key informants expressed the feelings of this group as a whole:

I think basically it is an unquestioned right to children ... Maybe it's true that they don't know how else to love ... The other problem with all this stuff is the differences in situations ... Ownership is there in the male's right to own the child's body or his wife's body. (Key Informant 'D-E').

It is an issue of power and sexual privilege ... That has also been the reaction against women who report wife assault and the reaction we are seeing now in the sexual abuse area ... Obviously you are never going to hear men talk about how they are going to maintain their power over women in the court system ... but I think the reaction ... and the ease with which they are able to keep women down ... in their place is both economically, as well as psychologically ... clear to me. (Key Informant 'H-E').

One key informant explained child sexual abuse in what could only be termed a classic 'family systems' model; when asked, 'Do you have any ideas about causal factors with respect to child sexual abuse?,' she replied:

Well ... if I look at some of the families I have dealt with and the dynamics ... the families where it occurs ... they tend to be ones where there are loose boundaries ... Communication between family members is very poor ... Usually the person in the mother-role is often emotionally and or physically unavailable to the members in the family ... and I guess that sort of sets up a situation whereby, I don't know ... the men are more likely to miss the closeness and security and look to a child to obtain those sorts of feelings. (Key Informant 'I-A')

Another key informant also expresses a very mainstream view about this problem. She appears to be ambivalent on the whole question, however. When asked how she conceptualizes the problem of child sexual abuse, she replied:

The ones I've seen are really screwed up psychiatrically ... I don't know ... unless it was invariably done to them ... It's a real circle ... a self-perpetuating cycle ... We have to consider power relationships ... Also, they tend to be the mothers of victims ... They condone it in some shape or form ... by denial ... and tend to choose people ... who, I don't know ... It's so prevalent maybe it's not all wrong ... but the reason I think it is wrong is because people are so screwed up in their adult lives ... We should be able to help adult survivors. On the other hand, there are obviously many adult women who have coped with that ... where, yes, it hasn't been great but its been okay ... and they have gone on and had good marriages ... or maybe they haven't ... Maybe they are in the divorce group ... the non-nurturing group ... I don't know how it tracks. (Key Informant 'N-A')

Here, the reader sees the unravelling of many of the doubts and ambivalences expressed by professionals who work in this area.

Levine and Estable (1983) speak to many of the issues raised here. They question why it is that society has permitted a woman's health and autonomy to be sacrificed for others and why women are forced to deny their own needs in favour of the well-being of their families. They question why is it assumed that women can or should provide all the nurturing for others and expect no nurturing for themselves.

Male Key Informants' Views on Child Sexual Abuse

The eight male key informants' responses to the question of why some men sexually abuse children are difficult to categorize. They range from 'I don't know' to long, thought-out answers.

One key informant said, 'That's something I can't comprehend because the thought to myself as well as to some of my colleagues is so repulsive ... I can't answer ... I don't know why' (Key Informant 'L-A').

Another answered in this manner: 'Yes ... well ... it is a dynamic I've really never understood ... Before the book *Lolita* ... it was supposed there was an age of sexual innocence ... I think the Lolita syndrome destroyed that ... ' (Key Informant 'G-B').

Another still suggested: 'I think there is a vast number of men who can have a sexual relationship with a woman but they might prefer a sexual relationship which would be very tender ... as well as very sexual ... This is where they would find their greatest satisfaction' (Key Informant 'J-B'). The above response from key informant 'J-B' gives the reader a sense of what informs the thinking of at least one child welfare expert who is engaged in developing policy and programs for women and children in cases of child sexual abuse.

One respondent seemed very confident in his reply: 'There seem to be at least two groups of men ... those who have courtship problems ... [who] simply do not know the boundaries of acceptable behaviour ... that would include men who are not that smart ... and another group of men who have real sexual preference problems ... They get aroused by children (Key Informant 'C-B').

The responses of the remaining two can be expressed in the following quote by one of them: 'I have trouble answering that one ... part of it stems from the absolute control ... that the law has chosen to give parents, particularly fathers, and ... males seek easy outlets for their sexual desires ... and if there is no perception that anything will happen to you ... that has some effect on your behaviour' (Key Informant 'K-C'). Only the two male key informants represented by this last quote responded in a similar way to that of the majority of the female key informants interviewed.

Traditional values seem to be protected by men in senior decision-making positions, as noted in some of the judges' comments in Chapter Seven.

9

Children's Aid Society Records

During the examination of files from seven different child welfare agencies, it became evident that the ideology of the family continued to play an important part in the investigation and management of child sexual abuse cases by child welfare authorities. This was evident in the content of the material examined, the agency forms, and the decision-making process of the case management plans that affected the lives of the women and children. Examples are taken from mental-health assessments, medical reports, and agency forms to illustrate this point.

Mental-Health Assessments

It is standard practice in this province for the courts, child welfare, or legal representatives of one of the parties involved to request an assessment of the mental health of members of the child's family in sexual abuse cases. These assessments are usually carried out by psychiatrists, psychologists, or social workers. The following examples will illustrate the impact of the assessments, conducted by professionals, on the mothers interviewed for this study.

The husband of Bridget Hesse was assessed by a psychiatrist after he sexually molested his step-daughter. These comments appeared in his psychiatric assessment: 'The behaviour is not exclusively a product of some aberration on his part, but rather an outcome of warped relationships within this family ... He is anxious ... [He has] significant feelings of inadequacy, immaturity present ... [As with the] classic dynamic in certain incestuous families, he felt himself treated as a person of significance [by the child].'

This assessment has normalized the offender's behaviour by reframing it. In other words, the psychiatrist found it understandable that if this man could not be treated as a person of significance by his partner or other adults in his environment, then he must use a child to bolster his self-esteem and to provide his emotional and sexual gratification. Some assessments appear to fulfil the task of protecting male privilege. This one falls into that category, in my opinion. Such assessments are at the basis of numerous feminist critiques of mental-health professionals (Armstrong 1995; Caplan 1989; Masson 1984; Levine 1982; Chesler 1972).

In some assessments, women were termed angry and hostile and referred for special counselling; in other instances, women were assessed as not able to protect their children because they were too passive to stand up to their partners, and were referred for special counselling. The following report from agency records is an example of such a psychiatric assessment. It was completed on Catharine Burns, a non-offending mother, by a male psychiatrist:

Given all that has been stated in this report to date, the natural question that arises is the part that mother has played up to the time of the discovery of the abuse ... [Catharine Burns] is a naive and trusting individual believing the best of all others, hoping for the best and tending to deny painful truths ... The second feature of [her] personality is her severe difficulty in both being able to experience subjectively and to express unequivocally feelings of anger, opposition and hostility ... In addition, there is also the laudable characteristic of desiring to help others which can also be a personal liability. The result of all of this is an individual who finds it very difficult to stand up for herself, to assert herself, to let her rising indignation and anger push her into definitive action that prevents further denigration and possible abuse. A more complete resolution requires therapy designed to foster genuine self-assertiveness for her 'Patsy' attitude.

For mothers such a Catherine Burns, there are only two choices; either they are referred for therapy for being 'too nice,' or referred for therapy for being 'too hostile.' But the focus of the child's victimization is on the mother and what she does or does not do, rather than on the father or male offender's behaviour. Mothers have no say in the rules that govern their lives. In this particular case, rules that have been constructed within the helping professions to protect male privilege (Caplan 1989; Chesler 1987; Dominelli 1986; Krane 1994; Levine 1982; MacKinnon 1987; Masson 1984).

In the Burns case, vicious and painful sexual attacks were made by the father on his preschool daughter. The case did not go to criminal trial because the judge deemed there was a lack of evidence, despite a medical report of harm to the child and a written confession in the offender's own handwriting. Feminist critiques such as that of Levine & Estable (1983) address such situations: 'The prevalent approach to incest indicates how fathers, husbands, men are viewed as relatively marginal actors in a form of male violence perpetrated against their own female children ... So it is that issues of male violence such as incest are assessed mainly in the light of what mothers and daughters have or have not done' (30).

Psychiatrists are informed by their training and by their own set of values, which they bring to bear in their decision-making and assessments of individuals for the courts (Leyton 1987; Masson 1984). In earlier chapters, the views and values reflected in mainstream psychiatric literature were examined. An important role played by psychiatrists and other mental-health professionals submitting assessments to the court system is reproducing and maintaining dominant ideology in the child welfare system.

The following example is from the recording of a professional social worker in a child welfare agency. It pertains to Gertrude Davis, whose husband sexually abused their daughter when she was between the ages of nine and eleven. In the words of the social worker (taken from the protection file):

The sexual *misconduct* also brought into light [Gertrude Davis's] own fears that she is getting older. Consequently, [Gertrude Davis] appears to have interpreted [her husband's] action as a clear indication that he no longer finds her attractive ... and she has not yet come to terms with the role she herself played in setting up the scenario that brought about the *misconduct* (emphasis added).

Mrs [Davis] has been encouraged to seek individual counselling (not yet done so) [as she] brought problems into [the] marriage re: her role as mother/wife.

Father physically and orally manipulated [his daughter's] breasts; fondled her genitals; and, performed cunnilingus. The abused child was in competition with the mother. Father thought his daughter was enjoying it [the sexual abuse] ... He did not mean to hurt her ... Mother is opinionated ... strong willed, angry and hostile.

Diagnostic Impressions
Family enmeshed, boundaries between various sub-systems diffused and easily crossed. One of the results of this enmeshment was a sexual one. Dad felt belittled and unwanted.

The language used in this assessment trivializes the sexual abuse, and the descriptions of the mother and child suggest they were the ones responsible. This child was severely traumatized by the sexual abuse and has been in therapy since the disclosure.

The social worker, like the psychiatrist, has presented the assessment in such a way as to confuse the issue of who has done something wrong here. Whose perspective is this assessment presenting? We learn that 'Dad felt belittled and unwanted,' and that he thought his daughter was enjoying the abuse. Such a family therapy type of assessment, with the abstract notions of 'enmeshment' and 'boundaries,' simply clouds the issue of a case of child sexual assault, which is a crime – a crime that gets reduced to a 'family problem,' by mental-health professionals.

The following assessment on Joan MacDonald's daughter, Fran, who was severely traumatized by a male boarder in the household where she lived, was written by a well-respected male psychologist/consultant to child welfare in Toronto. But first, the details as given by the mother of the child and from the agency files. The molestation took place when Fran was five years old, over a six to eight month period. The boarder took her to the basement while others in the house were sleeping and sexually penetrated her. He also forced her to perform fellatio on him, during which time he called her 'a dirty pig,' and splashed black paint over her. The medical report stated: 'The hymen gone ... area wet and murky ... large vaginal opening.' Fran suffered night screaming, regression, encopresis, and was described by her worker as 'having a deep seated fear uncommon for her age.' Fran was still in therapy during the time I interviewed her mother (nearly two years later). These behaviours did not start until after the child had been sexually molested by the male boarder. Joan MacDonald left the child's father when Fran was only two years of age because he was incarcerated for a criminal offence. The child was raised alternately by her grandmother and her mother throughout periods of her life.

In the psychological assessment report, the psychologist attributed the child's suffering '*primarily* to loss of adults in her life' (emphasis added). The assessment virtually ignores the brutal attack on the body and integrity of the child. This raises questions about the use of these types of assessments in such situations. Although Fran sustained the loss of her father, according to this child's mother, this was insignificant, given that her father had lived with Fran for only the first two years of her life and was uninvolved in her care. Also, during that time, Fran witnessed her father beating her mother. It might even be suggested that her father's leaving was a gain in the child's potential development and future life chances.

Assessments are used to help guide the courts and child welfare agencies in making decisions for families. The way in which the problem is conceptualized by mental-health experts determines the goals set by other professionals working with families. Part of the practitioner's role is to help bring about change in families. It appears, from reading twenty-two files in this study, that traditional values held by professionals regarding a father's supremacy in the family are reinforced and protected, thereby minimizing the serious effects of the abuse on the children, while blaming mothers for failing to meet the needs of their children and/or partners. Agencies and courts appear to be very 'pro-assessment,' with views grounded on a narrow definition of families.

The assessments examined in this research tend to perpetuate notions of the sexual division of labour, preserve family autonomy, and attribute causes and responsibility for sexual abuse to mothers instead of focusing on the offender's behaviour.

Medical Reports

Rose Foote took her nine-year-old daughter, Helen, to the doctor for an examination after a fifteen-year-old boy at school had attempted to rape her. This particular child had been sexually abused twice; once by a male teen on the school grounds and later by her own father. During the interview when Rose Foote told me about the first case of sexual abuse, I asked her when her daughter, Helen, was examined by the doctor, what he found. She replied, 'He told me that she was lucky ... there wasn't an indication of penetration [the hymen was still intact].'

Unnecessary emphasis is often placed on an 'intact' hymen, even when the child's emotional well being is at risk. This is part of the traditional concern expressed about the morality of young girls who have experienced sexual interference before they are legally, socially, and religiously sanctioned to do so. Up until fairly recently in both Canada and the United States, such practices frequently resulted in this type of young victim being placed in delinquency centres and training schools. According to the early writing of social workers Breckinridge and Abbott (1912), it was felt that a young girl who had lost her virginity was not an appropriate companion for the child who was still a virgin, and that child was therefore removed from her normal surroundings and placed with similar child-victims. Also, according to Gordon's (1988b) findings in her child welfare record survey conducted on files in Boston dating from 1880 to 1960, between 1910 and 1930: 'Incest and sexual abuse were fit into a new category, sexual delinquency. In this new understanding the victims, almost always girls, were labeled as sexually deviant and criminal, even when they had been raped or mistreated at young ages, and were often incarcerated in industrial schools' (22).

Similar action was taken against child-victims in the Canadian child welfare system. Indeed, the repeal of Section 8 of the *Training School Act* in Ontario only occurred in 1977. This change made it more difficult to continue this type of discrimination against sexually victimized female children, since they could no longer be placed in correctional institutions (training schools) through an administrative decision only (Ontario Ministry 1983). Such practices were only officially changed in the 1970s. The changes have not been fully integrated (or accepted) by some practitioners who persist in referring to traditional values, such as the importance of the protection of female virginity.

Agency Forms

The notion of the ideal family is maintained and perpetuated in agency forms. For example, one form examined in agency files suggested the underlying assumptions of those who set up crisis support groups for child victims. A number of agencies used the same form. The form listed forty-eight items for children to check off concerning the areas in which they would like to focus their work within the group. Included on the list were: '21. To get over a lot of really angry feelings I have towards my mother for letting this happen; 26. To get ready to tell the abuser how I feel about what he did to me and ask for an apology.'

There is an assumption here that mother is 'letting this happen' to her child. No other comments in the rest of the items referred to the offender. The absence of any mention of the child's father on this list (unless he was the offender) also assumes he has no part to play in the child's life with respect to protecting her or him from sexual abuse. Both the problem and the treatment have been socially constructed to fit dominant values which blame mothers, ignore fathers, and trivialize the role of abusers.

These examples from my examination of agency records illustrate ways in which family ideology is reproduced through assessments, case notes, and in agency forms. Every case file examined reproduced family ideology, through the written assessments, judgments made by workers, agency forms, underlying assumptions of existing programs, future goals for family members, treatment plans; and other actions or behaviours. No file I examined was free of institutionalized sexism. Any differences in the files were in the degree of sexism expressed.

10

A Feminist Analysis of Institutionalized Abuse

In the examination of mainstream or dominant views, an attempt was made to select concrete examples of what individuals within particular institutions do and say in their interventions, and how their attitudes, comments, and behaviours impacted on the day-to-day lives of the twenty-four mothers.

Institutionalized abuse of mothers clearly manifested itself during the post-disclosure period. No mother in this study escaped such an experience. Mothers of victims were castigated severely by members of the helping professions (medical, social work, psychiatry, psychology, child welfare, and other counsellors), many of whom informed the mothers that they were part of the problem and were at least partially responsible for their child's victimization.

A number of examples of the blaming of the mothers, which is tantamount to abuse of the women involved, were discussed throughout various chapters. These included instances involving school personnel who both overtly and covertly told mothers that they could not believe that they had been totally unaware the sexual abuse was occurring. Also included were illustrations of probation officers, police officers, and court officials (judges, Crown attorneys, and lawyers) who trivialized the children's experiences and discounted the negative effects upon the mothers through short or inappropriate sentences given to the offenders, a lack of follow-up regarding dangerous offenders at large in the community, and by their reluctance to lay criminal charges.

It became clear that in the majority of cases, the women's situation at disclosure was further encumbered by the interventions of authorities responsible for the investigation and assessment of child sexual abuse cases. To some degree, this outcome was expectable. What was not expected, however, was the responses of the significant others in these women's lives. These women experienced an almost total lack of emotional support and understanding from husbands/partners, family members, neighbours, friends, employers, and caseworkers..

Knowing that 'patriarchy's chief institution is the family' (Millett 1983, 45) should have prepared me for the manner in which this gendered violation of children would be handled, but it did not, as I was quite unprepared for the stories I heard. Many of the women felt betrayed by the responses they received from within their own families. Their own mothers (the children's grandmothers) made some of the most vitriolic attacks upon their daughters for going public with 'the secret' in their families; for marrying those particular men; for causing rifts within their families; and for allowing their children to cause such crises.

Husbands and partners, when they were not the offenders, gave little emotional support (with the exception of three) and preferred not to discuss the problems created by the sexual abuse. The fathers of the women in this study (grandfathers of the victims) were mostly silent and appeared uninterested, except in one case, where the mother's brother was the offender and the grandfather ordered his daughter, the child's mother, out of the home for even suggesting such an allegation (which was later admitted by the youth).

Another Canadian study found similar results. Fourteen women were interviewed in Saskatchewan with a focus on power in families and in the therapy session. Their families were described as 'uncaring, exploitative, uncommunicative, and abusive' (Newton 1996, 117). Unfortunately, many of their therapists were described in similar terms, especially male therapists. As well, Hooper (1992) found that the hoped-for family loyalty that her fifteen mothers sought was not always forthcoming. Dempster (1992) found that her thirty-four mothers described their extended families as unhelpful.

It became clear, during the course of this study, that the male role in families, in relationships, and in society was viewed very differently from that of the female in those situations. As discussed earlier, men have had particular expectations placed upon them to provide the economic support in families, to be involved in the public realm rather than in the private realm, and to be in control of the other members of the family. Although women have increasingly taken on work outside the home, the literature shows that women continue to provide the major caretaking role and the performance of household chores at home. Although research from the 1970s and onward suggests a slight increase in the amount of time men are spending with their children and in performing household tasks (Lamb 1986; Marsiglio 1994), the majority of this work continues to be done by women. According to a General Social Survey of adult Canadians, women spent two-and-a-half hours per day on housework chores, compared with one hour per day for men (Marshall 1994, 197). It is encouraging, however, to see in the literature that fathers are spending more time with their children. There is support for the notion that fathers need to expand their repertoire of parenting practices, given the increase in dual-earner families (Starrels 1994).[1]

The supremacy of men and the subordination of women are critical factors on which such an organization of relationships is based. Theories about how these differences have been socially constructed have been developed by feminist scholars during the 'second wave' of feminism (Baker Miller 1977; Belenky et al. 1986; Caplan 1989; Chesler 1987; Chodorow 1978; Devault 1991; Dominelli 1986; Gilligan 1982; Johnson 1992; Krane 1990; MacKinnon 1987; Van Den Bergh 1995). These differences and the resulting inequality became visible in this study.

Non-Offending Fathers

There were seventeen non-offending fathers in this study, ten of whom were active or semi-active in their children's lives at the time of the disclosure. Five non-offending fathers were sharing the same household with their children and the mothers of those children at the time of disclosure, while the remaining five fathers had legal access, and were therefore in touch with their children on a regular basis. The manner in which non-offending fathers responded to the disclosure of the sexual abuse of their children (as presented by the mothers, and through agency records, since no fathers were interviewed for this study), is analysed here to illustrate the point concerning fathers' role in a family-crisis situation.

As discussed earlier, Betsy Hamilton's daughter Gillian and son Allan were abused by a friend of the family. Ms Hamilton was divorced and remarried, so the children lived with their step-father and had regular visits with their biological father. During the interview, I asked Ms Hamilton about the fathers' responses to the sexual abuse disclosure. The following comments relate to the children's biological father:

Well ... initially he blamed me ... I guess that I didn't inform [the children] enough ... that I didn't protect them enough ... I didn't ... do enough ... He still hasn't come to grips with that. In a way, it's harder for him to deal with [Allan's] abuse ... It really shook him ... All of a sudden he was saying things like ... [he]

always noticed that [Allan] was a little soft ... he didn't like sports and he likes reading, and I said, 'well ... he's just a sensitive kind of person ... I mean ... you don't have to play football to be a boy ...' It was really hard for both [fathers] to talk about it ... like [Allan] should have known better.

A few months later, Allan and Gillian's step-father, in the course of an argument, slapped Gillian on the face a number of times and bruised her arms while telling her she was just using the sexual abuse incident to get out of doing her homework for school. Not only did these adult men give no emotional support regarding the painful experiences of their children and those of the mother, but they increased their anxiety and, indeed, attributed blame to them for what happened.

Anita Marshall's daughter Janet was molested by a next-door neighbour when she was between the ages of five and seven. Janet lived with her mother, father, and younger brother. Ms Marshall was worried about her daughter being closed off emotionally, and not wanting to discuss the abuse at all. When asked during the interview about Janet's relationship with her father, and whether they talk about the abuse, she replied: 'He has the same attitude as she does ... He says it's past, just don't keep going on about it ... He does not like to talk about it and she thinks very highly of her father, so it might be she is doing what she thinks he wants.'

Ms Marshall's concern about her daughter was based on Janet having told her mother after disclosure that she often thought about dying. Her mother was unable to determine what that feeling was connected to and therefore tried to open up communication with Janet in order to learn more about why her child was thinking about death. Her father's attempts to silence Janet might be interpreted as either a lack of awareness of the impact of the abuse on his daughter, or perhaps an inability to deal with his own guilt and feelings of inadequacy in protecting his daughter. In any event, his behaviour and attitude were clearly not in the best interests of his daughter's mental and/or emotional health.

A few men did appear more able to relate positively to their children after the sexual abuse disclosures. For example, Pamela Hill's son, Paul, as discussed earlier, was molested by an adolescent male relative at age five. The worker from the child welfare agency was trying to explain to Paul why it was important for him to go to court and testify because he was the only witness. During the interview, Pamela Hill said: 'Last week we were within seconds of being "creamed" by this car that smashed into a post ... [My husband] had to go to court because he was a witness of the accident. [We thought] it would be great for [Paul] to go with him [to court].'

It was felt that Paul would be able to see his own father in court, which might allay his own fears about testifying in the criminal trial of the offender. It was a helpful gesture on the part of this father to lessen his son's anxiety about his own upcoming appearance in criminal court as a witness.

This man did not emotionally support his wife, however. Pamela Hill attempted to explain her situation during the interview: 'I was trying so hard to be just normal for my kids ... and felt I was being ripped apart inside ... and nobody cared ... I didn't want to "bug" my husband because I knew it was hard for him ... I talk about things a lot and he is more withdrawn ... His way is not very good because he does not work it through ... I was getting angry at him because I couldn't communicate about it ... I have to talk.'

Interestingly, although sixteen of the twenty-four non-offending mothers attended crisis support groups, none of the non-offending fathers attended crisis support groups. This finding is not peculiar to my study, but rather appears to be the 'norm' in situations of child sexual abuse cases in this area.

From this study, it seems clear that the non-offending father sees himself and is seen by others as slightly removed from the painful experiences of the child and the mother after disclosure. Fathers did not give any indication that they felt responsible for providing emotional support to other family members, whereas the women were identified by others and identified themselves as central to the children's recovery from the traumatic experience, and also central to keeping family relationships in place. Fathers in this study were not highly involved in the emotional life of their families.

As discussed in earlier chapters, part of the explanation lies in the different socialization patterns of boys and girls raised in conventional families, where males are taught to develop skills, to be active, and to dominate others, while girls are taught to develop their nurturing abilities, to be passive, and to relate to and accommodate other's wishes (Baker Miller 1977; Belenky et al. 1986; Chowdorow 1978; Taylor et al. 1995). These differing assigned roles have maintained male supremacy in a patriarchal society and reinforced female subordination.

Examination and Analysis of the Emotional Support of Males

The interviews in this study revealed that men provided little emotional support for the mothers or the children after disclosure. Of the seventeen mothers who were married or had live-in partners, only three men were named as the most supportive persons in their lives at that time. Male friends of the sole support mothers were also not considered by the women to have been emotionally supportive. Brothers, fathers, and biological fathers of victims were equally invisible when it came to emotional support for women or children. The majority of men refused to discuss the subject and avoided post-disclosure responsibilities involving the children. This inability and/or unwillingness of men to provide emotional support for women is documented in the research findings of other studies as well (Baker 1984; Rubin 1976).

The work of Jean Baker Miller (1977), Chodorow (1978), Dinnerstein (1977), and Gilligan (1982) help to explain this phenomenon. Females, not because of their biological or inherent abilities, but because of the way they have been socialized, have acquired superior relationship skills, while males have received much less focus on this part of their personality development, both in infancy and in childhood.

Ruddick (1982), in her discussion of maternal thinking, gives an illustration of what a value it is to be able to show concern for another human being. She uses an example from Simone Weil's work: 'In the first legend of the Grail, it is said that the Grail ... belongs to the first comer who asks the guardian of the vessel, a king three quarters paralyzed by the most painful wound, "What are you going through?" The love of our neighbor in all its fullness simply means being able to say to him: 'What are you going through?' ... Only he who is capable of attention can do this (1951, 115).'

Ruddick argues that to ask the question, 'What are you going through?' is central to maternal practice. She believes maternal thought exists for all women in a very different way than it does for men, mainly because 'we are daughters, nurtured and trained by women' (89). The author does not suggest, however, that no males have maternal thoughts or capabilities, or that all women possess such abilities.

The women I interviewed were asked to describe the best relationship they had ever had in their life. Three women chose not to name such a relationship. Of the remaining twenty-one, fourteen named women and seven named men (nine girlfriends, four sisters, and one grandmother; three husbands, one boyfriend, one grandfather, one brother, and one brother-in law). It is interesting to note that twelve women were married or had a male live-in partner at the time I interviewed them, but only three of the twelve women named their husbands as their 'best relationship.'

When asked what the qualities of those 'best relationships' were, the most frequently named qualities were someone: I can count on, 'Who is always there for me,' 'Who is emotionally supportive,' 'Who is trust-worthy,' 'With whom I can share anything,' and 'Who likes and respects me. In this study, although women marry and/or share their lives with men, other women are named two to one as their most important emotional relationship.

How Males Protect Each Other

In this study, there were a number of examples of males protecting each other from criminal charges of molestation and/or from the serious consequences of this crime. This point was also documented by Jeffreys (1985) concerning the 'first wave' of feminism, as mentioned earlier. There have been a number of high-profile Canadian cases of male victims of sexual abuse under inquiry, including the cover-up at Mount Cashel orphanage in St John's, Newfoundland. The results indicated that those in senior management (male-dominated) positions of the judiciary, the child welfare system, and the police protected those in powerful positions in the Roman Catholic Church rather than the victimized children ('Judge's job' *Toronto Star* 1990, A11; Spears 1990).

In previous chapters, I have discussed male judges, their decision-making, and their comments in the court system. It became very clear that some male offenders walked away from courts free of any criminal charges whatsoever even when there was solid evidence to convict them. When judges did sentence the men in question, they handed down light sentences in relation to the crimes committed. For example, although ten years is the maximum for assault, it is rarely given. It is unusual, in my experience and those of my key informants, for a convicted offender to receive more than a two-year sentence for the crime of child sexual abuse.

When a key informant who specializes in this particular work was interviewed for this study, he said, 'I think that people who molest children are far, far more dangerous than bank robbers ... and bank robbers get serious jail sentences ... more than child molesters do on the average.' Since our laws reflect society's strongest values, it appears that in the hierarchy of rights, property rights take precedence over personal rights; adults' rights take priority over children's rights; and male rights take precedence over the rights of females and children.

In more than one case, police officers and Crown attorneys were more concerned about the age of elderly male offenders than the safety of young children, and made decisions not to lay charges. One particular offender had the added advantage of being a wealthy businessman in the community. During my interview with Anita Marshall, she described how the offender violated his court order eight days after it was made. She called the authorities to have him charged with breach of probation, since he appeared in her neighbourhood and posed a continued threat to her daughter's safety. The response she received speaks for itself: 'I questioned that through the police and through the probation officer and they told me that I should mind my own business and *not to bother the man anymore, and had I not caused him enough grief* ... I said: "He has broken his probation, I want you to act on it now ... " He said: "No, we have contacted the Crown attorney and this is what he wants me to do.'" (emphasis added).

Later, Ms Marshall called the supervisor of the probation officer. He called her back and said; 'We are not in the Gestapo.' Ms Marshall said the whole thing had made her feel as if she herself were the perpetrator. Ms Marshall and her daughter were, in fact, further victimized by the police system that was supposed to protect them.

The actions of most of the men in this study tended to preserve and perpetuate male privilege in our society at the expense of women and children.

The Double Bind for Mothers

Feminist Sandra Butler's comments (1978) capture the sense of the intolerable double-bind situation that women find themselves in when their children disclose sexual abuse. When the perpetrators are their partners and/or the children's biological fathers, women's conflicted position is intensified.

A woman's loving concern for herself often is seen as an abandonment of her family. A woman is not free to acknowledge her interests and her hungers and to attempt to act upon them ... She also is not free to be enraged, in pain, confused, or ambivalent about any of her socially assigned tasks, for that is seen as denial of her central role as a woman. She must not neglect her family's needs ... For if she does, and her family disintegrates, the full weight of the responsibility rests on her betrayal of her role. (116)

As we have seen, the theory and practice of the helping professions typically individualizes sexual abuse and privatizes it by defining it as a family problem. Since women are held responsible for the care of their children, it is assumed that they could have prevented the abuse by supervising the child more carefully. The fact that the abuse may be perpetrated by a biological or social father who is also in a position of trust and responsibility for the child is virtually ignored by professionals and the state.

Women are, of course, not allowed to express anger, according to the ideology of the family, but must be nurturing at all times. When they are nurturing and understanding, they are sometimes condemned for not being more assertive and able to take charge of the home and protect the child. The negative feelings that women are not allowed to express do not disappear, but often resurface as guilt and self-blame and are turned inward (Levine and Estable 1983).

Alternative literature, written mostly by feminists, shows that the needs and rights of women are gaining acceptance in the wider social context. There is still a great deal of controversy concerning motherhood and the need for women to be 'perfect mothers,' however.

In mainstream practice, in cases where the father of the child is the abuser, the mother is often considered '"weak and ineffectual," aware of the incest but unwilling or unable to stop it. Women in this situation are negatively assessed in a variety of ways, and are considered passive or as having little self-esteem' (Levine & Estable 1983, 29). Again, Sandra Butler nicely sums up the situation:

Two words which consistently intrude upon all theory and analysis concerning mothers in families in which incestuous assault occurs are 'abandoning' and 'colluding.' These are the names of their crimes, the reasons they are held responsible for the actions of others. If a mother is 'passive' she fails by not having provided her child with the strength to resist incestuous overtures. If she is 'aggressive,' she fails by having caused her husband to feel emasculated and therefore in need of turning to someone else for his emotional and sexual needs. (1978, 113)

There appears to be little recognition of the physical and economic dependence of women on men in this society, which contributes to a lack of understanding about the torment women endure in trying to decide how to respond to their children's disclosures of sexual abuse. Do they remove their children from the only source they have of economic support? Can they survive as sole-support parents without becoming impoverished? Can they get access to the kind of emotional support needed to make changes in their lives? There is little compassion for the mother facing multiple dangers if she does take action, and yet there are consequences (Levine and Estable 1983).

Reports made to authorities indicate that female children are sexually abused in greater numbers than male children (Sedlak and Broadhurst 1996), and that adult males are the majority of offenders (Badgley et al. 1984; Finkelhor 1984; Russell 1984; Canadian Panel 1993). This picture is changing rapidly, however, as more First Nations adults who attended residential schools in Canada as children are speaking out. Also, there are increased reports from males, including those who were sexually abused as children while attending choir practice in the Anglican Church in Kingston, Ontario; in religious schools, such as that run by the Roman Catholic Church in Newfoundland; and by those attending training schools, such as St John's Training School in Ontario. Other secrets recently hitting the media involve Canada's national sport, hockey. Junior hockey players who were abused by their coaches are now coming forward and reporting to the police about the years of molestation they suffered. Criminal charges are being laid against their abusers.

It is recognized that a small number of women do sexually abuse their children and that, in fact, some mothers may well fail to protect their children from abuse, intentionally and/or unintentionally (Matthers 1993). The research findings to date indicate clearly, however, that women are usually not the offenders in cases of child sexual abuse (Badgley et al. 1984; Faller 1987; Finkelhor 1986; Herman 1992; Canadian Panel 1993).

The Politics of Child Sexual Abuse

The research described here has brought into view the pervasiveness of the phenomenon of child sexual abuse. In addition to the thirty-one child-victims of the study, seventeen of the twenty-four mothers in this study revealed that they, too, had been sexually victimized as children. Also, three of the seven female key informants revealed that they or their own children had been victims of child sexual abuse. In total then, this study has uncovered fifty-one child-victims

There remains considerable resistance from some professionals and the public to accept the prevalence of child sexual abuse. Moreover, individuals in authority positions who hold with a more conventional approach to the victimization of children have difficulty acknowledging that such abuse arises out of the social legitimation of unequal power relations within families (Dominelli 1989).

These comments made by male key informants recognized for their expertise in child welfare are representative of a conventional (mainstream) point of view: 'My feeling is that child sexual abuse will come to an end in another couple of years or so and we will be off and running on something else (Key Informant 'A-D'); 'We are basically on a job-creation program for health and social service professionals' (Key Informant 'C-B').

These remarks could be characterized as a 'protect the sanctity and autonomy of the family' approach which, in practice, protects the rights and privileges of male heads of families, and reinforces a system which blames mothers and children for the abuse. This is not to suggest a conspiracy or an evil plot of men against women, but to make the point that such actions arise out of the gendered social organization of relationships in society.

Jane Gilgun (1983) studied the effects of child sexual abuse on child development and the life courses of twenty female children ages ten to fifteen and completed a survey of 117 boys and girls in the same age range from New York. On the basis of her findings, she makes the following statement:

These two themes [age and sex stratification] resulted in downplaying the role of the male, who is characterized as less culpable and more of a victim than the females [in child sexual abuse cases]. Only an historical context which is heavily sex and age stratified in favor of the male could permit these images to flourish. Otherwise, the female children and their mothers would have risen up in rebellion long ago. (195)

Challenging the dominant view so well expressed by Gilgun has proved to be a difficult and painful task for those working for change in this area. For example, a number of public cases in Canada illustrate the seriousness of child sexual abuse, and demonstrate how the 'status quo' is maintained by the major institutions responsible for dealing with it.

Making visible and casting the problem in terms of the unequal relations of gender and age enables the sexual abuse of children to be conceptualized as a crime against society, which can and should be prosecuted in the courts, rather than dealt with as a family problem. Linda Gordon's (1988b) major research on child welfare records over an eighty-year period in Boston revealed that professionals who intervened in families during that time (1880 to 1960) were not helpful in resolving the problem of violence against women and children. This was not because the cries for help from women and children were ignored by those mandated to help them, but because professionals reinterpreted the problem in two ways: as seductiveness on the part of the victim, or as the result of victimization by strangers. In both instances, young girls were deemed

delinquent. These re-definitions directed attention away from a consideration of sexual abuse within families, and away from the physical abuse of
women by their partners.

Mothers' Explanations for Sexual Abuse

During the interviews, mothers were asked to give their views on the causal
factors of child sexual abuse. When the twenty-four women were asked why
they thought this happened to their children, four said they simply did not
know. The responses of the remaining twenty can be divided into four
separate categories of explanation: gender issues, individual 'sickness' model,
societal values, and reflective comments on their own choices for partners.

Eight mothers felt that males in our society had problems with their
need to express power and to dominate those less powerful than themselves (i.e, women and children). Catharine Burns' words illustrate the
feelings of these eight mothers:

I have a lot of trouble with this ... I have trouble with the whole universe where this
could happen to little girls ... How do males do that? ... I can't figure it out ... I
know that little children are just so delightful and sweet and yummy ... I love to kiss
their little cheeks and hug them although it is not sexual ... Sometimes I think that
mothers like to generate and men like to destroy ... but not all men do. I think that
there are too many bad men ... and it can't just be pathological behaviour ... So
many are doing it ... I have trouble trying to sort out why or how.

In attempts to explain the causes of child sexual abuse on the basis of
their own experiences, seven mothers mentioned specific or individual
reasons which included the following: this man was sick, violent, perverted, lacking in morals, pedophilic, immature, and/or stressed. Bridget
Hesse's view about her husband reflects statements made by the other six
mothers:

I know his background growing up ... My mother-in law is a very cold woman and
very dominant ... My husband had no social skills ... He also never lived his teenaged life, so I think in some ways they [the offenders] try to relive what they never
had ... They know what they are doing is not right but [still do it] for some reason
... what I don't understand ... I have a healthy fear of going to jail ... breaking the
law [but] ... it doesn't seem to cross their minds and, of course, they justify it ...
Plus the fact that ... I had been sick and almost died once ... He had a lot of
responsibility, and a lot of stress on him.

This individualized perspective does not take into account such dimensions as sexual division of labour or male power and supremacy. Ms Hesse also blames her husband's mother for his behaviour, which is perhaps the most telling example of how deeply internalized mother-blaming is, not only in men, but also in women.

Two mothers took a broader conceptual view of the problem and suggested that public attitudes and laws do not get the correct message across to potential offenders, and that long-term sanctions against such behaviours are not yet in place; also, the silencing of women on the topic in the past has contributed to increased victimization. The following from Shelly Brown illustrates these views:

I think that men are taught to be in control and that they can do anything they want ... and when they find out they can't do anything they want ... they don't have the skills to deal with other people on a one-to-one basis ... They can pack up in a group and do macho things ... and relate that way ... He blames me for his confusion ... He can't take the responsibility for it himself. I think men sexually abuse children because they can get away with it ... because they are not mature enough and responsible enough to monitor themselves.

Three mothers reflected on their own behaviours and choices concerning the sexual abuse of their children and what might have been different. For example, Olga Kadishun said, 'I was very naive as to this problem ... We need to be better educated.' Betsy Hamilton expressed a somewhat similar view. She felt she had taught her children to be open and trusting with other human beings, and then they were taken advantage of by someone whom they were taught to respect. She questioned her own values and the values of society in general and decided maybe she should not have taught her children to be so trusting of others. Gertrude Davis said that the only way things might have been different for her daughter would have been if she herself had chosen a better father for her children. She blamed herself for marrying such a man: 'I wish I had done things differently in my life ... but I know I always did the best I could ... I'll try to make this up the best I can.'

Despite the fact that this mother suggests that mothers should not blame themselves, her quote clearly gives the message of self-blame, as do the words of other women in this study.

An attributional analysis of the child sexual abuse based on the responses of the mothers in this study indicate that ten women focused mainly on internal factors attributing the cause of the sexual abuse to individual characteristics of the offender (immature, perverted, pedophilic, and so on) or to their own personal characteristics (their choice of a mate), while ten women focused on broader external factors of society (male power, laws, and so on). Four of the women said they simply had no explanations to offer.

There were as many women who saw the situation as controllable as there were who viewed it as uncontrollable. Similarly, some women defined the stability dimension as stable, because the offence was connected to the offender's personality traits, while others viewed them as unstable, since they felt that they (the mothers) might have put more effort into choosing a better mate. The locus of causality was described mainly as an internal factor as related to the ability of the offender to harm children. To speculate on the four women who did not attempt to find meaning or explanation for their child's sexual abuse, perhaps they believed it was external to them and happened by chance.

This is somewhat encouraging of their understanding of the dynamics of sexual abuse, since half the women who responded viewed the patriarchal system responsible for condoning and allowing the sexual abuse of children to occur; however, the results of the other half do reflect the continued mainstream views, since ten women ascribed cause on an individual basis.

The women in this study did not sexually abuse their children, and yet they were held responsible by professionals, the public, and in some cases members of their own families, for allowing the abuse to occur. I call this institutionalized abuse of mothers.

11

Implications for Professionals, Social Action, and Change

When I first interviewed the twenty-four women for this research, I suggested to them that the telling of their stories could possibly help other women whose children had been abused to receive better services. Since I was committed to change in the child welfare delivery system, I planned to include a social action and change section in my final draft and distribute copies of the highlights of my results to relevant institutions in the province. I did follow through with that promise, but encountered a total lack of interest from relevant senior bureaucrats and ministry officials.

As agreed, I mailed each woman a two-page summary of my results in 1990. Following that mailing, I continued to have contact with nine of the twenty-four women by telephone and correspondence, and met with one woman for lunch.

After I moved away from the Toronto area where my research was conducted, I was interested in knowing how the women's lives had changed. I mailed a one-page letter to twelve of the twenty-four women, complete with a stamped self-addressed envelope, in July 1993, asking if there were any updates to their experiences they wished me to include in this book. Only four responded. Five of the envelopes were 'returned to sender' due to the lack of forwarding addresses, and I heard nothing from the remaining three.

The comments from the four mothers who responded are discussed throughout this chapter and will illustrate to the reader just how deep and lasting were the effects of the sexual abuse and disclosure events on the lives of the children and their mothers.

In this final chapter, I summarize the main findings of the research with various implications for policy, practice, research, and education. I will revisit the literature and research as required, and provide updates from the four mothers about their current circumstances. Finally, I will discuss ideas for change.

An area of women's oppression that often seems to be ignored by society has been opened up by the women themselves during the interviews for this study. Women were given the space to say what happened to them after their children disclosed, and the freedom to define their experiences in their own words. The major theme of the study is mother-blaming; indeed, blaming becomes the unifying theme that links all the chapters in this book.

Implications for Policy, Practice, Research, and Training, and Suggestions for Action and Change

Since families and family life are under major scrutiny in this study, I will begin with the implications for mothers and children living in the types of families where they are frequently subordinated and at risk for violence.

Family Issues

In examining the prevailing ideologies and everyday realities in this study, it becomes clearer how institutions charged with assisting families are affected. One critical factor is the normative definition of 'the' family, which has persisted over time, and which has negative consequences for women and children. A key informant identifying with alternative ideology said, 'The concept of "the" family we know now has to be shattered.' A similar suggestion is made by Linda Gordon (1988b), who states that we must rid ourselves of the notion of a 'proper family.' The 'nuclear' family is just one of many types of families in existence today. It is important for policy-makers and other experts to recognize that both children and adults can be loved, nurtured, and supported in a variety of living arrangements, and that an increasing number of these do not conform to the idealized notion of 'the' family. More important, these decision-makers must rethink the notion that preserving 'the' family in cases of child sexual abuse is always desirable.

Laws

Given the current norms in society for the appropriate care of children, it is clear that terms such as 'parent' or 'the person having charge of the child' assume that these responsibilities will be borne by mothers in the present residual model of child welfare. The legislation reinforces this presumption. The women who took part in this study felt blamed by the wording of child welfare legislation, which implies that mothers know or *should know* of their child's victimization: that they have either colluded in the crime by allowing the sexual abuse to continue, or have been negligent in not discovering it. As one mother put it after her experience with the institutions mandated to help: 'It was like a stint in hell ... Now I feel like I should be able to charge somebody with mental cruelty ... Somebody should pay for what they do to mothers.'

Consideration should be given to re-examining any sections of provincial child welfare acts worded in such a way that they appear to blame mothers for the sexual abuse of their children. For example, in the Ontario Child and Family Services Act (1984): '(c) The child has been sexually molested or sexually exploited, by the person having charge of the child or by another person where the person having charge of the child *knows or should know* of the possibility of sexual molestation or sexual exploitation and fails to protect the child' (emphasis added).

Governments create situations that can only result in feelings of fear and mistrust from the very women they wish to assist in caring for their children. It would therefore make a great deal of sense if mothers were not placed in such a negative position with those mandated to implement child welfare legislation.

The Courts

This research indicates how court-ordered assessments tend to minimize the actions of perpetrators and focus instead on the actions of mothers, which are held up to intense and biased scrutiny by 'experts.' The harm done to children by the perpetrators of the sexual abuse is frequently trivialized in this process. The silencing of women and children, and the amplifying, instead, of experts tends to reinforce the views of an already 'gender-biased court system' (Wilson 1990).

This situation could be corrected by the state, by insisting that assessment reports be more sensitive. This would require that professionals providing assessments to the courts listen to and be informed by the experiences of women and children. This would probably require training.

Mothers in this study felt 'put down' and blamed by most mental-health professionals engaged by the courts to complete assessments. A major revamping of the curricula at the university level that challenges mainstream theories for social workers, psychologists and psychiatrists is over-due. Existing theories of family relationships do not address the diverse social, economic, and political problems that women and children face.

Future trends indicate that mediation services will become more and more the norm in child welfare and family courts in the 1990s. It is therefore critical that the professionals providing such services are made aware that sexist attitudes should not inform their practice with women and children.

Custody and Access

Mothers in this study described how their children were court-ordered to visit their fathers and were subsequently sexually abused by them. These women stated that although they had expressed fears for the safety of their children, their concerns were ignored by the courts. In order to protect their children, some women gave up financial support in exchange for no further access to the children by their fathers.

The Vancouver Custody and Access Support and Advocacy Association has published a book, *Women and Children Last* (1996), in which woman after woman tells of her experiences with mediators and the court system. These experiences, most of which were devastating, support those of the women interviewed for this study.

In one particular family in my study, a father used every known manipulation to get access to his daughter (even bringing video equipment to the school). Laws that favour males but encourage the harassment of women and children need to be rescinded by governments in order to preserve the safety and protection of women and children.

Court Orders in Child Welfare Court

Non-offending mothers in this study were court-ordered into treatment groups as part of a supervision order with child welfare agencies. The assumptions underlying such court-orders are that mothers allowed the abuse to occur. Women who were able to engage their own legal counsel did not have to accept such directives from the courts. Such a double standard of legal rights should not be allowed to continue.

Perpetrators in the Community

Offenders who were released back into the community with minimal supervision created 'nightmare situations' for a number of the women and their children in this study. Since the courts have no further interest in those set free owing to lack of evidence to convict, this is undoubtedly one of the most difficult problems to correct. Unsuspecting children can come into contact with these individuals in any location. Women have no way of knowing whether a man (such as her next-door neighbour) has been involved with the law on this account. Men who are criminally charged and given light sentences create a similar problem for the safety of children in the community.

The search for alternative methods for dealing with these situations should be given a high priority. A recent situation in North Vancouver in which a pedophile was released back into the community (*Yeager* 1995) was responsible for mobilizing parents to insist he move out of their area. After protesting and confronting the offender, that community was successful in their attempts to protect their children from a known pedophile. I realize it is not the best solution to have these sex offenders hounded from the city when they are released from prison. Naturally, I don't accept this 'NIMBY' approach, however, I think it appalling and outrageous to wait until he commits another serious crime before he is safely behind bars. I would have to say if I err it would be on the side of the child. In truth, we have as yet no answer to this problem.

One of the four mothers who provided an update of her circumstances focused on the danger of the perpetrator remaining in her community. Before the disclosure, Rachel Cohen worked full time as an office manager to support her son and daughter. Although her ex-husband lived nearby and paid some child support, he had demonstrated little interest in or involvement with his children.

Rachel Cohen's son was sexually abused by a family friend over a period of three or four years. It took the form of sexual fondling and attempted anal intercourse. The disclosure took place when the boy was ten. The offender was a married professional, with children, and lived in the same neighbourhood. Because he had been a trusted friend, he had had access to the child on a regular basis.

Rachel Cohen's son was seriously traumatized by the abuse and attended therapy sessions and a group for a couple of years following the disclosure. The offender was given ninety days in jail for his offence, forty-five of which were to be served on weekends. Ms Cohen felt upset that the offender was not given a sentence that reflected the seriousness of the crime he had committed. Although the offender was ordered by the court to not approach children under age sixteen, he continued to live in their midst, and therefore posed a continued risk. In Ms Cohen's estimation, her children were put at risk by the court's decision, as they had to pass the offender on the street and in local stores daily.

The Criminal Injuries Board awarded her son a reasonably large amount of money (his mother did not reveal the amount) to be kept in trust until he turned eighteen.

Ms Cohen was forced to seek psychiatric help for herself after the disclosure, as she was depressed and suffered from severe panic attacks. She decided to take a month's sick leave from work, but that month turned into two years of disability leave, with weekly and biweekly therapy sessions. Ms Cohen says she now manages her panic attacks about 90 per cent of the time and is no longer on medication. She wrote: 'For the first time in my life I am starting to take care of me.'

With respect to her two children, she is less confident about their futures. Her son, who was victimized, is skipping school, fighting on the school grounds, and generally presenting aggressive behaviour at home, while her daughter has ended her studies at school against her mother's wishes.

Ms Cohen does not know if the changes in her son's behaviour have anything to do with the effects of the sexual abuse, but his relationship with her has changed significantly. Rachel Cohen has upgraded her education and is now job hunting with the hope of regaining some of the stability and more positive aspects of family life she lost during and after the disclosure.

It seems clear from the experiences described by the majority of mothers in this study that judges need a different form of training, one which would expose them to the complex issues in child sexual abuse situations, in order to help them develop a fuller understanding on which to base their decisions. Women's groups lobbying against inappropriate sentencing for offenders and inappropriate comments made in court about women and children by judges have exposed these incidents publicly and demanded change.

Civil Proceedings against Offenders

Six of the mothers in this study were involved in civil court proceedings regarding custody and access issues, however, no mother indicated that she pursued a civil suit in court for monetary damages from the offender. Maybe the reason why they did not pursue civil damages on behalf of their children was directly related to the lack of financial resources of the offenders. It is now becoming more common, however, to have such cases before the courts, if the offender can pay.

The standard of proof is lower in civil proceedings than in criminal cases, requiring only 'proof on the balance of probabilities' rather than 'proof beyond a reasonable doubt,' as in criminal cases. It is not necessary to have had a successful criminal case outcome in order for compensation to be granted or even to have had criminal charges laid (Bala 1991; Bernstein 1990).

Various provincial governments such as Ontario, Nova Scotia, New-foundland, and New Brunswick have attempted to avoid litigation by setting up various mediated settlements for those who had been sexually abused as children while in foster care, group homes, or institutions (Ouston 1998a, 1998b). Other provinces such as British Columbia, have at least sixty civil suits at various stages in the courts, but is attempting to work on a mediation settlement to cover all potential costs of the 200,000 children and youths who might have been abused in the provincial system of foster homes, correctional facilities and residential facilities between 1940 and 1992 (Ouston 1998a). The federal government has awarded a $100-million package to Aboriginal peoples for various forms of abuse including sexual abuse suffered in the various schools systems (Tibbetts 1998). The Roman Catholic Church has paid more than US$400 million in damages for priests sexually abusing children ('Misconduct' 1993).

Individual awards have included a case in Ontario where a woman was awarded $50,000 in 1989 against a man who had sexually abused her during seven years of her childhood (Bernstein 1990); $1 million awarded by the BC Supreme Court to two step-children for physical and sexual abuse suffered between 1966 and 1974 by their step-father, John Battye, who was the former director of education for the Juan de Fuca Hospitals ('Public Access' 1998); and, in a Maple Ridge, BC case, a man was ordered to pay his step-daughter $200,000 for sexual abuse inflicted on her between 1978 and 1982. No previous criminal penalty was ever imposed (Hall 1998).

Knowledge that offenders of sexual abuse may be ordered to pay large sums of money in civil court cases may prove to change some of the sex practices of those seeking sexual gratification from children, but were previously not concerned about losing their savings, business, house, or future employment earnings to pay the lawsuit.

Child Welfare

The child welfare agencies were the pivotal point in the context of the experiences of mothers in this study. Social workers, who are the majority of child welfare workers, are trained to keep families together. How can there be change, given the type of training workers are receiving; the residual mandate of child welfare legislation; the limited resources made available to do this work; the outdated perspective on 'the' family that continues to inform service delivery in the 1990s; and last but not least, a majority of male decision-makers dominating the senior administrative positions of every child welfare system in Canada? It is not surprising that few workers are able to challenge the current unwieldy system in order to effect change for women and children.

The threat of having the state remove the child from her or his mother's care was the most frightening possibility for the women in this study, and demonstrates the need for Societies to treat clients respectfully in these situations and with an awareness of the impact that their presence and power have on women.

Although women and children are the major clients of child protection, and women are the main caseworkers in direct service with families, there appears to be a lack of mutual understanding and respect, as evidenced in the records and in the interviews with the twenty-four women in this study. It is suggested here that child welfare definitions of families need to be updated, and that anti-sexist programs should be instituted within all child welfare systems, as with the anti-racist programs now being made available to workers and senior management in some of the agencies.

Women want the assistance of child welfare workers; sixteen of the twenty-four interviewed called the agencies themselves for help. Women are also requesting more respect, sensitivity and validation, from workers regarding their own experiences, however.

Consciousness-Raising Groups

As discussed in previous chapters, mothers and child-victims are routinely referred to crisis support groups. Some of these operate as consciousness-raising groups, and some do not. Approximately one-half of the mothers referred to groups in one program did attend on a regular basis. Although many of the women made positive remarks about the groups, others were less well served, and it is clear from the relevant literature that one of the major goals in the groups is to help mothers better protect their children from sexual abuse. While protecting children is critical, this focus can be better achieved by dealing with women's anger and rage. All twenty-four women interviewed described an all-consuming rage, which they said made them want to kill the perpetrator in question. The women could not relate to or understand these strong feelings and were frightened by them. Dealing with this rage should be a prerequisite in helping them deal effectively with their own children's problems.

Consciousness-raising groups, which served women well in the 1970s could be reclaimed by more agencies as the major type of healing and support program and awareness model for women. Recent research completed by Russell et al. (1996) revealed how an approach utilizing a feminist philosophy transformed the lives of women who participated in adult women's support groups in the Vancouver area, by bringing about the social awareness needed for them to change their own life situations.

By applying Kelly's (1988a) continuum of violence theory, blaming mothers can be viewed as yet another form of committing violence against women. The potential for women to resist blaming themselves (when their children are sexually abused) lies in the raising of consciousness and awareness. This change could happen in the crisis support group process.

As noted, however, the major focus of most of these support groups has been 'how mothers can better protect their children.' Some groups have, therefore, delivered a contradictory message to women: 'It's not your fault *but* here is how to *better* protect your child.' This is not to suggest that the groups were not helpful, but to point out that the groups in this study could have helped to empower women more if there had been a special focus on consciousness-raising. None of the twenty-four mothers interviewed understood or recognized that the blaming was an integral part of a socially constructed phenomenon.

One of the four mothers who responded to my last request for an update of her life derived a great deal from the groups she attended. The following provides a brief glance at her current family situation.

Pamela Hill, a mother of two sons, in her mid-thirties, did not work outside the home at the time of the interview. Much of the family life revolved around both extended families, where there appeared to be a great deal of warmth and caring. Her youngest son was six years old when his teenaged cousin attempted anal intercourse with him. After the child disclosed to his mother, the Society and the police became involved, and a criminal investigation began. The teen offender pleaded not guilty in court and was found not guilty. Ms Hill was disappointed with the outcome. She felt her nephew needed to be mandated into counselling sessions, which did not happen.

Pamela Hill's letter reflects her thoughtful, caring, and optimistic personality. In 1993, she wrote:

A fair bit has happened since I last talked with you. The most positive thing is that both my son and I, as well as our family, have been able to put the abuse behind us and get on with our lives. This is not to say that we have forgotten it, but only that it no longer rules our every waking moment. My son is now almost 12 years old and is in grade seven. He is an excellent student and has many friends.

We still attend family reunions and functions but if there is any chance that the offender and his family will be there we do not take our boys.

While things are pretty calm in our family right now, I am sure that will not last forever ... I am confident that we can get through anything now. Maybe the abuse has made us stronger as a family but it sure was a huge price to pay. It still surprises me to discover that so many lives can be affected and for such a long time because of the act of one person.

This mother was involved in a group for non-offending mothers, which she attended regularly, and which she found provided an excellent source of support for her. She later became a volunteer leader for the groups to support other mothers whose children had been sexually abused.

Barry Levy (1995) in his article 'Violence Against Women' quotes Kamen (1991), who suggests that CR groups should be revived and expanded for both men and women with an appreciation of the cultural diversity of their experiences. I concur with his suggestion.

Police Departments

In addition to the need to recruit more women on police forces to handle sexual abuse cases, this study brought to light the lack of training available for police officers working in the area of child sexual abuse. Police officers appeared to be more sympathetic to the males who committed the offences than to the women and children, and also appeared to be reluctant to lay charges in some cases. The women who reported their children's sexual abuses expected the police to prosecute, and were confused when charges were not laid immediately. The women felt they received less attention and concern (with respect to their complaints) from the police than the perpetrators received. One of the four mothers who responded when asked for an update of her current circumstances emphasized the importance of the police response to protect children.

Dorothy White is a woman in her fifties raising her granddaughter, whom she legally adopted at age four. She called the police after her daughter, then twenlve, disclosed sexual abuse by her step-father, Ms White's husband. The police were reluctant to lay criminal charges because of his advanced age (seventy-three), but Ms White obtained support from an advocate group and changes were eventually laid. The perpetrator was incarcerated for six months.

Since the abuse had started when Ms White's step-daughter was approximately four, the abuse was well entrenched in her repertoire of behaviours by age twelve. Using the Finkelhor and Browne (1985) framework, this child was sexually traumatized by the experience. Her sexuality was shaped in a developmentally inappropriate manner (i.e., not in the service of the child but for the gratification of her step-father). Consequently, she was having difficulty in most areas of her life and especially in school.

After the disclosure, Ms White's adopted daughter was involved in both one-to-one therapy sessions and in groups, but she continued to experience difficulty in focusing her concentration on her school work. She could not get along with peers, was generally fearful and unhappy, and had expressed suicidal thoughts to her adopted mother.

Later, Ms White's adopted daughter was sexually assaulted by five boys in the school stairwell. One young offender was criminally charged with sexual assault, one was charged with common assault, and two others had their charges dropped. One was never apprehended. Her daughter was out of school for more than a month because of the assault. Ms White was fearful of further violence following her daughter's testimony in court against the boys.

In response to the looming threats to her daughter's life, Ms White made some very common sense decisions. She enrolled her daugher in karate lessons, body building, and gymnastics, which greatly improved her daughter's self-esteem.

I was very touched by a letter from Dorothy White's step-daughter, who is now seventeen and in her last year of school. She described herself as having difficulty making friends. She wrote that she would like to be a police officer when she finishes school so she can protect children from child abuse, and help put their offenders behind bars.

Ms White now works part-time and does some volunteer work with seniors. She says she is reluctant to take a chance on having any more men in her life, since the two men she married were both violent to her and to her children.

The women were frustrated that the police were of little help in making public areas safer for children, especially the school and the schoolground area. Increased priority and emphasis by police forces in protecting children from revictimization is critical.

Social Class

Based on my own experience in this work, and on prevailing theories, I would argue that economically advantaged women would have had different experiences with the social and justice systems than the mothers I interviewed. It appears that in more economically advantaged families, the sexual abuse of children does not get reported to mandated agencies for investigation. It is, however, known that sexual abuse takes place in all classes. In fact, Russell's study (1986) indicates that girls reared in high-income families were more frequently victimized than girls reared in low-income families (102). The so-called 'privacy' of such families is protected because they can afford to engage their own lawyers, psychiatrists, psychologists, and other experts. This hypothesis needs to be tested in Canadian research.

The Workplace

The fact that women lose their jobs and/or feel they must resign because of the need to attend to their traumatized children after disclosure, or because of the need to heal themselves emotionally, raises the question of the need to have child sexual abuse identified as an issue for consideration in the workplace. The women in this study told of such experiences. One woman was asked for her resignation, and three other women felt they had to quit their jobs because of the stress created by their children's victimization.

There is a precedent for this issue to be considered, since a wide range of issues for quality of working life are currently being addressed by employers; the development of fitness programs and employee assistance programs are other examples. If child sexual abuse were identified as an issue by human resources departments, perhaps programs could be developed based on the employee assistance model for dealing with substance abuse. Attention by unions to this question as they develop their benefit requirements might be considered, given the prevalence of child sexual abuse.

Women should be entitled to paid time off when they are required to attend to their traumatized children, or when their own emotional state (as a result of these events) leaves them temporarily unable to function in the workplace. Health and social leave benefits could be written into union contracts, human rights acts, and employment contracts.

Hospitals and the Medical Profession

Not all of the physicians who examined the children in this study reported their suspicions of sexual abuse to the appropriate agencies, even though the law in this particular province states: 'Despite the provisions of any other Act, a person referred to in subsection (4) who, in the course of his or her professional or official duties, has reasonable grounds to suspect that a child is or may be suffering or may have suffered abuse shall forthwith report the suspicion and the information on which it is based to a society.'

The *Child Welfare Act* in Ontario, then, requires that those who perform professional or official duties with respect to children have a special duty to report.

Failure to report in some provinces in Canada can result in charges being laid and, upon conviction, doctors can be fined. There should be increased pressure placed upon medical doctors (as well as other professionals) in Ontario to report sexual abuse, through an increased focus on awareness and education programs on the legal duty to report. If this fails to change the reporting patterns of child sexual abuse, then the implementation of sanctions as in other provinces may be necessary. Based on my own experience in this work, I know that the credibility of child welfare system needs to be addressed before some professionals will agree to make referrals.

Less than half of the thirty-one child-victims in this study were medically examined after disclosure. There were delays in getting appointments for those who were seen, and overly long waiting periods for anxious mothers with small children. One child was not examined until six months after she had been molested. As well, there were insufficient female doctors trained in this area and available to perform the necessary examinations, because female and small children appear to be more comfortable being examined by them.

Hospitals could place a priority on the immediate medical examination of child-victims. Special training is critical, and this should be considered when hospitals are hiring specialists for this area.

Some doctors in this study were highly insensitive and focused almost exclusively on whether or not there was vaginal penetration, and advised mothers how lucky they were when penetration had not occurred, despite severe trauma to the child. Medical-school curricula in pediatrics should reflect the new knowledge of sexual abuse and how it can be diagnosed. As well, knowledge of the psycho-social components of such a diagnosis are critical, as a social history is still the most important part of the medical examination.

Housing

Women who chose to leave their partners after the disclosure found it difficult to obtain affordable housing and had to live in substandard quarters in order to protect their children from revictimization. Women whose children have been sexually abused should be placed on a priority listing for safe, affordable housing, in order to protect their children from further sexual abuse. This type of housing policy would allow women to more easily make choices about who they will live with and where they will live. Alternatively, the perpetrator should be required to leave the home, and hostel accommodations provided pending final disposition of the case. The child-victims should not be removed from their homes, as this gives them the message that they have done something wrong. More provincial legislation is reflecting such a position (such as the *Child, Family and Community Service Act* of British Columbia 1994).

Schools

The children in this study suffered considerable trauma from the sexual abuse, and the majority of them did not do well in school because of fear, isolation, low self-esteem and anger caused by the abuse. School boards could be encouraged to continue and/or develop education programs that create a safe environment in which children can disclose. Three children in this study disclosed after participating in sexual-abuse prevention programs conducted in their schools. Such programs appear to be effective. In addition to continuing with these types of prevention programs on reporting, boards of education could also provide training for teachers and school personnel that would increase their ability to understand and support children and mothers in such situations.

Child-Care Policy

A lack of choice in arranging child-care sometimes forces women to leave their children with people or in situations that they otherwise would not choose; this was evident in this survey. Thus, accessible, affordable, quality child-care options must finally become a reality in Canadian society. A progressive national child-care policy would not only foster equality for women, but provide early education, child-development services, and increased protection for all children, provided those hired were police screened before being employed in child-care systems.

The Invisibility of Men as Parents and Partners

An important finding in this study was the invisibility of non-offending fathers in the lives of children and women. Men did not (nor were they expected to) attend crisis or support groups if they were non-offending fathers. Only three mothers named their husbands or partners as emotionally supporting them after the disclosure of the sexual abuse. The majority of men did not want to discuss the sexual abuse or any of the circumstances surrounding it.

Greater expectations must be placed on men by both families and professionals to provide care and nurturing for children. Men were excused from most of the tasks following the disclosure of sexual abuse, such as treatment, court, and child-welfare sessions, on the grounds that this involvement would interfere with their work. This is a gender issue that is too complex and too deeply engrained in the conscious and unconscious minds of both men and women to be resolved without major changes in the educational and socialization patterns of boys and girls in our society. Special attention is needed to focus on gender attitudes in elementary schools and the modeling of equity in the classroom is critical to bring about long-term change.

Age

Both the age of the child-victims and that of the offenders influenced the handling of the alleged sexual abuse by police and Crown attorneys. Some children in this study were considered to be too young for police officials to proceed with criminal charges against the offender and, in some cases, the offenders were too old, in the estimation of those enforcing the law, to lay criminal charges against them. Police officers involved in this work were much more lenient with youth than with adult offenders, and this is understandable in terms of how criminal charges would affect the life chances for such youths; however, research shows that these youths benefit from mandated counselling programs.

This study focused on mothers of children in the four to twelve age range. The experiences of mothers of children under the age of four and over the age of twelve would constitute further and different areas of research that might well reveal different effects upon mothers durng the post-disclosure period.

Resources and Programs

Programs should be defined, designed, and implemented by persons sensitive to the needs and rights of both women and children. Provincial governments might benefit by committing financial resources to a wider range of programs and services than exist at present. For example, during the time of this research, women who were adult survivors were unable to access appropriate free and affordable counselling to accommodate their own healing process. Over 95 per cent of the (female) adult incest survivors in a study in Ontario had to wait anywhere from three months to a year for services that would allow them to function better in mothering their own children (Guberman 1989). More recently, a study conducted in British Columbia with seventy professional counsellors of adult survivors of sexual abuse reported that waiting lists of three months to a year or more for such services are not uncommon (SPAN 1997).

The Compensation Board for Injuries

All mothers of sexually abused children could be encouraged to seek financial compensation for their children's injuries. Only one woman in this study had this type of support. More and better education about the rights of citizens to this fund should be made available to the general public through promotion programs in the media.

The Child Abuse Register

The Register, or a similar central method of recordkeeping, could have the potential to protect children from sexual abuse if it were used as a screening mechanism for those who apply for positions to work with children, as suggested in the Bala Report of 1987. As it operated during this research, the Register appeared to be less than effective to anyone concerned with the safety of children. The majority of agencies examined in this study no longer held reporting to the Register as an important priority.

Because of 'turf' wars between agencies, one mother in this study was delayed in getting treatment services to her small daughter because the name of the offender had not been placed on the Register. The treatment centre indicated it did not accept referrals for treatment unless the offenders names were placed on the Register. Child-victims should not be penalized because of inter-agency differences about reporting to the Child Abuse Register.

Lack of sound decision-making with respect to issues concerning the Register and its operation has harmed children. Provincial governments must take responsibility for their inaction when policy originally developed to protect children has produced unintended negative consequences.

Training – Universities/Colleges/Schools

Training in the health and social sciences, education, law, and police departments should stress equality of the sexes, and examine violence against women and children from a more egalitarian and political perspective, as validated by the Charter of Rights of the Canadian Constitution, rather than promoting ideology that supports men's unquestioned rights to women and children and theories that are family-systems focused.

The last of the four mothers who provided an update of her current life and circumstances in relation to the impact of the sexual abuse illustrates two important examples of how curriculum and training affected her experiences.

Catherine Burns is a mother of two children whose husband had anally penetrated their four-year-old daughter with objects for several months. Ms Burns was working outside the home part-time during the disclosure period. She took her daughter to the emergency department at the hospital after noticing anal bleeding and the sexual abuse was validated. The first call she made to a Children's Aid Society intake worker was not successful, since she was told to think it over carefully before she reported such a serious allegation.

She called one of the other Societies, an intake worker and police officer investigated the incident, and criminal charges were proceeded with. The child-victim was unable to testify, however, and began to cry when she saw her father in court. Criminal charges were therefore dismissed. Ms Burns was very disappointed in the judge's decision to dismiss charges without hearing other evidence that could have been used. She pointed out the need for judges to have a different training and exposure to the complex issues in child abuse situations in order to allow them to develop a full understanding on which to base their decisions.

Catherine Burns had returned to her studies in graduate school when she wrote her update letter. She expressed feelings of anger toward an older, male social-work professor in a course she was taking, whose comments in class on incest were quoted in her letter: 'What are those mothers doing while their children are being sexually abused?' She did not like what she termed his 'mother-blaming' attitude, but said she was unable to confront him in class because of his power over her in marking assignments.

Her daughter was in therapy for quite a long time, but is now doing very well in school and with friends. Her son, who had not been sexually abused, but had been badly affected by his sister's abuse, is also doing much better now.

The Burns family has relocated. Catherine Burns was awarded full custody of the two children with no access visits. The last she had heard about her former husband, the offender, was that he had a new partner who was expecting their baby. There were no mandated therapy sessions or negative sanctions from the court system toward this offender. The chances of his harming another small child are high, if we consider the guideline used in high-risk assessment models (British Columbia, 1996).

She says her life has taken on a very different focus, as she is working on a doctoral program and teaching part-time, and is the sole supporter of her family. Ms Burns sounded very optimistic about the future for herself and her children, and said that she would arrange future counselling for her daughter if and when she needs it as she enters puberty.

It seems clear that many of the women have completed their healing and are on their way to a reasonable recovery. Not all of the children are in such good shape, but this outcome is hardly surprising. The children would naturally take longer to heal than the mothers, since they are on different sides of the sexual abuse experience (Johnson 1992).

Two-thirds of the mothers in my research were themselves victims of child sexual abuse, and many had not dealt with their own healing process until their children disclosed. Many were involved along with their children in therapy and group sessions.

When the trauma of childhood sexual abuse remains unresolved, it can, and frequently does, produce long-term negative effects for the adult survivors (Alexander 1993; Bass and Davis 1988; Briere and Runtz 1993; Courtois 1988; Finkelhor et al. 1986; Herman 1992; Rodriguez et al. 1996; Russell 1986).

The secondary traumatization of mothers is developing a growing body of practice knowledge that identifies the vulnerably of mothers following child sexual abuse disclosure (Figley 1983; Green et al. 1995). Symptoms of secondary trauma are equal to those of post-traumatic stress disorder Bettcher (1996); Carter (1993); Dempster (1992); Hooper (1992).

Our social services, unfortunately, do not provide sufficient and adequate counselling services for women and children experiencing this trauma in their lives. The work of feminist counsellors has provided the backbone of this service, as sexual abuse counselling for children or adults has not been totally incorporated into mainstream services. The service delivery system has been slow to respond and many agencies are forced to depend on grants and unstable funding to provide group counselling for survivors. This problem is further exacerbated by the manner in which the Canadian health system operates. Many private-practice counsellors are not covered by existing medical fees, and therefore many women must pay for their own counselling services. This clearly discriminates against poor women who need this service. In agencies where the service is provided, the waiting lists are long, forcing women to delay their own healing process.

Current mainstream literature is biased towards mother blaming with respect to interpretations of the survivor's ability to mother her children. Such mothers are often seen as negligent and inadequate. The results of my study do not support such findings. Nor does the research of Callahan et al. (1994); Caplan (1989); Dempster (1992); Gilgun (1984); Holten (1990); Hooper (1989); Johnson (1992); Loewen (1995); or Swift (1995). All twenty-four mothers in this study were managing their mothering tasks with unbelievable courage and care, but not necessarily without difficulties and struggles. I was greatly impressed by the women's strength, endurance, and ability to survive such horrific circumstances.

Language

Being able to name what has been done to you is an empowering act. Encouraging women and children to speak out about violence committed against them helps them to take control of their lives. Expressions that obscure the nature and direction of the abuse create confusion and mask the situation. For example, the phrase 'incestuous families' does not accurately apply to all members of the family, as it typically describes the sexual abuse of a daughter by her father. Women in this study were frequently included in this labelling. Professionals involved with sexually abused children and mothers of these children should be sensitive and clear in the language they use in writing their assessments and case recordings.

Future Research Funding

Governments and other funding bodies need to encourage alternative approaches in research that move away from traditional models that reproduce notions of gendered division of labour and conventional methods of defining problems and families. Women-centred researchers should be given priority for future research grants in order to bring about a reasonable balance of views toward women, since they constitute slightly more than one-half of the population.

Concluding Comments

Women in this study were blamed (and blamed themselves) for their children's victimization. It was documented how institutionalized sexism contributed to the 'ethic of blame' experienced by the mothers interviewed. Implications for policies, programs, and research were outlined, stating the need for consciousness-raising not only for mothers but for professionals working with them, and for male professionals in particular. The need for social action to bring about change in policies and programs focused on attitudes of those in decision-making positions.

Important themes that emerged in this study included the mother-blaming that exists in child-welfare legislation and policies, and in the practices following the intervention process; the amount and degree of violence perpetrated against women and children; the insensitivity of some key informants to the rights and needs of women and children; the inadequacies of the child-welfare system with respect to service delivery and agency policies, the lack of priority in hospitals for immediate physical examination of sexually abused children; the lack of training and awareness in schools, the workplace, and the courts; the frequent reluctance of the police and the courts to protect children from sexual abuse; and the invisibility of men as supportive helpers to women and children in cases of sexual abuse.

Although this work has stressed the importance of ideology in keeping women in their place, it has also pointed out the material and economic considerations that make it difficult for women to leave abusive situations. It is essential that changes in areas such as employment, education, child care, and housing be available to support women when their children are sexually abused, so that they can make realistic and positive choices.

Until laws are more just; treatment programs are more available, accessible, and relevant; public and professional attitudes toward women and children are changed; institutions reflect more sensitive and respectful approaches to working with women and children; the issue of sexual abuse must remain on the political agenda.

Notes

1. One of the first workshops held in Metropolitan Toronto for those working in the child sexual abuse area was held at the University of Toronto on 16 February 1981. Dr Henry (Hank) Giarretto and his wife, Ana Giarretto, spoke of their program in California (CSATP), which covered Santa Clara County with a population of approximately one million. They talked about the increases in child sexual abuse reported in Santa Clara County, from 31 cases in 1973 to 800 cases in 1981. The attendees at the workshop at the time could identify only 100 cases of child sexual abuse in Toronto for the year 1980. Giarretto suggested that extrapolating from his statistics, Metropolitan Toronto (with a population of 2.5 million, at the time) should have anywhere from 1,500 to 2,000 cases of sexual abuse reported. In 1989, the largest agency, the Children's Aid Society of Metropolitan Toronto, reported that they opened approximately 637 new cases of child sexual abuse (Byrne 1990, A9). Although there were no published statistics for the other two agencies at the time (the Catholic Children's Aid Society of Metropolitan Toronto, and the Jewish Children's Aid), my discussions with experienced protection caseworkers in those agencies convinced me that my guesstimate of 300 newly opened cases of child sexual abuse for the Catholic Children's Aid Society and 70 for the Jewish Children's Aid would be realistic estimates for 1989. The only agency where cases were validated and documented, however, were those of the Children's Aid Society of Metropolitan Toronto (with approximately 637 cases). Giarretto's prediction of 1,500 to 2,000 cases of child sexual abuse in the Metropolitan Toronto area within a ten year period was based on his own experiences in San José, California, on his number of validated cases of sexual abuse. It is reasonable to assume that about one-

third of the reported cases of CAS would not be substantiated (Trocme et al. 1995), resulting in a reporting estimate of approximately 1,500 cases which could result in 1,000 validated for Metropolitan Toronto for the year of 1989.

The Metropolitan Toronto Police reported an average of 520 incidents of sexual offences against children reported per year between 1977 and 1980 (Metropolitan Toronto 1982, B-2). These would not have been all validated cases reported to child welfare authorities.

2. See, for example, on retrospective adult accounts of sexual abuse: Bagley and Ramsay 1986; Wyatt 1985; The Canadian Panel 1993; Russell 1986; Williams 1994; on child-victims: Badgley et al. 1984; Faller 1988; Gilgun 1983; on adult incest survivors: Butler 1978; Herman and Hirschman 1982; Women's Research Centre 1989; on female perpetrators: Elliott 1993; Faller 1987; Matthers 1993; Wolfers 1993; Young 1993; on male perpetrators: Conte et al. 1982; Groth et al. 1982; Groth and Birnabaum 1981.

Chapter 3

1. For more detail on the alternative perspective critiques on caregiving in the family and what it does to women, see Carol Baines et al. (1991, chapters 1, 8, and 9); Finch and Groves (1983); Chodorow (1978, chapters 1 and 2); DeVault (1991, chapters 4 and 5); Levine (1982); on celebration of child-birth, see O'Brien (1981, chapter 6); on arguments against women bearing children, see Firestone (1970).

2. Ironically, despite Rousseau's teachings on the importance of family life and child care and his advice in *Emile* (Trans. A. Bloom 1979, Book 1, 49) that 'He who cannot fulfill the duties of a father has no right to become one,' Rousseau violated his own principles in both the duties of a father and the importance of child development. In volume two of his *Confessions* (Trans. Niklaus 1971, Book VIII, 9) he writes of deliberately abandoning five of his own illegitimate children to the Foundling Hospital, and of sharing the sexual favours of small female children 'not yet eleven years of age' (Book VIII, 6; Book X, 177).

3. See Ehrenreich and English's *For Her Own Good* (1979) for a more detailed discussion on Watson's views, as well as the views of other 'experts' on child rearing and development during the early 1900s.

4. My computer search yielded numerous studies about mothers and childhood sexual abuse, but most were clinically focused doctoral dissertations that examined various traits and characteristics of women whose children were victimized. Since I did not wish to perpetuate the mainstream stance on this topic, I rejected most of them for my review. The studies cited in my text are

considered to be alternative or feminist views, and are closely related to the work of Sandra Butler, Judith Herman, David Finkelhor, and Diana Russell.

For an example of mainstream literature on mothers whose children were sexually abused, see Lydia Tinling, 'Perpetuation of Incest by Significant Others: Mothers Who Do Not Want to See' (1990, Sept. *Individual-Psychology,* 46(3), 280–97) or Martha Wilson 'A Preliminary Report on Ego Development in Non-offending Mothers of Sexually Abused Children' (1995, April, *Child Abuse and Neglect,* Vol. 19(4), 511–18).

5. Although feminism can be traced back to the fifteenth century, there were only two periods in history where women were able to turn their protests into full-scale movements. The first period was from the nineteenth to the early twentieth century which was referred to as the 'first wave' of feminism. The 'second wave' of feminism began in the late 1960s and is considered an important movement today, despite a developing anti-feminist counter-movement. For further discussion on this period, see Hester Eisenstein's *Contemporary Feminist Thought* (1983). Before that time period (1920–70), no *strong* feminist movement existed, according to Elizabeth Wilson in *What's to Be Done about Violence against Women?* (1983, 88).

6. In her book *The Spinster and Her Enemies: Feminism and Sexuality, 1880–1930,* Sheila Jeffreys discusses the subject of child sexual abuse from the first wave of feminism. She mentions that this problem was introduced in the House of Lords in 1884–5, but no action was taken as 'Shaftsbury said that physical cruelty to children was too private and domestic and beyond the reach of the legislature' (77).

Chapter 4

1. Statistics Canada, in its random study (1993), included only physical or sexual violence in its definition, whereas my study included those two categories as well as emotional, verbal, and psychological abuse, as indicated in the women's stories.

Chapter 6

1. Two books published in the 1970s by Goldstein, Freud, and Solnit, *Beyond the Best Interests of the Child* (1973) and *Before the Best Interests of the Child* (1979), had a tremendous impact on the development of legislation and policy in Canadian Child Welfare. The ideas expressed in these books helped to shape the principles in new child welfare legislation with respect to 'the best interests of the child,' later translated into practice. The child's need for

continuity of care emphasized the importance of child welfare's work with the biological parents to resolve concerns but, if separation from the family was necessary, this was guided by the notion that psychological parents could provide the necessary care, as it was the psychological parents or the parent(s) the child was bonded to that was important to the child's development. The psychological parents and the biological parents could play different roles in the child's life.

2. This represents a selection of some of the standards relevant in child sexual abuse cases from the Ontario Ministry of Community and Social Services's *Standards and Guidelines* (1986).

INS-01.1 The worker shall respond to an allegation of child abuse by seeing the child immediately to ensure the child's safety ... There shall be no deviation from the requirement that the child be seen immediately except in rare situations where a decision to defer seeing the child is related to the best interests of the child in the circumstances.

INS-02.1 Activities in Investigation include:
   – a check of CAS records and Child Abuse Register
   – informing of police
   – interview of referral source, the abused child, the parent(s), the person who had charge of the child, siblings of alleged victim, the alleged abuser (unless circumstances preclude this)
   – medical attention, if required.

INS-02.2 The Worker Shall:
   a) document each finding made and each action taken in responding to an allegation of child abuse as soon as possible within 24 hours of the finding or action, except as required
   b) maintain this information in a form that is legible, understandable and accessible as needed.

The Finding:

ENS-01.1 On the basis of the initial investigation, the worker shall reach one of the following conclusions:
   a) the allegation of child abuse appears unfounded
   b) child abuse is suspected to have occurred
   c) the investigation has verified the information of the allegation of child abuse.

ENS-02.1 Where no evidence of child abuse can be substantiated, the Society shall:

a) advise the family of the disposition immediately
b) provide written confirmation within 14 days
c) if the child is not at risk and the family does not wish to accept voluntary services, the Society shall close the case, and document the reasons.

Chapter 10

1. See, for example, the issue of the *Journal of Family Issues* devoted to fatherhood (Vol. 15(1), March 1994), including paternal roles and involvement, based on the results of national surveys.

References

Abramovitz, M. (1995). From Tenement Class to Dangerous Class to Underclass: Blaming Women for Social Problems. In A. Van den Berg (Ed.). *Feminist Practice in the 21st Century* (pp. 211–231), Washington, DC: NAWS Press.

Aguilera, D.C., and Messick, J.M. (1982). *Crisis Intervention: Therapy for Psychological Emergencies.* New York: Mosby.

Akabas, S. (1995). The World of Work. In Nan Van Den Bergh, (Ed.), *Feminist Practice in the 21st Century* (pp. 105–25). Washington, DC: NASW Press.

Alexander, P.C. (1993). The Differential Effects of Sexual Abuse Characteristics and Attachment in the Prediction of Long-Term Effects of Sexual Abuse. *Journal of Interpersonal Violence,* 8 (3) (September), 346–62.

Araji, S., and Finkelhor, D. (1986). Abusers: A Review of the Research. In D. Finkelhor and Associates, (Eds.), *A Sourcebook on Child Sexual Abuse* (pp. 89–118). Beverly Hills: Sage.

Arcana, J. (1979). *Our Mother's Daughters.* Berkeley: Shameless Hussy Press.

Armstrong, L. (1978). *Kiss Daddy Goodnight: A Speak-Out on Incest.* New York: Pocket Books.

– (1995). *Of 'Sluts' and 'Bastards': A Feminist Decodes the Child Welfare Debate.* Monroe, Maine: Common Courage Press.

Armstrong, P., and Armstrong, H. (1981). *The Double Ghetto.* Toronto: McClelland and Stewart.

Arnup, K. (Ed.). (1995). *Lesbian Parenting: Living with Pride and Prejudice.* Charlottetown, PEI: Gynergy.

Aronson, J.H. (1988). Women's Experience in Giving and Receiving Care: Pathways to Social Change. Unpublished doctoral dissertation, University of Toronto.

Babbie, E. (1983). *The Practice of Social Research* (3rd ed.). Belmont, California: Wadsworth.

Badgley, R., Allard, H., McCormick, N., Proudfoot, P. Fortin, D., Ogilvie, D., Rae-Grant, Q., Gelinas, P., Pepin, L., and Sutherland, S. [Committee on Sexual Offences Against Children and Youths] (1984). *Sexual Offences Against Children* (Vols. 1 & 2). Ottawa: Supply and Services Canada.

Badinter, E. (1981). *Mother Love: Myth and Reality*. New York: Macmillan.

Bagley, C. (1985). Child Sexual Abuse: A Child Welfare Perspective. In K. Levitt and B. Wharf (Eds.), *The Challenge of Child Welfare* (pp. 66–91). Vancouver: University of British Columbia Press.

Bagley, C., and King, K. (1990). *Child Sexual Abuse*. London: Tavistock/ Routledge.

Bagley, C., and Ramsay, R. (1986). Sexual Abuse in Childhood: Psychosocial Outcomes and Implications for Social Work Practice. *Journal of Social Work and Human Sexuality*, *4*, 33–47.

Baines, C. Evans, P., and Neysmith, S. (Eds.), (1991). *Women's Caring: Feminist Perspectives on Social Welfare*. Toronto: McClelland and Stewart.

Baker, M. (Ed.). (1984). *The Family: Changing Trends in Canada*. Toronto: McGraw-Hill Ryerson.

Baker Miller, J. (1977). *Toward a New Psychology of Women*. Boston: Beacon Press.

Bala, N.C. (1987). *Review of the Ontario Child Abuse Register*. Kingston, Ontario: Queen's University Press.

– (1991). An Introduction to Child Protection Problems. In N. Bala, J. Hornick, and R. Vogl (Eds.). *Canadian Child Welfare Law* (pp. 1–23). Toronto: Thompson

Barrett, M., and McIntosh, M. (1982). *The Anti-Social Family*. London: Verso.

Bart, P. (1983). Review of Chodorow's *The Reproduction of Mothering*. In J. Trobilcot (Ed.), *Mothering: Essays in Feminist Theory* (pp. 147–52). Totowa, New Jersey: Rowman and Allanheld.

Bass, E., and Davis, L. (1988). *The Courage to Heal*. New York: Harper and Row.

Belenky, M. Clinchy, B., Goldberger, N., and Tarule, J. (1986). *Women's Ways of Knowing: The Development of Self, Voice and Mind*. New York: Basic Books.

Benjamin, J. (1988). *The Bonds of Love*. New York: Pantheon Books.

– (1992). Discussion on the Relational Self. *Contemporary Psychotherapy Review*, *7*, 82–92.

Berliner, L., and Stevens, D. (1982). Clinical Issues in Child Sexual Abuse. In J. Conte and D. Shore (Eds.), *Social Work and Child Sexual Abuse* (pp. 93–108). New York: The Haworth Press.

Bernard, J. (1974). *The Future of Motherhood*. New York: Penguin Books.

Bernstein, C., (1990, March 25). Sexual Abusers Now Pay Big Money. *Toronto Star*. p. F4.

Bettcher, C. (1996). Vicarious Traumatization: The Unintended Consequences of Political Action and Caring. Unpublished master's thesis, University of British Columbia.

Bleier, R. (1984). *Science and Gender: A Critique of Biology and Its Theories on Women.* New York: Pergamon Press.

Bogdon, R.C., and Biklen, S.K. (1982). *Qualitative Research for Education.* Boston: Allyn and Bacon.

Bograd, M. (1984). Family Systems Approaches to Wife Battering: A Feminist Critique. *American Journal of Orthopsychiatry, 54* (4), 558–68.

Bowker, L.H., Arbitell, M., and McFerron, J.R. (1988). On the Relationship between Wife Beating and Child Abuse. In K. Yllo and M. Bograd (Eds.), *Feminist Perspectives on Wife Abuse* (pp. 158–74). Newbury Park, California: Sage Publications.

Bowlby, J. (1963). *Attachment and Loss* (Vol. 1). New York: Penguin Books.

Boyd S. (1995). Comments on back cover of K. Arnup, *Lesbian Parenting: Living with Pride & Prejudice.* Charlottetown, PEI: gynergy books.

Breckinridge, S.P., and Abbott, E. (1970). *The Delinquent Child and the Home.* New York: Arno Press. (Originally published 1912).

Breines, W., and Gordon, L. (1983). The New Scholarship on Family Violence. *Signs: Journal of Women in Culture and Society, 8* (3), 490–531.

Bridenthal, R. (1982). The Family: The View from a Room of Her Own. In B. Thorne with M. Yalom (Eds.), *Rethinking the Family: Some Feminist Questions* (pp. 225–39). New York: Longman.

Briere, J., and Runtz, M. (1993). Childhood Sexual Abuse: Long Term Sequelae and Implications for Psychological Assessment. *Journal of Interpersonal Violence, 8* (3) (September) 321–45.

British Columbia (1994). Child, Family and Comunity Services Act. Victoria: Author.

British Columbia, Ministry of Children and Families, Child Protection Consultation Services. (1996). *The High Risk Model Assessment for Child Protection British Columbia.* Victoria: Author.

Browning, D.H., and Boatman, B. (1977). Incest: Children at Risk. *American Journal of Psychiatry, 134,* 69–72.

Bunch, C. (1986). *Passionate Politics.* New York: St Martin's Press.

Burgess, A., Groth, A.N., Holmstrom, Lynda L., and Sgroi, S. (1985). *Sexual Assault of Children and Adolescents.* Toronto: Lexington Books.

Butler, S. (1978). *Conspiracy of Silence: The Trauma of Incest.* San Francisco: Volcano Press.

Byrne, C. (1990, May 2). Poverty, Drugs Cited as Cases of Child Abuse Climb by 14%. *Toronto Star.* p. A9

Caldwell, G. (1983). Great Expectations. In *OACAS Journal, 27* (6) (June), 1–5.

Callahan, M. (1993). Feminist Approaches: Women Recreate Child Welfare. In B. Wharf (Ed.), *Rethinking Child Welfare in Canada*. Toronto: McClelland and Stewart.

Callahan, M., Lumb, C., and Wharf, B. (1994). *Strengthening Families by Empowering Women*. Victoria: Ministry of Social Services and the School of Social Work, University of Victoria, BC.

Canada, Department of Justice. (1988). Criminal Code of Canada.

Canadian Panel on Violence against Women. (1993). *Changing the Landscape: Ending Violence – Achieving Equality*. Ottawa: Minister of Supply and Services.

Caplan, P. (1984). *The Myth of Women's Masochism*. New York: E.P. Dutton.

– (1989). *Don't Blame Mother*. New York: Harper and Row.

Caplan, P., and Hall-McCorquodale, I. (1985). Mother-Blaming in Major Clinical Journals. *American Journal of Orthopsychiatry, 55* (3), 345–53.

Carniol, B. (1995). *Case Critical: Challenging Social Work in Canada*. (3rd ed.). Toronto: Between the Lines.

Carter, B. (1987a). What Impact Has the Women's Movement Had on Child Welfare's Approach to Child Abuse? Unpublished comprehensive paper, Faculty of Social Work, University of Toronto.

– (1987b). *Child Abuse: A Child Protection Manual for Hospitals of Ontario*. Toronto: Ontario Hospital Association.

– (1993, Spring). Child Sexual Abuse: Impact on Mothers. Affilia: *Journal of Women and Social Work, 8*(1), 72–90.

Carter, B., and Zanutto, K. (1984). Development of a Multi-Agency Treatment Network for Families Where Sexual Abuse Has Occurred. In *Ontario Collection* (pp. 321–33). Toronto: Ontario Ministry of Community and Social Services.

Chester, P. (1987). *Mothers on Trial*. Washington: McGraw-Hill.

Chodorow, N. (1978). *The Reproduction of Mothering*. Berkeley: University of California Press.

Chodorow, N., and Contratto, S. (1982). The Fantasy of the Perfect Mother. In B. Thorne with M. Yalom (Eds.), *Rethinking the Family: Some Feminist Questions* (pp. 54–75). New York: Longman.

Christian, B. (1994). An Angle of Seeing: Motherhood in Buchi Emecheta's *Joys of Motherhood* and Alice Walker's *Meridian*. In E. Glenn, G. Chang, and L. Forcey (Eds.), *Mothering Ideology, Experience, and Agency*. New York: Routledge.

Cohen, T. (1983). The Incestuous Family Revisited. *Social Casework* (March) 154–61.

Cohen-Schlanger, M., Fitzpatrick, A., Hulchanski, J., and Raphael, D. (1995). Housing as a Factor in Admissions of Children to Temporary Care: A Survey. *Child Welfare, 74* (3), 547–62.

'Common Sense Says: Lock Up Sex Offenders' (1997 November 1) *Vancouver Sun*. p. A18.

Conte, J., and Shore, D. (1982). (Eds.), *Social Work and Child Sexual Abuse*. New York: The Haworth Press.

Cormier, B.M., Kennedy, M., and Sangowicxz, J. (1962). Psychodynamics of Father-Daughter Incest. *Canadian Psychiatric Association Journal*, 7, 203–17.

Courtois, C.A. (1988). *Healing the Incest Wound: Adult Survivors in Therapy*. New York: W.W. Norton.

– (1991). Theory, Sequencing, and Strategy in Treating Adult Survivors. In J. Briere (Ed.), *Treating Victims of Child Sexual Abuse* (pp. 47–60). San Francisco: Jossey-Bass.

Coutis, J. (1994). Ontario May Screen for Abusers. *Globe and Mail*, 28 May, p. A1.

Crean, S. (1988). *In the Name of the Fathers: The Story behind Child Custody*. Toronto: Amanita Publications.

Cummerton, J.M. (1986). *A Feminist Perspective on Research: What Does It Help Us See?* In N. Van Den Bergh and L.B. Cooper (Eds.), *Feminist Visions for Social Work* (pp. 80–100). Silver Springs, Maryland: National Association of Social Workers.

Danica, E. (1990). *Don't: A Woman's Word*. Toronto: McClelland and Stewart.

De Beauvoir, S. (1953). *The Second Sex*. New York: Knoff.

Dempster, H.L. (1992). *The Aftermath of Child Sexual Abuse: The Woman's Perspective*. London: HMSO.

Deutsch, H. (1973). *The Psychology of Women* (Vol. 11). New York: Bantam Books.

DeVault, M.L. (1991). *Feeding the Family*. Chicago: University of Chicago Press.

Dietz, C.A., and Craft, J.L. (1980). Family Dynamics of Incest: A New Perspective. *Social Casework*, *61*, 602–9.

Dinnerstein, D. (1977). *The Mermaid and the Minotaur: Sexual Arrangements and Human Malaise*. New York: Harper and Row.

Dinsmore, C. (1991). *From Surviving to Thriving*. Albany: State University of New York Press.

Dobash, R.E., and Dobash, R.P. (1979). *Violence against Wives: A Case against the Patriarchy*. New York: The Free Press.

– (1983). Patterns of Violence in Scotland. In R. Gelles and C. P. Cornell. (Eds.), *International Perspectives on Family Violence* (pp. 147–57). Lexington, Massachusetts: Lexington Books.

– (1988). Research as Social Action: The Struggle for Battered Women. In K. Yllo and M. Bograd (Eds.), *Feminist Perspectives on Wife Abuse* (pp. 51–74). Newbury Park, California: Sage Publications.

Dominelli, L. (1986). Father-Daughter Incest: Patriarchy's Shameful Secret. *Critical Social Policy*, 6 (1), 8–22.

– (1989, August). Betrayal of Trust: A Feminist Analysis of Power Relationships in Incest Abuse and Its Relevance for Social Work Practice. *British Journal of Social Work*, *19* (4), 291–307.

Dominelli, L., and McLeod, E. (1989). *Feminist Social Work*. London: Macmillan.

Donzelot, J. (1979). *The Policing of Families*. New York: Pantheon Books.

Dreikurs, R. (1964). *Children: The Challenge*. New York: Hawthorn Books.

Dulude, L. (1984). *Love, Marriage and Money: An Analysis of Financial Relations between the Spouses*. Ottawa: Canadian Advisory Council on the Status of Women.

Durant, W., and Durant, A. (1967). *Rousseau and Revolution*. New York: Simon and Schuster.

Ehrenreich, B., and English, D., (1979). *For Her Own Good*. New York: Anchor Press.

Eichler, M. (1983). *Families in Canada Today*. Toronto: Gage Publishing.

– (1997). *Family Shifts*. Toronto: Oxford University Press.

Eichler, M., and Lapointe, J. (1985). *On the Treatment of the Sexes in Research*. Ottawa: Social Sciences and Humanities Research Council of Canada.

Eisenstein, H. (1983). *Contemporary Feminist Thought*. Boston: G. K. Hall and Co.

Eisenstein, Z. (1984). *Feminism and Sexual Equality: Crisis in Liberal America*. New York: Monthly Review Press.

Ellerstein, N.S., and Canavan, W. (1980). Sexual Abuse of Boys. *American Journal of Diseased Children, 134*, 225–57.

Engels, F. (1972). *The Origin of the Family, Private Property and the State*. New York: Pathfinder Press.

Erikson, E.H. (1963). *Childhood and Society* (2nd ed.). New York: W.W. Norton and Company Inc.

Faller, K.C. (1987, July). Women Who Sexually Abuse Children: A Descriptive Study. Paper presented at the Third National Family Violence Research Conference. Durham, New Hampshire.

– (1988). *Child Sexual Abuse: An Interdisciplinary Manual for Diagnosis, Case Management and Treatment*. New York: Columbia University Press.

– (1989). Why Sexual Abuse: An Exploration of the Intergenerational Hypothesis. *Child Abuse and Neglect, 13*, 543–9.

Figley, C.R. (1995). Compassion Fatigue: Coping with Secondary Traumatic Stress Disorder in Those Who Treat the Traumatized. In C.R. Figley (Ed.). *Compassion Fatigue as Secondary Traumatic Stress Disorder: An Overview*. (pp. 1–20). New York: Brunner/Mazel.

Finkel, K. (1983). *Recognition and Assessment of the Sexually Abused Child: Guidelines for Physicians*. Toronto: Ontario Medical Foundation.

Finkelhor, D. (1984). *Child Sexual Abuse: New Theory and Research*. New York: Free Press.

– (1994). Current Information on the Scope and Nature of Child Sexual Abuse. *The Future of Children, 4*, (2), 31–53.

Finkelhor, D, and Associates. (1986). *A Sourcebook on Child Sexual Abuse*. Beverly Hills: Sage Publications.

Finkelhor, D., and Browne, A. (1985). The Traumatic Impact of Child Sexual Abuse: A Conceptualization. *American Journal of Orthopsychiatry, 55* (4), 530–41.

Finkelhor, D., Moore, D., Hamby, S., and Straus, M. (1997). Sexually Abused Children in a National Survey of Parents: Methodological Issues. *Child Abuse & Neglect, 21* (1), 1–9.

Firestone, S. (1970). *The Dialectic of Sex*. New York: Morrow.

Flax, J. (1978). The Conflict between Nurturance and Autonomy in Mother-Daughter Relationships and within Feminism. *Feminist Studies, 2*, 171–189.

– (1986). Gender as a Problem: In and for Feminist Theory. *American Studies* (June), 193–213.

Fraser, P., Clark, S., Eberts, M., Gilbert, J.P. McLaren, J., and Ruffo, A. [Special Committee on Pornography and Prostitution] (1985). *Pornography and Prostitution in Canada*. (Vols. 1 and 2). Ottawa: Minister of Supply and Services.

Fraser, S. (1987). *My Father's House: A Memoir of Incest and of Healing*. Toronto: Doubleday.

Freeman, D. (1985). The Involvement of Children in Family Therapy, *Canadian Social Work Review*, 30–41.

Freud, A. (1981). A Psychoanalyst's View of Sexual Abuse by Parents. In P.B. Mrazek and C.H. Kempe, (Eds.), *Sexually Abused Children and Their Families* (pp. 33–4). Oxford: Pergamon Press.

Freud, S. (1950). *Beyond the Pleasure Principle* Trans. J. Strachey. New York: Liveright. (Originally published 1920).

Friday, N. (1977). *My Mother/My Self*. New York: Delacorte.

Gaddini, R. (1983). Incest as a Developmental Failure. *Child Abuse and Neglect, 7*, 357–8.

Garbarino, J. (1995). *Raising Children in a Socially Toxic Environment*. San Francisco: Jossey-Bass Publishers.

Gelles, R., and Cornell, C. (1983). Introduction: An International Perspective on Family Violence. In R. Gelles and C. Cornell (Eds.), *International Perspectives on Family Violence* (pp. 1–22). Lexington, Mass.: Lexington.

Ghalam, N. (1994). Women in the Workplace. In *Canadian Social Trends* (Vol. 2). Toronto: Thompson Educational Publishing.

Giarretto, H. (1982). *Integrated Treatment of Child Sexual Abuse: A Treatment and Training Manual*. Palo Alto, California: Science and Behavior Books.

Giarretto, H., and Giarretto, A. (1981). Incest and Treatment. Workshop held at University of Toronto, 16 February, sponsored by Citytv.

Gil, E. (1993). *Treatment of Adult Survivors of Childhood Abuse*. Walnut Creek: Launch Press.

Gilgun, J.F. (1983). Does the Mother Always Know? Alternatives to Blaming Mothers of Child Sexual Abuse Victims. *Response, 7*, 2–4.

– (1984). The Sexual Abuse of the Young Female in Life Course Perspective.

Dissertation Abstracts International, 44, 3058. (University Microfilms International No. DEQ84–10713).

– (1987, July). Research Interviewing in Child Sexual Abuse. Paper presented at the Third National Family Violence Research Conference. Durham, New Hampshire.

Gilligan, C. (1982). *In a Different Voice.* Cambridge, Mass.: Harvard University Press.

Gimenez, M.E. (1984). Feminism, Pronatalism and Motherhood. In J. Trebilcot (Ed.), *Mothering: Essays in Feminist Theory* (pp. 287–314). Totowa, New Jersey: Rowman and Allanheld.

Giovannoni, J. (1985). Child Abuse and Neglect: An Overview. In J. Laird and A. Hartman (Eds.), *A Handbook of Child Welfare: Context, Knowledge and Practice.* (pp. 193–212). London: The Free Press.

Goldsmith, J. (1982). The Postdivorce Family System. In F. Walsh (Ed.). *Normal Family Processes.* (pp. 297–330). New York. The Guildford Press.

Goldstein, J., Freud, A., and Solnit, A. (1973). *Beyond the Best Interests of the Child.* New York: The Free Press.

Goldstein, J., Freud A., and Solnit, A. (1979). *Before the Best Interests of the Child.* New York: The Free Press.

Gondolf, E. (1987, July). Who Are These Guys? Paper presented at the Third National Family Violence Research Conference. Durham, New Hampshire.

Goode, W.J. (1964). *The Family.* New Jersey: Prentice Hall.

Gordon, L. (1985). Child Abuse, Gender, and the Myth of Family Independence: A Historical Critique. *Child Welfare,* 64 (3), 213–23.

– (1988a, December). The Frustrations of Family Violence Social Work: An Historical Critique. *Journal of Sociology and Social Welfare, 15* (4), 139–60.

– (1988b). *Heroes of Their Own Lives: The Politics and History of Family Violence.* New York: Viking Penguin.

Gordon, T. (1974). *Parent Effectiveness Training.* New York: Peter H. Wyden.

Graham, H. (1983). Caring: A Labour of Love. In J. Finch and D. Groves (Eds.), *A Labour of Love: Women, Work and Caring* (pp. 13–30). London: Routledge and Kegan Paul.

Grams, A. (1970, September). Fatherhood and Motherhood in a Changing World. *International Child Welfare Review,* 18–27.

Green, A.H., Coupe, P., Fernandez, R., and Stevens, B. (1995). Incest Revisited: Delayed Post-Traumatic Stress Disorder in Mothers Following the Sexual Abuse of Their Children. *Child Abuse and Neglect, 19* (10), 1275–82.

Groth, A.N., and Birnbaum, H.J. (1981). *Men Who Rape.* New York: Plenum Press.

Groth, A.N., Hobson, W.F., and Gary, T.S. (1982). The Child Molester: Clinical

Observations. In J.R. Conte and D.A. Shore (Eds.), *Social Work and Child Sexual Abuse* (pp. 129–44). New York: The Haworth Press.

Guba, E., and Lincoln, Y. (1989). *Effective Evaluation*. San Francisco: Jossey-Bass.

Guberman, C. (1989, December). *Services/Funding for Adult Incest Survivors Within Ontario: An Overview*. Toronto: Ontario Women's Directorate.

Guberman, C., and Wolfe, M. (Eds.). (1985). *No Safe Place: Violence against Women and Children*. Toronto: Women's Press.

Gutierrez, L.M. (1987, Summer). Social Work Theories and Practice with Battered Women: A Conflict-of-Values Analysis, *Affilia: Journal of Women and Social Work*. 2 (2), 36–52.

Hagens, S., Thomas, H., and Byles, J. (1986). *A Review and Assessment of Protocols for Interagency Collaboration in Reporting, Investigation and Managing Child Abuse in Ontario*. Hamilton: McMaster University.

Hall, N. (1997, November 20). Parents File Complaint over Judge's Sex-Case Comments. *Vancouver Sun*, p. A3c.

Hall, N. (1998, April 8). Judge Awards $200,000 for Abuse. *Vancouver Sun*, p. B5c.

Harding, S. (Ed.) (1987). *Feminism and Methodology*. Bloomington, Ind.: Open University Press.

Hawkesworth, M.E. (1989). Knowers, Knowing, Known: Feminist Theory and Claims of Truth. *Signs: Journal of Women in Culture and Society, 14* (3), pp. 535–57.

Hartmann, H. (1992). Capitalism, Patriarchy, and Job Segregation by Sex. In M. Humm (Ed.), *Modern Feminisms: Political, Literacy, Cultural* (pp. 99–103). New York: Columbia University Press.

Heger, A.H. (1996). Twenty Years in the Evaluation of the Sexually Abused Child: Has Medicine Helped or Hurt the Child and the Family? *Child Abuse and Neglect, 20* (10), 893–7.

Henderson, J.D. (1972). Incest: A Synthesis of Data. *Canadian Psychiatric Association Journal, 17*, 299–313.

– (1983, February). Is Incest Harmful? *Canadian Journal of Psychiatry, 28*, 34–9.

Heriot, J. (1991). Factors Contributing to Maternal Protectiveness Following the Disclosure of Intra-Familial Child Sexual Abuse: A Documentary Study Based on Reports of Child Protective Service Workers. Unpublished doctoral dissertation, School of Social Work and Community Planning, University of Maryland, Baltimore.

Herman, J. (1992). *Trauma and Recovery*. New York: Basic Books.

Herman, J., and Hirschman, L. (1977). Father-Daughter Incest. *Signs: Journal of Women in Culture and Society, 2*, 735–56.

– (1982). *Father-Daughter Incest*. Cambridge, Mass.: Harvard Universtiy Press.

Herman-Giddens, M., and Frothingham T. (1987). Prepubertal Female Genitalia. *Pediatrics, 80*, 203–8.

Holten, J.D. (1990). When Do We Stop Mother-Blaming? *Journal of Feminist Family Therapy*, *2* (1), 53–60.

hooks, b. (1989). *Talking Back.* Toronto: Between the Lines.

Hooper, C. (1989). Alternatives to Collusion: The Response of Mothers to Child Sexual Abuse in the Family. *Educational and Child Psychology*, *6* (1) 22–9.

– (1992). *Mothers Surviving Child Sexual Abuse.* London: Tavistock/Routledge.

Hudson, K. (1989, December 13). Murdered Son Was 'An Ideal Boy' His Father Says. *Toronto Star*, p. A7.

Jeffreys, S. (1985). *The Spinster and Her Enemies: Feminism and Sexuality, 1880–1936.* London: Pandora.

Johnson, J.T. (1992). *Mothers of Incest Survivors.* Bloomington: Indiana University Press.

– (1993). *Sexualized Children: Assessment of Sexual Behavior Problems in Preschool and Latency-aged Children.* Passadena, California: Child and Adolescent Psychiatric Clinics of North America.

Jordan, J. (1995). A Relational Approach to Psychotherapy. *Women and Therapy*. 16, 51–61.

– (Ed.). (1997). *Women's Growth in Diversity: More Writings from the Stone Center.* New York: The Guilford Press.

Jordan, J.V. Kaplan, A.G., Miller, J.B., Stiver, I.P., and Surrey, J.L. (Eds.). (1991). *Women's Growth in Connection: Writings from the Stone Center.* New York: Guilford Press.

Judge's Job Said On Line, Probe Told. (1990, March 17). The *Toronto Star*, p. A11.

Justice, B., and Justice, R. (1979). *The Broken Taboo: Sex in the Family.* New York: Human Sciences Press.

Kadushin, A., and Martin, J. (1981). *Child Abuse: An Inter-actional Event.* New York: Columbia University Press.

Kelly, L. (1988a). How Women Define Their Experiences of Violence. In K. Yllo and M. Bograd (Eds.), *Feminist Perspectives on Wife Abuse* (pp. 114–32). Newbury Park, California: Sage Publishing.

– (1988b). *Surviving Sexual Violence.* Minneapolis: University of Minnesota Press.

Kempe, C.H., and Kempe, R. (1984). *The Common Secret: Sexual Abuse of Children and Adolescents.* New York: W. H. Freeman and Company.

Kempe, C.H., Silverman, F.N., Steele, B.F., Droegemuller, W., and Silver, K. (1962). The Battered-Child Syndrome. *Journal of the American Medical Association*. *181* (1), 105–12.

Kenna, K. (1989, November 28). Judge Who blamed Tot in Sex Case Criticized. *Toronto Star*, p. A2.

Kinsey, A.C., Pomeroy, W.B., and Martin, C.E. (1948). *Sexual Behavior in the Human Male.* Philadelphia: W.B. Saunders.

Kinsey, A.C., Pomeroy, W.B., Martin, C.E., and Gebhard, P.H. (1953). *Sexual Behavior in the Human Female*. Philadelphia: W.B. Saunders.

Kirst-Ashman, J., and Hull, G. (1995). *Understanding Generalist Practice*. Chicago: Nelson-Hall Publishers.

Klein, M. (1953). Love, Guilt and Reparation. In M. Klein and J. Riviere (Eds.), *Love, Guilt and Reparation and Other Papers, 1921–1946*. London: Hogarth.

Kramarae, C., and Treichler, P. (1992). *Amazons, Bluestockings and Crones*. Hammersmith, Eng. Pandora.

Krane, J. (1990, Summer). Patriarchal Biases in the Conceptualization of Child Sexual Abuse: A Review and Critique of Literature from a Radical Feminist Perspective. *Canadian Social Work Review, 7* (2), 183–96.

– (1994). The Transformation of Women into Mother Protectors: An Examination of Child Protection Practices in Cases of Child Sexual Abuse. Unpublished doctoral dissertation, University of Toronto.

Krugman, R. (1986). Recognition of Sexual Abuse in Children. *Pediatric Review, 8*, 25–30.

Lahey, K.A. (1984). Research on Child Abuse in Liberal Patriarchy. In J.M. Vickers (Ed.), *Taking Sex into Account* (pp. 156–84). Ottawa: Carleton University Press.

Lamb, M.E. (1986). The Emergent American Father. In M.E. Lamb (Ed.), *The Father Role: Applied Perspectives* (pp. 3–25). New York: John Wiley and Sons.

Landis, J. (1956). Experiences of 500 Children with Adult Sexual Deviants. *Psychiatric Quarterly Supplement, 30*, 91–109.

Lane, M.E. (1982). *A Background Paper: The Legal Response to Sexual Abuse of Children*. Toronto: Metropolitan Chairman's Special Committee on Child Abuse.

Lasch, C. (1979). *Haven in a Heartless World: The Family Beseiged*. New York: Basic Books.

Leach, P. (1994). *Children First*. New York: Alfred A. Knopf.

Levine, H. (1982). The Personal Is Political: Feminism and the Helping Professions. In A. Miles and G. Finn (Eds.), *Feminism in Canada: From Pressure to Politics* (pp. 175–209). Montreal: Black Rose Books.

Levine, H., and Estable, A. (1983). 'The Deprivation of Mothers: A Feminist Perspective.' In *The Power Politics of Motherhood: A Feminist Critique of Theory and Practice*. (pp. 48–51). Ottawa: Centre for Welfare Studies. Carleton University.

Levy, B. (1995). Violence against Women. In N. Van Den Bergh (Ed.), *Feminist Practice in the 21st Century* (pp. 312–29). Washington, DC: NASW Press.

Levy, D. (1943). *Maternal Overprotection*. New York: Columbia University.

Leyton, E. (1986). *Hunting Humans: The Rise of the Modern Multiple Murderer*. Toronto: McClelland and Stewart.

Light, L. (1992 February). *Is Anyone Listening? Report of the British Columbia Task Force on Family Violence.* Victoria: Ministry of the Attorney General.

Loewen, H. (1995). The Experience of Mothering Children for Women Who Were Sexually Abused in Childhood. Unpublished master's thesis, University of British Columbia.

Lustig, N., Dresser, J.W., Spellman, S.W., and Murray, T.B. (1966, January). Incest: A Family Group Survival Pattern. *Archives of General Psychiatry, 14,* 31–40.

MacKinnon, C.A. (1987). *Feminism Unmodified: Discourses on Life and Law.* Cambridge, Mass: Harvard University Press.

MacLeod, L. (1987). *Battered but Not Beaten: Preventing Wife Battering in Canada.* Ottawa: Ministry of Supply and Services. Canadian Advisory Council on the Status of Women.

Makin, K. (1990, May 11). Paroled Sex Offenders to Receive Specialized Treatment, CSC Says. *Globe and Mail,* p. A10.

Man Must Pay $1 Million for Sex Abuse. (1998, April 16). *Vancouver Sun,* p. B4cc.

Manion, I.G., McIntyre, J., Firestone, P., Ligezinska, M., Ensom, R., and Wells, G. (1996). Secondary Traumatization in Parents Follwing the Disclosure of Extra-familial Child Sexual Abuse: Initial Effects. *Child Abuse and Neglect, 20* (11), 1095–1109.

Marshall, K. (1994). *Household Chores.* Canadian Social Trends (Vol. 2). Toronto: Thompson Educational Publishing.

Marshall, W.L., and Maric, A. (1996). Cognitive and Emotional Components of Generalized Empathy Defects in Child Molesters. *Journal of Child Sexual Abuse, 5*(2), 101–17.

Marsiglio, W. (1994). Fatherhood: Results from National Surveys. *Journal of Family Issues, 15* (1) (March), 1–166.

Masson, J. (1984). *The Assault on The Truth: Freud's Supression of the Seduction Theory.* Toronto: Farrar and Straus and Giroux.

Matthers, J. (1993). Working with Female Sexual Abusers. In M. Elliott, (Ed.), *Female Sexual Abuse of Children* (pp. 61–78). Colchester, Essex: Longmans.

McCann, I.L., and Pearlman, L.A. (1990). Vicarious Traumatization: A Contextual Model for Understanding the Effects of Trauma on Helpers. *Journal of Traumatic Stress, 3* (1), 131-49.

McIntyre, K. (1981). Role of Mothers in Father-Daughter Incest: A Feminist Analysis. *Social Work, 26* (2), pp. 462–6.

Media Fact Sheet. (1989, 16 February). Toronto: Children's Aid Society of Metropolitan Toronto.

Meiselman, K. (1978). *Incest: A Psychological Study of Causes and Effects with Treatment Recommendations.* San Francisco: Jossey-Bass.

Metropolitan Toronto Special Committee on Child Abuse. (1982, October). *Developing a Comprehensive Response to Child Sexual Abuse.* Toronto: Author.
– (1983, November). *Child Sexual Abuse Protocol.* Toronto: Author.
– (1986, June). *Child Sexual Abuse Protocol.* Toronto: Author.
– (1988). *Crisis Support Group Program, Program Statistics and Analysis.* Toronto: Author.
Miller, J. (1994). Women's Psychological Development: Connections, Disconnections and Violations. In M. Berger (Ed.), *Women Beyond Freud: New Concepts of Feminine Psychology* (pp. 79–97). New York: Brunner/Mazel Publishers.
Millett, K. (1979). *The Basement: Meditations on a Human Sacrifice.* New York: Simon and Schuster.
– (1983). *Sexual Politics.* New York: Ballantine Books.
Ministry of the Attorney General, Ministry for Children and Families, Ministry of Education, Skills and Training, Ministry of Health, and Ministry of Women's Equality (1998). *The B.C. Handbook for Action on Child Abuse and Neglect.* Victoria, B.C.: Ministry for Children and Families.
Misconduct – Vatican Blames Society for Sex Abuse by Priests. (June 24, 1993). *Vancouver Sun,* p. A14.
Misenheimer, E.E. (1981). *Rousseau on the Education of Women.* Washington, DC: University Press of America.
Mitchell, A. (1985). Child Sexual Assault. In C. Guberman and M. Wolfe (Eds.), *No Safe Place: Violence against Women and Children* (pp. 87–110). Toronto: The Women's Press.
Mohr, J.W., Turner, R.E., and Jerry, M.B. (1964). *Pedophilia and Exhibitionism.* Toronto: University of Toronto Press.
Morgan, D.H.J. (1985). *The Family, Politics and Social Theory.* London: Routledge and Kegan Paul.
Morgan vs. Foretich. (1989, September 4). *Toronto Star,* p. C6.
Mrazek, D. (1985). The Child Psychiatric Examination of the Sexually Abused Child. In P.B. Mrazek and C.H. Kempe, (Eds.), *Sexually Abused Children and Their Families.* (pp. 143–54). Oxford: Pergamon Press.
Mrazek, P.B. (1985). Definitions and Recognition of Sexual Abuse: Historical and Cultural Perspectives. In P.B. Mrazek and C.H. Kempe (Eds.), *Sexually Abused Children and Their Families* (pp. 5–16). Oxford: Pergamon Press.
Myer, M. (1984/5). A New Look at Mothers of Incest Victims. *Journal of Social Work and Human Sexuality, 3,* 47–58.
National Council of Welfare. (1988). *Poverty Profile.* Ottawa: Author.
– (1990). *Poverty Profile.* Ottawa: Author.
Nelson, B.J. (1984). *Making an Issue of Child Abuse: Political Agenda Setting for Social Problems.* Chicago: University of Chicago Press.

Newton, E. (1996, Fall). Power in Families and Power in Therapy: Child Sexual Abuse Survivors' Experiences. *Canadian Journal of Community Mental Health, 15* (2), 109–21.

Ni Carthy, G., Merriam, K., and Coffman, S. (1984). *Talking It Out.* Seattle: The Seal Press.

Oakley, A. (1981). *Subject Women.* New York: Pantheon Books.

– (1982). Interviewing Women: A Contradiction in Terms. In H. Roberts (Ed.), *Doing Feminist Research* (pp. 30–61). London: Routledge and Kegan Paul.

O'Brien, M. (1983). *The Politics of Reproduction.* Boston: Routledge and Kegan Paul.

Okun, L. (1986). *Woman Abuse: Facts Replacing Myths.* Albany, New York: State University of New York Press.

Olesen, V. (1994). Feminisms and Models of Qualitative Research. In N. Denzin and Y. Lincoln (Eds.), *Handbook of Qualitative Research.* Thousand Oaks, California: Sage Publications.

Ontario. (1965). *The Child Welfare Act.* Toronto: Queen's Printer for Ontario.

– (1978). *The Child Welfare Act.* Toronto: Queen's Printer for Ontario.

– (1984). *The Child and Families Services Act.* Toronto: Queen's Printer for Ontario.

Ontario Association of Children's Aid Societies. (1966, February). *Journal, 9* (2), p. 1.

– (1989). Fact Sheet. Ontario: Author.

Ontario Legislature. (1989). *Bill 124: An Act to Amend the Children's Law Reform Act.* Toronto: Queen's Printer for Ontario.

Ontario Ministry of Community and Social Services. (1974, September). *Procedures for Investigating and Reporting Physical Abuse.* Toronto: Author.

– (1978a). *Report of the Task Force on Child Abuse* (Garber Report). Toronto: Queen's Printer for Ontario.

– (1978b). *Report on the Child Abuse Survey.* Toronto: Author.

– (1979, November). *Standards and Guidelines for Management of Child Abuse Cases.* Toronto: Author.

– (1981, February). *Guidelines for Reporting to the Register.* Toronto: Author.

– (1981, February). *Standards and Guidelines: Child Abuse.* Toronto: Author.

– (1982). *The Child Abuse Register: Guidelines for Expunction.* Toronto: Author.

– (1983, November). *Three Decades of Change.* Toronto: Author.

– (1986). *Standards and Guidelines for Management of Child Abuse Cases.* Toronto: Author.

Ouston, R. (1998a, January 5). Potential Cost of Sex-Abuse Suits Has B.C. on Defensive. *Vancouver Sun*, p. A3.

– (1998b, January 7). Trial-free Compensation Urged for People Abused as Children. *Vancouver Sun*, p. B8.

Pagelow, M.D. (1984). *Family Violence.* New York: Praeger Publishers.

Parke, R.D. (1982). Theoretical Models of Child Abuse: Their Implications for Prediction, Prevention and Modification. In R.H. Starr (Ed.), *Child Abuse Prediction: Policy Implications* (pp. 31–66). Cambridge, Mass.: Ballinger Publishing.

Parton, N. (1985). *The Politics of Child Abuse.* London: Macmillan.

Pasick, P.L., and Pasick, R.S. (1985). The Developing Child. In J. Laird and A. Hartman (Eds.), *A Handbook of Child Welfare: Context, Knowledge and Practice* (pp. 178–92). London: The Free Press.

Pincus, A., and Minahan, A. (1973). *Social Work Practice: Model and Method.* Itasca, IL: F.E. Peacock Publishers.

Platiel, R. (1989, April 15). Sexual Abuse of Children Called an Epidemic. *Globe and Mail,* p. A2.

Porter, F.S., Blick, L.C., and Sgroi, S.M. (1982). Treatment of the Sexually Abused Child. In S. Sgroi, (Ed.), *Handbook of Clinical Intervention in Child Sexual Abuse* (pp. 109–45). Lexington, Mass.: Lexington Books.

Public Access to Names, Locations of Pedophiles Mulled. (1998, July 17). *Vancouver Sun,* p. A10.

Rabuzzi, K.A. (1988) *Motherself: A Mythic Analysis of Motherhood.* Bloomington: Indiana University Press.

Radwanski, G. (1987). *Ontario Study of the Relevance of Education, and the Issue of Dropouts.* Toronto: Ontario Ministry of Education.

Rapoport, R., Rapoport, R.N., and Strelitz, Z. (1977). *Fathers, Mothers and Others.* London: Routledge and Kegan Paul.

Rapp, R. (1982). Family and Class in Contemporary America: Notes Toward an Understanding of Ideology. In B. Thorne and M. Yalom (Eds.), *Rethinking the Family: Some Feminist Questions* (pp. 168–87). New York: Longman.

Raycroft, M. (1991). Abuse and Neglect Allegations in Child Custody and Protection Cases. In N. Bals, J. Harnich, and Robin Vogl, *Canadian Child Welfare Law* (pp. 225–36). Toronto: Thompson Educational Publishing.

Reed, E. (1972). Introduction. In F. Engels, *The Origin of the Family, Private Property and the State* (pp. 7–24). New York: Pathfinder Press.

Reimer, M. (1995). Downgrading Clerical Work in Textually Mediated Labour Process. In M. Campbell and A. Manicom (Eds.), *Knowledge, Experience, and Ruling Relations* (pp. 193–208). Toronto: University of Toronto Press.

Reinharz, S. (1992). *Feminist Methods in Social Research.* New York: Oxford University Press.

Report of the Social Assistance Review Committee (SARC), Transitions. (Thompson Report). (1988). Prepared for the Ontario Ministry of Community and Social Services. Toronto: Queen's Printer of Ontario.

Report of the Special Advisor to the Minister of National Health and Welfare on

Child Sexual Abuse in Canada (1990). [Rix Rogers] *Reaching for Solutions.* Ottawa: Ministry of Supply and Services.

Rheingold, J.C. (1964). *The Fear of Being a Woman: A Theory of Maternal Destructiveness.* New York: Greene and Straton.

Rich, A. (1986). *Of Woman Born: Motherhood as Experience and Institution.* New York: W.W. Norton and Company.

Ridgely, E. (1998/99) Family Treatment. In F.J. Turner (Ed.). *Social Work Practice: A Canadian Perspective* (pp. 195–205). Scarborough, Ontario: Prentice Hall.

Roberts, H. (1985). *The Patient Patients.* London: Pandora Press.

Robertshaw, C. (1981). *Child Protection in Canada.* Ottawa: Health and Welfare Canada.

Rodriguez, N., Ryan, S., Rowan, A., and Foy, D. (1996). Posttraumatic Stress Disorder in a Clinical Sample of Adult Survivors of Chldhood Sexual Abuse. *Child Abuse and Neglect, 20* (10), 943–52.

Rosaldo, M.Z., and Lamphere, L. (Eds.). (1974). *Woman Culture and Society.* Stanford, California: Stanford University Press.

Ross, M.S. (1996). Risk of Physical Abuse to Children of Spouse Abusing Parents. *Child Abuse and Neglect, 20* (7), 589–98.

Rossi, A.S. (1973). Maternalism, Sexuality and the New Feminism. In J. Zubin and J. Money (Eds.), *Contemporary Sexual Behavior.* Baltimore: Johns Hopkins University Press.

Rothman, B.K. (1995). Beyond Mothers and Fathers: Ideology in a Patriarchal Society. In E.N. Glenn, G. Chang and L.R. Farcey (Eds.). *Mothering Ideology, Experience, and Agency* (pp. 139–57). New York: Routledge.

Rousseau, J.J. (1971). *Confessions.* New York: Dutton (Everyman's Library). (Originally published 1749).

– (1979). *Emile.* Introduction, trans. and notes A. Bloom. New York: Basic Books. (Originally published 1762).

Royal Commission on the Status of Women in Canada, Report of. (1970). Government of Canada. Ottawa: Information Canada.

Rubin, L.B. (1976). *Worlds of Pain.* New York: Basic Books.

Ruddick, S. (1982). Maternal Thinking. In B. Thorne with M. Yalom (Eds.), *Rethinking the Family: Some Feminist Questions* (pp. 76–94). New York: Longman.

Rush, F. (1980). *The Best Kept Secret: Sexual Abuse of Children.* New York: McGraw-Hill.

Russell, D.E.H. (1983). The Incidence and Prevalence of Intrafamilial and Extrafamilial Sexual Abuse of Female Children. *Child Abuse and Neglect: The International Journal, 7* (2), 133–46.

– (1984). *Sexual Exploitation: Rape, Child Sexual Abuse, and Workplace Harassment.* Beverly Hills: Sage Publications.

– (1986). *The Secret Trauma: Incest in the Lives of Girls and Women.* New York: Basic Books.

Russell, M., Carter, B., Zuk, G., Saunders, M., Ehren-Lis, N., amd Wood, C. (1996). Transformational Experiences of Women in Sexual Abuse Survivors Groups: The Women's Voices. Research paper presented at the Annual Conference of the Association of Women in Psychology, Portland, Oregon, 16 March 1996.

Sanday, P.R. (1986). *Female Power and Male Dominance: On the Origins of Sexual Inequality.* London: Cambridge University Press.

Schorr, A.L. (1986, June). Why We Care about Child Abuse. *Readings: A Journal of Reviews and Commentary in Mental Health, 1* (2), 10–11.

Sedlak, A.J., and Broadhurst, D.D. (1996). *Third National Incidence Study of Child Abuse and Neglect.* Washington, DC: Department of Health and Human Services.

Sgroi, S. (1982). An Approach to Case Management. In S. Sgroi (Ed.), *Handbook of Clinical Intervention in Child Sexual Abuse* (pp. 81–108). Lexington, Mass.: Lexington Books.

– (1988). *Vulnerable Populations* (Vol. 1). Lexington, Mass.: Lexington Books.

Shulman, L. (1984). *The Skills of Helping* (2nd ed.). Itasca, Illinois: F.E. Peacock Publishers.

Siedman, I.E. (1991). *Interviewing as Qualitative Research.* New York: Teachers College Press.

Smith, D.E. (1987). *The Everyday World as Problematic: A Feminist Sociology.* Toronto: University of Toronto Press.

SPAN. [The Counselling Standards Committee Service Providers Adult/ Advocacy Network] (1997, August). A Report of Counselling Services Being Provided for Adult Survivors of Child Sexual Abuse. Vancouver: Author.

Spears, J. (1990, March 31). 'Clues to Mount Cashel cover-up Locked in Graves.' The *Toronto Star*, p. D4.

Spender, D. (1985). *For the Record.* London: The Women's Press.

Spiegel, D. (1982). Mothering, Fathering and Mental Illness. In B. Thorne with M. Yalom (Eds.), *Rethinking the Family: Some Feminist Questions* (pp. 95–110). New York: Longman.

Spitz, R. (1965). *The First Years of Life: A Psychoanalytic Study of Normal and Deviant Development of Object Relations.* New York: International University Press.

Spock, B. (1957). *The Pocket Book of Baby and Child Care.* New York: Penguin.

Stanko, E.A. (1986). *Intimate Intrusions: Women's Experience of Male Violence.* London: Routledge and Kegan Paul.

– (1988). Fear of Crime and the Myth of the Safe Home: A Feminist Critique of Criminology. In K. Yllo and M. Bograd (Eds.), *Feminist Perspectives on Wife Abuse* (pp. 75–88). Newbury Park, California: Sage Publications.

Stanley, L., and Wise, S. (1983). *Breaking Out: Feminist Consciousness and Feminist Research.* London: Routledge and Kegan Paul.

Starrels, M.E. (1994, March). Gender Differences in Parent-Child Relations. *Journal of Family Issues, 15* (1) 148–65.

Statistics Canada. (1985, March). *Women in Canada: A Statistical Report.* Ottawa: Ministry of Supply and Services.

– (1990a). *Women in Canada: A Statistical Report* (2nd ed.). Ottawa: Ministry of Supply and Services.

– (1990b). *Canada Year Book 1990.* Ottawa: Ministry of Supply and Services.

Stewart, C. (1987, December). Understanding the New Law on Child Sexual Abuse. Toronto: Institute for the Prevention of Child Abuse.

Straus, M.A., Gelles, R.J., and Steinmetz S. (1981). *Behind Closed Doors.* New York: Anchor Press.

Strauss, A. (1987). *Qualitative Analysis for Social Scientists.* Cambridge: Cambridge University Press.

Strauss, A., and Corbin, J. (1990). *Basics of Qualitative Research.* Newbury Park, California: Sage Publications.

Studio D of the National Film Board of Canada (Producer), B. Shaffer, and S. Turcotte (Directors) (1987). *To a Safer Place* [Film]. Montreal: National Film Board of Canada.

Surrey, J. (1991). The Self-in-Relation: A Theory of Women's Development. In J. Jordan et al., *Women's Growth in Connection: Writings from the Stone Center,* (pp. 51–66). New York: The Guilford Press.

Swift, K. (1995). *Manufacturing 'Bad Mothers.'* Toronto: University of Toronto Press.

Swigonski, M.E. (1993, Summer). Feminist Standpoint Theory and the Questions of Social Work Research. *Affilia: Journal of Women and Social Work, 8* (2), 171–83.

Taylor, J., Gilligan, C., and Sullivan A. (1995). *Between Voice and Silence.* Cambridge, Mass.: Harvard University Press.

Terr, L. (1991). *Too Scared to Cry.* New York: Harper and Row.

Thompson Educational Publishing. (1994). *Canadian Social Trends* (Vol 2). Toronto: Author.

Thompson, G. (1983). Judging Judiciously. In R.S. Abella and C. L'Heureux-Dubé (Eds.). *Dimensions of Justice.* Toronto: Butterworth.

Thompson, G. (1987, February). *Judicial Response to Child Abuse.* Presentation given in graduate course entitled 'Violence in Families: An Interdisciplinary Perspective', Facult of Social Work, University of Toronto.

Thorne, B. (1982). Feminist Rethinking of the Family: An Overview. In B. Thorne with M. Yalom (Eds.) *Rethinking the Family: Some Feminist Questions* (pp. 1–24). New York: Longman.

Thorne B., with Yalom, M. (1982). (Eds.). *Rethinking the Family: Some Feminist Questions.* New York: Longman.

Tibbetts, J. (1998, January 5). Aboriginals Await $100-million Package for Abuse at Schools. *Vancouver Sun,* p. A7.

Tomm, W. (1995). *Bodied Mindfulness.* Waterloo, Ontario: Wilfrid Laurier University Press.

Trainor, C., Normond, J., and Verdon, L. (1995). Women and the Criminal Justice System. In *Women in Canada: A Statistical Report* (3rd ed.) (pp. 101–16). Ottawa: Statistics Canada.

Trocme, N, McPhee, D., and Tam, K.K. (1995, May/June). Child Abuse and Neglect in Ontario: Incidence and Characteristics. *Child Welfare, 74* (3), 563–86.

Turner, F.J. (1986). Theory in Social Work Practice. In J. Turner (Ed.). *Social Work Treatment.* (pp. 1–18). New York: The Free Press.

Vale Allen, C. (1980). *Daddy's Girl.* Toronto: McClelland and Stewart.

Van Den Bergh, N. (1995). (Ed.). *Feminist Practice in the 21st Century.* Washington, DC: NASW Press.

Vancouver Custody and Access Support and Advocacy Association. (1996). *Women and Children Last.* Vancouver: Author.

Vienneau, D. (1990, February 16). BC Judge Cleared in Fuss about His Remarks. *Toronto Star,* p. A13.

Vogel, A. (1997, December 31). Child Development Key to Society's Well-Being. *Vancouver Sun,* p. B6.

Voysey, M. (1975). *A Constant Burden: The Reconstruction of Family Life.* London: Routledge and Kegan Paul.

Walsh, F. (1982). Conceptualizations of Normal Family Functioning. In F. Walsh (Ed), *Normal Family Processes.* (pp. 3–42). New York: The Guilford Press.

Ward, M. (1994). *The Family Dynamic.* Scarborough, Ontario: Nelson.

Washburne, C.K. (1981, July). A Feminist Analysis of Child Abuse and Neglect. Paper presented at National Conference on Family Violence, Durham, New Hampshire.

Watson, J. (1928). *Psychological Care of Infant and Child.* New York: W.W. Norton.

Wattenburg, E. (1985). In a Different Light: A Feminist Perspective on the Role of Mother in Father-Daughter Incest. *Child Welfare, 64* (3), 205–11.

Weil, S. (1951). *Waiting on God.* New York: Putnam.

Weinberg, S.K. (1955). *Incest Behavior.* New York: Citadel Press.

Weiner, B. (1986). *An Attributional Theory of Motivation and Emotion.* New York: Springer-Verlag.

Wells, M. (1990). *Canada's Law on Child Sexual Abuse: A Handbook.* Ottawa: Minister of Supply and Services.

Westkott, M. (1978). Mothers and Daughters in the World of the Fathers. *Frontiers, 2* (3), 16–21.

– (1997). *Women, Men, and Gender: Ongoing Debates.* New Haven: Yale University Press.

White, B.L. (1975). *The First Three Years of Life.* Englewood Cliffs, NJ: Prentice Hall.

Williams, L.M. (1994). Recall of Childhood Trauma: A Prospective Study of Women's Memories of Child Sexual Abuse. *Journal of Consulting and Clinical Psychology, 62* (6), 1167–76.

Williams, M. (1993). Sexual Abuse. *The Journal of Child Sexual Abuse, 2,* 41–59.

Wilson, Madam Justice B. (1990, February). Will Women Judges Really Make a Difference? An address given at Osgoode Hall Law School, Toronto.

Wilson, E. (1977). *Women and the Welfare State.* London: Tavistock Publications.

– (1983). *What Is To Be Done about Violence Against Women?* Middlesex: Penguin Books.

Winnicott, D.W. (1957). *The Child and the Family: First Relationships.* London: Tavistock Publications.

Wolfers, O. (1993). The Paradox of Women Who Sexually Abuse Children. In M. Elliott (Ed.), *Female Sexual Abuse of Children.* (pp. 99–106). Colchester, Eng.: Longman.

Women's Research Centre. (1989). *Recollecting Our Lives.* Vancouver: Press Gang Publishers.

Worell, J., and Etaugh, C. (1994). Transforming Theory and Research with Women. *Psychology of Women Quarterly, 18,* 443–50.

Wyatt, G.E. (1985). The Sexual Abuse of Afro-American and White-American women in Childhood. *Child Abuse and Neglect, 9,* 507–19.

Wyatt, G.E., and Peters, S.D. (1986). Issues in the Definition of Child Sexual Abuse in Prevalence Research. *Child Abuse and Neglect: The International Journal, 10,* 231–40.

Wyatt, G.E., and Powell, G.J. (Eds.). (1988). *Lasting Effects of Child Sexual Abuse.* Newbury Park, California: Sage Publications.

Yeager, S. (1995, August 11). Treatment Shortfall. *Vancouver Sun,* p. B1.

Young, V. (1993). Women Abusers: A Feminist View. In M. Elliott (Ed.), *Female Sexual Abuse of Children* (pp. 107–21). Colchester, Eng. Longman.

Zastrow, C. (1995). *The Practice of Social Work.* (5th. ed.). Belmont, California: Brooks/Cole Publishing.

Index